O for a lodge in some vast wilderness,
Some boundless contiguity of shade,
Where rumour of oppression and deceit,
Of unsuccessful or successful war,
Might never reach me more.

PART II.

CONTAINING

HYMNS:

TRANSLATIONS FROM MADAME GUION

TRANSLATIONS FROM MILTON:

MINOR POEMS:

AND

ADAM; A SACRED DRAMA:

FROM THE ITALIAN OF GIO. BATTISTA ANDREINI.

CONTENTS OF PART SECOND.

CONTAINING HYMNS: TRANSLATIONS FROM MADAME GUION; TRANSLATIONS FROM MILTON: AND MINOR POEMS.

HYMNS.

TRANSLATIONS FROM THE FRENCH OF MADAME DE LA MOTHE GUION.

TRANSLATIONS OF THE LATIN AND ITALIAN POEMS OF MILTON.

TRANSLATIONS FROM VINCENT BOURNE.

MINOR POEMS.

TRANSLATIONS OF GREEK VERSES.

EPIGRAMS TRANSLATED FROM THE LATIN OF OWEN.

TRANSLATIONS FROM THE FABLES OF GAY.

COMPLIMENTARY POEMS TO MILTON,

Translated from the Latin and Italian.

HYMNS.

I. WALKING WITH GOD.—Gen. v. 24.

OH! for a closer walk with God,
  A calm and heavenly frame;
A light to shine upon the road
  That leads me to the Lamb!

Where is the blessedness I knew
  When first I saw the Lord?
Where is the soul-refreshing view
  Of Jesus and his word?

What peaceful hours I once enjoy'd!
  How sweet their memory still!
But they have left an aching void,
  The world can never fill.

Return, O holy Dove, return!
  Sweet messenger of rest:
I hate the sins that made thee mourn,
  And drove thee from my breast.

The dearest idol I have known,
  Whate'er that idol be,
Help me to tear it from thy throne,
  And worship only thee.

So shall my walk be close with God,
  Calm and serene my frame;
So purer light shall mark the road
  That leads me to the Lamb.

B

II. JEHOVAH-JIREH. THE LORD WILL PROVIDE.—Gen. xxii. 14.

THE saints should never be dismay'd,
  Nor sink in hopeless fear;
For when they least expect his aid,
  The Saviour will appear.

This Abraham found: he raised the knife;
  God saw, and said, 'Forbear!
Yon ram shall yield his meaner life;
  Behold the victim there.'

Once David seem'd Saul's certain prey;
  But hark! the foe's at hand;*
Saul turns his arms another way,
  To save the invaded land.

When Jonah sunk beneath the wave,
  He thought to rise no more;†
But God prepared a fish to save,
  And bear him to the shore.

Blest proofs of power and grace divine,
  That meet us in his word!
May every deep-felt care of mine
  Be trusted with the Lord.

Wait for his seasonable aid,
  And though it tarry, wait:
The promise may be long delay'd,
  But cannot come too late.

III. JEHOVAH-ROPHI. I AM THE LORD THAT HEALETH THEE.—Exod. xv. 26.

HEAL us, Emmanuel, here we are,
  Waiting to feel thy touch:
Deep-wounded souls to thee repair,
  And, Saviour, we are such.

* 1 Sam. xxiii. 27 † Jonah i. 17

Our faith is feeble, we confess
 We faintly trust thy word;
But wilt thou pity us the less?
 Be that far from thee, Lord!

Remember him who once apply'd
 With trembling, for relief;
'Lord, I believe,' with tears he cried,*
 'Oh, help my unbelief!'

She too, who touch'd thee in the press,
 And healing virtue stole,
Was answer'd, 'Daughter, go in peace,†
 Thy faith hath made thee whole.'

Conceal'd amid the gathering throng,
 She would have shunn'd thy view;
And if her faith was firm and strong,
 Had strong misgivings too.

Like her, with hopes and fears we come,
 To touch thee, if we may;
Oh! send us not despairing home,
 Send none unheal'd away.

IV. JEHOVAH-NISSI. THE LORD MY BANNER.

Exod. xvii. 15.

By whom was David taught
 To aim the deadly blow,
When he Goliah fought,
 And laid the Gittite low
Nor sword nor spear the stripling took,
But chose a pebble from the brook.

'Twas Israel's God and king
 Who sent him to the fight;
Who gave him strength to sling,
 And skill to aim aright.
Ye feeble saints, your strength endures,
Because young David's God is yours.

* Mark ix. 24 † Mark v. 34.

Who order'd Gideon forth,
To storm the invaders' camp,
With arms of little worth,
A pitcher and a lamp?*
The trumpets made his coming known,
And all the host was overthrown.

Oh! I have seen the day,
When with a single word,
God helping me to say,
My trust is in the Lord,
My soul hath quell'd a thousand foes,
Fearless of all that could oppose.

But unbelief, self-will,
Self-righteousness, and pride,
How often do they steal
My weapon from my side
Yet David's Lord, and Gideon's friend;
Will help his servant to the end.

V. JEHOVAH-SHALOM. THE LORD SEND PEACE.—Judges vi. 24.

Jesus, whose blood so freely stream'd
To satisfy the law's demand;
By thee from guilt and wrath redeem'd,
Before the Father's face I stand.

To reconcile offending man,
Make Justice drop her angry rod:
What creature could have form'd the plan,
Or who fulfil it but a God?

No drop remains of all the curse,
For wretches who deserved the whole;
No arrows dipt in wrath to pierce
The guilty, but returning soul.

* Judges vii. 9, and 20.

Peace by such means so dearly bought,
What rebel could have hoped to see?
Peace, by his injured Sovereign wrought,
His Sovereign fasten'd to a tree.

Now, Lord, thy feeble worm prepare!
For strife with earth and hell begins;
Confirm and gird me for the war,
They hate the soul that hates his sins.

Let them in horrid league agree!
They may assault, they may distress;
But cannot quench thy love to me,
Nor rob me of the Lord my peace.

VI. WISDOM.—Prov. viii. 22—31.

Ere God had built the mountains,
Or raised the fruitful hills;
Before he fill'd the fountains
That feed the running rills
In me, from everlasting,
The wonderful I am,
Found pleasures never wasting,
And Wisdom is my name.

When like a tent to dwell in,
He spread the skies abroad,
And swathed about the swelling
Of Ocean's mighty flood;
He wrought by weight and measure,
And I was with him then:
Myself the Father's pleasure,
And mine the sons of men.

Thus wisdom's words discover
Thy glory and thy grace
Thou everlasting lover
Of our unworthy race!
Thy gracious eye survey'd us
Ere stars were seen above;
In wisdom thou hast made us,
And died for us in love.

And could'st thou be delighted
  With creatures such as we,
Who, when we saw thee, slighted,
  And nail'd thee to a tree?
Unfathomable wonder,
  And mystery divine!
The voice that speaks in thunder,
  Says, 'Sinner, I am thine!'

VII. VANITY OF THE WORLD.

God gives his mercies to be spent;
  Your hoard will do your soul no good;
Gold is a blessing only lent,
  Repaid by giving others food

The world's esteem is but a bribe,
  To buy their peace you sell your own;
The slave of a vain-glorious tribe,
  Who hate you while they make you known

The joy that vain amusements give,
  Oh! sad conclusion that it brings!
The honey of a crowded hive,
  Defended by a thousand stings.

'Tis thus the world rewards the fools
  That live upon her treacherous smiles:
She leads them blindfold by her rules,
  And ruins all whom she beguiles.

God knows the thousands who go down
  From pleasure into endless woe;
And with a long despairing groan
  Blaspheme their Maker as they go.

O fearful thought! be timely wise;
  Delight but in a Saviour's charms,
And God shall take you to the skies,
  Embraced in everlasting arms.

VIII. O LORD, I WILL PRAISE THEE.

Isaiah xii. 1.

I WILL praise thee every day
Now thine anger's turn'd away!
Comfortable thoughts arise
From the bleeding sacrifice.

Here, in the fair gospel-field,
Wells of free salvation yield
Streams of life, a plenteous store,
And my soul shall thirst no more.

Jesus is become at length
My salvation and my strength;
And his praises shall prolong,
While I live, my pleasant song.

Praise ye, then, his glorious name,
Publish his exalted fame!
Still his worth your praise exceeds,
Excellent are all his deeds.

Raise again the joyful sound,
Let the nations roll it round!
Zion, shout, for this is he,
God the Saviour dwells in thee!

IX. THE CONTRITE HEART.—Isaiah lvii. 15.

THE Lord will happiness divine
  On contrite hearts bestow;
Then tell me, gracious God, is mine
  A contrite heart or no?

I hear, but seem to hear in vain,
  Insensible as steel;
If ought is felt, 'tis only pain,
  To find I cannot feel.

E

I sometimes think myself inclined
  To love thee, if I could;
But often feel another mind,
  Averse to all that's good.

My best desires are faint and few,
  I fain would strive for more;
But when I cry, 'My strength renew,'
  Seem weaker than before.

Thy saints are comforted, I know,
  And love thy house of prayer;
I therefore go where others go,
  But find no comfort there.

O make this heart rejoice or ache;
  Decide this doubt for me;
And if it be not broken, break,
  And heal it if it be.

X. THE FUTURE PEACE AND GLORY OF THE CHURCH.—Isaiah ix. 15—20.

Hear what God the Lord hath spoken,
'O my people, faint and few,
Comfortless, afflicted, broken,
Fair abodes I build for you;
Thorns of heart-felt tribulation
Shall no more perplex your ways:
You shall name your walls, Salvation,
And your gates shall all be praise.

'There, like streams that feed the garden,
Pleasures without end shall flow;
For the Lord, your faith rewarding,
All his bounty shall bestow;
Still in undisturb'd possession
Peace and righteousness shall reign;
Never shall you feel oppression,
Hear the voice of war again.

'Ye no more your suns descending,
Waning moons no more shall see;
But, your griefs for ever ending,
Find eternal noon in me:
God shall rise, and shining o'er you,
Change to day the gloom of night;
He, the Lord, shall be your glory,
God your everlasting light.'

XI. JEHOVAH OUR RIGHTEOUSNESS

Jer. xxiii. 6.

My God, how perfect are thy ways!
  But mine polluted are;
Sin twines itself about my praise
  And slides into my prayer.

When I would speak what thou hast done
  To save me from my sin,
I cannot make thy mercies known,
  But self-applause creeps in.

Divine desire, that holy flame
  Thy grace creates in me;
Alas! impatience is its name,
  When it returns to thee.

This heart, a fountain of vile thoughts,
  How does it overflow!
While self upon the surface floats,
  Still bubbling from below.

Let others in the gaudy dress
  Of fancied merit shine,
The Lord shall be my righteousness,
  The Lord for ever mine.

XII. EPHRAIM REPENTING.—Jer. xxxi. 18—20.

My God, till I received thy stroke,
  How like a beast was I!
So unaccustom'd to the yoke,
  So backward to comply.

With grief my just reproach I bear,
  Shame fills me at the thought;
How frequent my rebellions were!
  What wickedness I wrought!

Thy merciful restraint I scorn'd,
  And left the pleasant road;
Yet turn me, and I shall be turn'd,
  Thou art the Lord my God.

'Is Ephraim banish'd from my thoughts,
  Or vile in my esteem?
No,' saith the Lord, 'with all his faults,
  I still remember him.

'Is he a dear and pleasant child?
  Yes, dear and pleasant still;
Though sin his foolish heart beguiled,
  And he withstood my will.

'My sharp rebuke has laid him low,
  He seeks my face again;
My pity kindles at his woe,
  He shall not seek in vain.'

XIII. THE COVENANT.—Ezek. xxxvi. 25—28.

The Lord proclaims his grace abroad!
Behold, I change your hearts of stone;
Each shall renounce his idol-god,
And serve, henceforth, the Lord alone,

My grace, a flowing stream, proceeds
To wash your filthiness away;
Ye shall abhor your former deeds,
And learn my statutes to obey.

My truth the great design ensures,
I give myself away to you;
You shall be mine, I will be yours,
Your God unalterably true.

Yet not unsought, or unimplored,
The plenteous grace shall I confer;*
No—your whole hearts shall seek the Lord,
I'll put a praying spirit there.

From the first breath of life divine,
Down to the last expiring hour,
The gracious work shall all be mine,
Begun and ended in my power.

XIV. JEHOVAH-SHAMMAH.—Ezek. xlviii. 35

As birds their infant brood protect,†
And spread their wings to shelter them,
Thus saith the Lord to his elect,
'So will I guard Jerusalem.'

And what then is Jerusalem,
This darling object of his care?
Where is its worth in God's esteem?
Who built it? who inhabits there?

Jehovah founded it in blood,
The blood of his incarnate Son;
There dwell the saints, once foes to God,
The sinners whom he calls his own.

There, though besieged on every side,
Yet much beloved and guarded well,
From age to age they have defied
The utmost force of earth and hell.

* Verse 37. † Isaiah xxxi. 5.

Let earth repent, and hell despair,
This city has a sure defence;
Her name is call'd, The Lord is there,
And who has power to drive him thence?

XV. PRAISE FOR THE FOUNTAIN OPENED.

Zec. xiii. 1.

There is a fountain fill'd with blood
Drawn from Emmanuel's veins;
And sinners, plunged beneath that flood,
Lose all their guilty stains.

The dying thief rejoiced to see
That fountain in his day;
And there have I, as vile as he,
Wash'd all my sins away.

Dear dying Lamb, thy precious blood
Shall never lose its power,
Till all the ransom'd church of God
Be saved to sin no more.

E'er since, by faith, I saw the stream
Thy flowing wounds supply,
Redeeming love has been my theme,
And shall be till I die.

Then in a nobler, sweeter song,
I'll sing thy power to save;
When this poor lisping stammering tongue
Lies silent in the grave.

Lord, I believe thou hast prepared
(Unworthy though I be)
For me a blood-bought free reward,
A golden harp for me!

'Tis strung, and tuned, for endless years,
And form'd by power divine,
To sound in God the Father's ears
No other name but thine.

XVI. THE SOWER.—Matt. xiii. 3.

Ye sons of earth, prepare the plough,
  Break up your fallow ground;
The sower is gone forth to sow,
  And scatter blessings round.

The seed that finds a stony soil,
  Shoots forth a hasty blade:
But ill repays the sower's toil,
  Soon wither'd, scorch'd, and dead.

The thorny ground is sure to baulk
  All hopes of harvest there;
We find a tall and sickly stalk,
  But not the fruitful ear.

The beaten path and highway side
  Receive the trust in vain;
The watchful birds the spoil divide,
  And pick up all the grain.

But where the Lord of grace and power
  Has bless'd the happy field,
How plenteous is the golden store
  The deep-wrought furrows yield!

Father of mercies, we have need
  Of thy preparing grace;
Let the same hand that gives the seed
  Provide a fruitful place.

XVII. THE HOUSE OF PRAYER.—Mark xi. 17

Thy mansion is the Christian's heart,
  O Lord, thy dwelling-place secure!
Bid the unruly throng depart,
  And leave the consecrated door.

Devoted as it is to thee,
  A thievish swarm frequents the place;
They steal away my joys from me,
  And rob my Saviour of his praise.

There, too, a sharp designing trade
  Sin, Satan, and the world maintain
Nor cease to press me, and persuade
  To part with ease, and purchase pain.

I know them, and I hate their din,
  Am weary of the bustling crowd;
But while their voice is heard within,
  I cannot serve thee as I would.

Oh! for the joy thy presence gives,
  What peace shall reign when thou art here!
Thy presence makes this den of thieves
  A calm delightful house of prayer.

And if thou make thy temple shine,
  Yet, self-abased, will I adore;
The gold and silver are not mine,
  I give thee what was thine before.

XVIII. LOVEST THOU ME?—John xxi. 16

HARK, my soul! it is the Lord:
'Tis thy Saviour, hear his word;
Jesus speaks, and speaks to thee:
'Say, poor sinner, lov'st thou me?

'I deliver'd thee when bound,
And when bleeding, heal'd thy wound:
Sought thee wandering, set thee right,
Turn'd thy darkness into light.

'Can a woman's tender care
Cease towards the child she bare?
Yes, she may forgetful be,
Yet will I remember thee.

'Mine is an unchanging love,
Higher than the heights above;
Deeper than the depths beneath,
Free and faithful, strong as death.

'Thou shalt see my glory soon,
When the work of grace is done:
Partner of my throne shalt be:—
Say, poor sinner, lov'st thou me?'

Lord, it is my chief complaint,
That my love is weak and faint;
Yet I love thee and adore:
Oh! for grace to love thee more!

XIX. CONTENTMENT.—Phil. iv. 11.

Fierce passions discompose the mind,
  As tempests vex the sea:
But calm content and peace we find,
  When, Lord, we turn to thee.

In vain by reason and by rule
  We try to bend the will;
For none but in the Saviour's school
  Can learn the heavenly skill.

Since at his feet my soul has sat,
  His gracious words to hear,
Contented with my present state,
  I cast on him my care.

'Art thou a sinner, soul?' he said,
  'Then how canst thou complain?
How light thy troubles here, if weigh'd
  With everlasting pain!

'If thou of murmuring wouldst be cured,
  Compare thy griefs with mine;
Think what my love for thee endured,
  And thou wilt not repine.

''Tis I appoint thy daily lot,
  And I do all things well;
Thou soon shalt leave this wretched spot,
  And rise with me to dwell.

In life my grace shall strength supply,
Proportion'd to thy day;
At death thou still shalt find me nigh,
To wipe thy tears away.'

Thus I, who once my wretched days
In vain repinings spent
Taught in my Saviour's school of grace,
Have learnt to be content.

XX. OLD TESTAMENT GOSPEL.--Heb. iv. 2.

Israel, in ancient days,
Not only had a view
Of Sinai in a blaze,
But learn'd the Gospel too;
The types and figures were a glass,
In which they saw a Saviour's face.

The paschal sacrifice,
And blood-besprinkled door,*
Seen with enlighten'd eyes,
And once applied with power,
Would teach the need of other blood,
To reconcile an angry God.

The Lamb, the Dove, set forth
His perfect innocence,†
Whose blood of matchless worth
Should be the soul's defence;
For he who can for sin atone,
Must have no failings of his own.

The scape-goat on his head‡
The people's trespass bore,
And to the desert led,
Was to be seen no more:
In him our Surety seem'd to say,
' Behold, I bear your sins away.'

* Exod. xii. 13. † Lev. xii. 6. ‡ Lev. xvi. 21.

Dipt in his fellow's blood,
  The living bird went free;*
The type, well understood,
  Express'd the sinner's plea;
Described a guilty soul enlarged
And by a Saviour's death discharged.

Jesus, I love to trace,
  Throughout the sacred page
The footsteps of thy grace,
  The same in every age!
O grant that I may faithful be
To clearer light vouchsafed to me!

XXI. SARDIS.—Rev. iii. 1—6

'Write to Sardis,' saith the Lord,
  And write what he declares,
He whose Spirit, and whose word,
  Upholds the seven stars:
'All thy works and ways I search,
  Find thy zeal and love decay'd;
Thou art call'd a living church,
  But thou art cold and dead.

Watch, remember, seek, and strive
  Exert thy former pains;
Let thy timely care revive
  And strengthen what remains:
Cleanse thine heart, thy works amend,
  Former times to mind recall,
Lest my sudden stroke descend,
  And smite thee once for all.

Yet I number now in thee
  A few that are upright;
These my Father's face shall see,
  And walk with me in white.

* Lev. xiv. 51—53.

When in judgment I appear,
  They for mine shall be confest;
Let my faithful servants hear
  And woe be to the rest.

XXII. PRAYER FOR A BLESSING.

Bestow, dear Lord, upon our youth
  The gift of saving grace;
And let the seed of sacred truth
  Fall in a fruitful place.

Grace is a plant, where'er it grow
  Of pure and heavenly root;
But fairest in the youngest shows,
  And yields the sweetest fruit.

Ye careless ones, O hear betimes
  The voice of sovereign love!
Your youth is stain'd with many crimes,
  But mercy reigns above.

True, you are young, but there's a stone
  Within the youngest breast;
Or half the crimes which you have done
  Would rob you of your rest.

For you the public prayer is made,
  Oh! join the public prayer!
For you the secret tear is shed,
  O shed yourselves a tear!

We pray that you may early prove
  The Spirit's power to teach;
You cannot be too young to love
  That Jesus whom we preach.

XXIII. PLEADING FOR AND WITH YOUTH.

SIN has undone our wretched race,
  But Jesus has restored,
And brought the sinner face to face
  With his forgiving Lord.

This we repeat, from year to year,
  And press upon our youth;
Lord, give them an attentive ear,
  Lord, save them by thy truth.

Blessings upon the rising race!
  Make this a happy hour,
According to thy richest grace,
  And thine almighty power.

We feel for your unhappy state,
  (May you regard it too)
And would awhile ourselves forget
  To pour out prayer for you.

We see, though you perceive it not,
  Th' approaching awful doom;
O tremble at the solemn thought
  And flee the wrath to come

Dear Saviour, let this new-born year
  Spread an alarm abroad;
And cry in every careless ear,
  'Prepare to meet thy God!'

XXIV. PRAYER FOR CHILDREN

GRACIOUS Lord, our children see,
By thy mercy we are free;
But shall these, alas! remain
Subjects still of Satan's reign?

Israel's young ones, when of old
Pharaoh threaten'd to withhold;*
Then thy messenger said, 'No;
Let the children also go.'

When the angel of the Lord
Drawing forth his dreadful sword,
Slew, with an avenging hand,
All the first-born of the land;†
Then thy people's doors he pass'd,
Where the bloody sign was placed;
Hear us, now, upon our knees,
Plead the blood of Christ for these!

Lord, we tremble, for we know
How the fierce malicious foe,
Wheeling round his watchful flight
Keeps them ever in his sight:
Spread thy pinions, King of kings!
Hide them safe beneath thy wings;
Lest the ravenous bird of prey
Stoop, and bear the brood away

XXV. JEHOVAH JESUS.

My song shall bless the Lord of all,
  My praise shall climb to his abode;
Thee, Saviour, by that name I call,
  The great, supreme, the mighty God.

Without beginning or decline,
  Object of faith, and not of sense;
Eternal ages saw him shine,
  He shines eternal ages hence.

As much, when in the manger laid,
  Almighty ruler of the sky,
As when the six days' work he made
  Fill'd all the morning stars with joy.

* Exod. x. 9. † Exod. xii. 12.

Of all the crowns Jehovah bears,
  Salvation is his dearest claim;
That gracious sound well pleased he hears,
  And owns Emmanuel for his name.

A cheerful confidence I feel,
  My well-placed hopes with joy I see;
My bosom glows with heavenly zeal,
  To worship him who died for me.

As man, he pities my complaint,
  His power and truth are all divine;
He will not fail, he cannot faint,
  Salvation's sure, and must be mine.

XXVI. ON OPENING A PLACE FOR SOCIAL PRAYER.

Jesus! where'er thy people meet,
There they behold thy mercy-seat;
Where'er they seek thee, thou art found
And every place is hallow'd ground.

For thou, within no walls confined
Inhabitest the humble mind;
Such ever bring thee where they come,
And going, take thee to their home.

Dear Shepherd of thy chosen few!
Thy former mercies here renew;
Here to our waiting hearts proclaim
The sweetness of thy saving name.

Here may we prove the power of prayer
To strengthen faith, and sweeten care;
To teach our faint desires to rise,
And bring all heaven before our eyes

Behold, at thy commanding word
We stretch the curtain and the cord;*
Come thou, and fill this wider space,
And bless us with a large increase.

* Isaiah liv. 2.

Lord, we are few, but thou art near;
Nor short thine arm, nor deaf thine ear;
Oh, rend the heavens, come quickly down,
And make a thousand hearts thine own.

XXVII. WELCOME TO THE TABLE.

This is the feast of heavenly wine
And God invites to sup;
The juices of the living vine
Were press'd to fill the cup.

Oh! bless the Saviour, ye that eat,
With royal dainties fed;
Not heaven affords a costlier treat
For Jesus is the bread.

The vile, the lost, he calls to them,
Ye trembling souls, appear!
The righteous in their own esteem
Have no acceptance here.

Approach, ye poor, nor dare refuse
The banquet spread for you;
Dear Saviour, this is welcome news,
Then I may venture too.

If guilt and sin afford a plea,
And may obtain a place,
Surely the Lord will welcome me,
And I shall see his face.

XXVIII. JESUS HASTING TO SUFFER.

The Saviour, what a noble flame
Was kindled in his breast,
When hasting to Jerusalem,
He march'd before the rest

Good will to men, and zeal for God
  His every thought engross;
He longs to be baptized with blood,*
  He pants to reach the cross!

With all his sufferings full in view,
  And woes to us unknown,
Forth to the task his spirit flew;
  'Twas love that urged him on.

Lord, we return thee what we can:
  Our hearts shall sound abroad,
Salvation to the dying Man,
  And to the rising God!

And while thy bleeding glories here
  Engage our wondering eyes,
We learn our lighter cross to bear
  And hasten to the skies.

XXIX. EXHORTATION TO PRAYER.

What various hindrances we meet
In coming to a mercy-seat!
Yet who that knows the worth of prayer,
But wishes to be often there?

Prayer makes the darken'd cloud withdraw,
Prayer climbs the ladder Jacob saw,
Gives exercise to faith and love,
Brings every blessing from above.

Restraining prayer, we cease to fight;
Prayer makes the Christian's armour bright
And Satan trembles when he sees
The weakest saint upon his knees.

While Moses stood with arms spread wide,
Success was found on Israel's side;
But when through weariness they fail'd,
That moment Amalek prevail'd.†

* Luke xii. 50. † Exodus xvii. 11.

Have you no words? Ha! think again,
Words flow apace when you complain,
And fill your fellow-creature's ear
With the sad tale of all your care.

Were half the breath thus vainly spent
To Heaven in supplication sent,
Your cheerful song would oftener be,
'Hear what the Lord has done for me.

XXX. THE LIGHT AND GLORY OF THE WORD.

The Spirit breathes upon the Word,
  And brings the truth to sight;
Precepts and promises afford
  A sanctifying light.

A glory gilds the sacred page,
  Majestic like the sun;
It gives a light to every age,
  It gives, but borrows none.

The hand that gave it still supplies
  The gracious light and heat:
His truths upon the nations rise,
  They rise, but never set.

Let everlasting thanks be thine,
  For such a bright display,
As makes a world of darkness shine
  With beams of heavenly day.

My soul rejoices to pursue
  The steps of him I love,
Till glory breaks upon my view
  In brighter worlds above.

XXXI. ON THE DEATH OF A MINISTER.

His master taken from his head,
  Elisha saw him go;
And in desponding accents said,
  'Ah, what must Israel do?'

But he forgot the Lord who lifts
  The beggar to the throne;
Nor knew, that all Elijah's gifts
  Will soon be made his own.

What! when a Paul has run his course
  Or when Apollos dies,
Is Israel left without resource?
  And have we no supplies?

Yes, while the dear Redeemer lives
  We have a boundless store,
And shall be fed with what he gives,
  Who lives for evermore.

XXXII. THE SHINING LIGHT.

My former hopes are fled,
  My terror now begins;
I feel, alas! that I am dead
  In trespasses and sins.

Ah, whither shall I fly!
  I hear the thunder roar;
The law proclaims destruction nigh,
  And vengeance at the door.

When I review my ways,
  I dread impending doom:
But sure a friendly whisper says,
  'Flee from the wrath to come.'

I see, or think I see;
  A glimmering from afar;
A beam of day, that shines for me,
  To save me from despair.

Forerunner of the sun,*
  It marks the Pilgrim's way;
I'll gaze upon it while I run,
  And watch the rising day.

XXXIII. SEEKING THE BELOVED.

To those who know the Lord, I speak,
  Is my beloved near?
The bridegroom of my soul I seek,
  Oh! when will he appear?

Though once a man of grief and shame,
  Yet now he fills a throne,
And bears the greatest, sweetest name,
  That earth or heaven have known.

Grace flies before, and love attends
  His steps where'er he goes;
Though none can see him but his friends
  And they were once his foes.

He speaks—obedient to his call
  Our warm affections move:
Did he but shine alike on all,
  Then all alike would love.

Then love in every heart would reign,
  And war would cease to roar;
And cruel and blood-thirsty men
  Would thirst for blood no more.

Such Jesus is, and such his grace,
  Oh, may he shine on you!
And tell him, when you see his face,
  I long to see him too.†

* Psalm cxxx. 6. † Cant. v. 8

XXXIV. LIGHT SHINING OUT OF DARKNESS.

God moves in a mysterious way
His wonders to perform;
He plants his footsteps in the sea,
And rides upon the storm.

Deep in unfathomable minds
Of never-failing skill,
He treasures up his bright designs,
And works his sovereign will.

Ye fearful saints, fresh courage take,
The clouds ye so much dread
Are big with mercy, and shall break
In blessings on your head.

Judge not the Lord by feeble sense
But trust him for his grace:
Behind a frowning providence
He hides a smiling face.

His purposes will ripen fast,
Unfolding every hour;
The bud may have a bitter taste,
But sweet will be the flower.

Blind unbelief is sure to err,*
And scan his work in vain:
God is his own interpreter,
And he will make it plain.

XXXV. WELCOME CROSS.

'Tis my happiness below
Not to live without the cross,
But the Saviour's power to know,
Sanctifying every loss:

* John xiii. 7.

Trials must and will befall;
  But with humble faith to see
Love inscribed upon them all,
  This is happiness to me.

God in Israel sows the seeds
  Of affliction, pain, and toil;
These spring up and choke the weeds
  Which would else o'erspread the soil:
Trials make the promise sweet,
  Trials give new life to prayer;
Trials bring me to his feet,
  Lay me low, and keep me there.

Did I meet no trials here,
  No chastisement by the way:
Might I not, with reason, fear
  I should prove a cast-away?
Bastards may escape the rod,*
  Sunk in earthly vain delight;
But the true-born child of God
  Must not, would not, if he might.

XXXVI. AFFLICTIONS SANCTIFIED BY THE WORD.

O HOW I love thy holy word,
Thy gracious covenant, O Lord!
It guides me in the peaceful way;
I think upon it all the day.

What are the mines of shining wealth,
The strength of youth, the bloom of health!
What are all joys compared with those
Thine everlasting word bestows!

Long unafflicted, undismay'd,
In pleasure's path secure I stray'd;
Thou madest me feel thy chastening rod,†
And straight I turn'd unto my God.

* Hebrews xii. 8.   † Psalm cxix. 71.

What though it pierced my fainting heart,
I bless'd thine hand that caused the smart;
It taught my tears awhile to flow,
But saved me from eternal woe.

Oh! hadst thou left me unchastised
Thy precept I had still despised;
And still the snare in secret laid
Had my unwary feet betray'd.

I love thee, therefore, O my God,
And breathe towards thy dear abode;
Where, in thy presence fully blest,
Thy chosen saints for ever rest.

XXXVII. TEMPTATION.

The billows swell, the winds are high,
Clouds overcast my wintry sky;
Out of the depths to thee I call,—
My fears are great, my strength is small.

O Lord, the pilot's part perform,
And guard and guide me through the storm,
Defend me from each threatening ill,
Control the waves,—say, 'Peace, be still.'

Amidst the roaring of the sea
My soul still hangs her hope on thee;
Thy constant love, thy faithful care,
Is all that saves me from despair.

Dangers of every shape and name
Attend the followers of the Lamb,
Who leave the world's deceitful shore,
And leave it to return no more.

Though tempest-toss'd and half a wreck,
My Saviour through the floods I seek;
Let neither winds nor stormy main
Force back my shatter'd bark again.

XXXVIII. LOOKING UPWARDS IN A STORM

God of my life, to thee I call,
Afflicted at thy feet I fall;
When the great water-floods prevail,*
Leave not my trembling heart to fail!

Friend of the friendless and the faint!
Where should I lodge my deep complaint?
Where but with thee, whose open door
Invites the helpless and the poor!

Did ever mourner plead with thee,
And thou refuse that mourner's plea?
Does not the word still fix'd remain,
That none shall seek thy face in vain

That were a grief I could not bear,
Didst thou not hear and answer prayer;
But a prayer-hearing, answering God
Supports me under every load.

Fair is the lot that's cast for me;
I have an Advocate with thee;
They whom the world caresses most
Have no such privilege to boast.

Poor though I am, despised, forgot,†
Yet God, my God, forgets me not:
And he is safe, and must succeed,
For whom the Lord vouchsafes to plead.

XXXIX. THE VALLEY OF THE SHADOW OF DEATH.

My soul is sad, and much dismay'd,
  See, Lord, what legions of my foes,
With fierce Apollyon at their head,
  My heavenly pilgrimage oppose!

* Psalm lxix. 15. † Psalm xl. 17

See, from the ever-burning lake,
  How like a smoky cloud they rise!
With horrid blasts my soul they shake,
  With storms of blasphemies and lies.

Their fiery arrows reach the mark,*
  My throbbing heart with anguish tear;
Each lights upon a kindred spark,
  And finds abundant fuel there.

I hate the thought that wrongs the Lord;
  Oh! I would drive it from my breast,
With thy own sharp two-edged sword,
  Far as the east is from the west.

Come, then, and chase the cruel host,
  Heal the deep wounds I have received!
Nor let the powers of darkness boast,
  That I am foil'd, and thou art grieved!

XL. PEACE AFTER A STORM.

When darkness long has veil'd my mind,
  And smiling day once more appears;
Then, my Redeemer, then I find,
  The folly of my doubts and fears.

Straight I upbraid my wandering heart,
  And blush that I should ever be
Thus prone to act so base a part,
  Or harbour one hard thought of thee!

Oh! let me then at length be taught
  What I am still so slow to learn;
That God is love, and changes not,
  Nor knows the shadow of a turn.

Sweet truth, and easy to repeat!
  But when my faith is sharply tried,
I find myself a learner yet,
  Unskilful, weak, and apt to slide.

* Ephes. vi. 16.

But, O my Lord, one look from thee
Subdues the disobedient will;
Drives doubt and discontent away,
And thy rebellious worm is still.

Thou art as ready to forgive
As I am ready to repine;
Thou, therefore, all the praise receive;
Be shame and self-abhorrence mine.

XLI. MOURNING AND LONGING.

The Saviour hides his face!
My spirit thirsts to prove
Renew'd supplies of pardoning grace,
And never-fading love.

The favoured souls who know
What glories shine in him,
Pant for his presence as the roe
Pants for the living stream!

What trifles tease me now!
They swarm like summer flies
They cleave to every thing I do,
And swim before my eyes.

How dull the Sabbath day,
Without the Sabbath's Lord!
How toilsome then to sing and pray,
And wait upon the word!

Of all the truths I hear,
How few delight my taste!
I glean a berry here and there,
But mourn the vintage past.

Yet let me (as I ought)
Still hope to be supplied;
No pleasure else is worth a thought,
Nor shall I be denied.

Though I am but a worm
 Unworthy of his care,
The Lord will my desire perform,
 And grant me all my prayer.

XLII. SELF-ACQUAINTANCE.

Dear Lord! accept a sinful heart,
 Which of itself complains,
And mourns, with much an frequent smart,
 The evil it contains.

There fiery seeds of anger lurk,
 Which often hurt my frame;
And wait but for the tempter's work,
 To fan them to a flame.

Legality holds out a bribe
 To purchase life from thee;
And discontent would fain prescribe
 How thou shalt deal with me.

While unbelief withstands thy grace
 And puts the mercy by;
Presumption, with a brow of brass,
 Says, 'Give me, or I die.'

How eager are my thoughts to roam
 In quest of what they love!
But ah! when duty calls them home,
 How heavily they move!

Oh, cleanse me in a Saviour's blood,
 Transform me by thy power,
And make me thy beloved abode,
 And let me roam no more.

XLIII. PRAYER FOR PATIENCE.

Lord, who hast suffer'd all for me,
  My peace and pardon to procure,
The lighter cross I bear for thee,
  Help me with patience to endure.

The storm of loud repining hush,
  I would in humble silence mourn;
Why should th' unburnt, though burning bush,
  Be angry as the crackling thorn?

Man should not faint at thy rebuke,
  Like Joshua falling on his face,*
When the cursed thing that Achan took
  Brought Israel into just disgrace.

Perhaps some golden wedge suppress'd,
  Some secret sin offends my God;
Perhaps that Babylonish vest,
  Self-righteousness, provokes the rod.

Ah! were I buffeted all day,
  Mock'd, crown'd with thorns, and spit upon;
I yet should have no right to say,
  My great distress is mine alone.

Let me not angrily declare
  No pain was ever sharp like mine,
Nor murmur at the cross I bear,
  But rather weep, remembering thine.

XLIV. SUBMISSION.

O Lord, my best desire fulfil,
  And help me to resign
Life, health, and comfort to thy will,
  And make thy pleasure mine.

* Joshua vii. 10, 11.

Why should I shrink at thy command,
  Whose love forbids my fears?
Or tremble at the gracious hand
  That wipes away my tears?

No, rather let me freely yield
  What most I prize to thee;
Who never hast a good withheld,
  Or wilt withhold from me.

Thy favour, all my journey through,
  Thou art engaged to grant;
What else I want, or think I do,
  'Tis better still to want.

Wisdom and mercy guide my way,
  Shall I resist them both?
A poor blind creature of a day,
  And crush'd before the moth!

But ah! my inward spirit cries,
  Still bind me to thy sway;
Else the next cloud that veils the skies,
  Drives all these thoughts away.

XLV. THE HAPPY CHANGE.

How blest thy creature is, O God,
  When, with a single eye,
He views the lustre of thy word
  The dayspring from on high!

Through all the storms that veil the skies,
  And frown on earthly things,
The Son of Righteousness he eyes,
  With healing on his wings.

Struck by that light, the human heart,
  A barren soil no more,
Sends the sweet smell of grace abroad
  Where serpents lurk'd before.*

* Isaiah xxxv. 7.

The soul a dreary province once
  Of Satan's dark domain,
Feels a new empire form'd within,
  And owns a heavenly reign.

The glorious orb, whose golden beams
  The fruitful year control,
Since first obedient to thy word,
  He started from the goal,

Has cheer'd the nations with the joys
  His orient rays impart;
But, Jesus, 'tis thy light alone
  Can shine upon the heart.

XLVI. RETIREMENT.

Far from the world, O Lord, I flee
  From strife and tumult far;
From scenes were Satan wages still
  His most successful war.

The calm retreat, the silent shade,
  With prayer and praise agree;
And seem, by thy sweet bounty made
  For those who follow thee.

There if thy Spirit touch the soul,
  And grace her mean abode,
Oh, with what peace, and joy, and love,
  She communes with her God!

There like the nightingale she pours
  Her solitary lays;
Nor asks a witness of her song,
  Nor thirsts for human praise.

Author and guardian of my life,
  Sweet source of light divine,
And (all harmonious names in one)
  My Saviour, thou art mine!

What thanks I owe thee, and what love,
  A boundless, endless store,
Shall echo through the realms above
  When time shall be no more.

XLVII. THE HIDDEN LIFE.

To tell the Saviour all my wants,
  How pleasing is the task!
Nor less to praise him when he grants
  Beyond what I can ask.

My labouring spirit vainly seeks
  To tell but half the joy;
With how much tenderness he speaks,
  And helps me to reply.

Nor were it wise, nor should I choose,
  Such secrets to declare;
Like precious wines their taste they lose,
  Exposed to open air.

But this with boldness I proclaim,
  Nor care if thousands hear,
Sweet is the ointment of his name,
  Not life is half so dear.

And can you frown, my former friends,
  Who knew what once I was;
And blame the song that thus commends
  The man who bore the cross?

Trust me, I draw the likeness true,
  And not as fancy paints;
Such honour may he give to you,
  For such have all his saints.

XLVIII JOY AND PEACE IN BELIEVING.

Sometimes a light surprises
  The Christian while he sings;
It is the Lord who rises
  With healing on his wings:
When comforts are declining
  He grants the soul again
A season of clear shining,
  To cheer it after rain.

In holy contemplation,
  We sweetly then pursue
The theme of God's salvation,
  And find it ever new;
Set free from present sorrow,
  We cheerfully can say,
E'en let th' unknown to-morrow*
  Bring with it what it may.

It can bring with it nothing,
  But he will bear us through;
Who gives the lilies clothing,
  Will clothe his people too;
Beneath the spreading heavens,
  No creature but is fed;
And he who feeds the ravens,
  Will give his children bread.

Though vine nor fig-tree neither†
  Their wonted fruit shall bear,
Though all the field should wither,
  Nor flocks nor herds be there:
Yet God the same abiding,
  His praise shall tune my voice;
For, while in him confiding
  I cannot but rejoice.

* Matthew vi. 34. † Habakkuk iii. 17, 18.

XLIX. TRUE PLEASURES.

LORD, my soul with pleasure springs
  When Jesus' name I hear;
And when God the Spirit brings
  The word of promise near:
Beauties too, in holiness,
  Still delighted I perceive;
Nor have words that can express
  The joys thy precepts give.

Cloth'd in sanctity and grace,
  How sweet it is to see
Those who love thee as they pass,
  Or when they wait on thee!
Pleasant too, to sit and tell
  What we owe to love divine;
Till our bosoms grateful swell,
  And eyes begin to shine.

Those the comforts I possess,
  Which God shall still increase,
All his ways are pleasantness,*
  And all his paths are peace.
Nothing Jesus did or spoke,
  Henceforth let me ever slight;
For I love his easy yoke,†
  And find his burden light.

L. THE CHRISTIAN.

HONOUR and happiness unite
  To make the Christian's name a praise;
How fair the scene, how clear the light,
  That fills the remnant of his days!

A kingly character he bears,
  No change his priestly office knows;
Unfading is the crown he wears,
  His joys can never reach a close.

* Prov. iii. 17. † Matt. xi. 30.

Adorn'd with glory from on high,
  Salvation shines upon his face;
His robe is of th' ethereal dye,
  His steps are dignity and grace.

Inferior honours he disdains,
  Nor stoops to take applause from earth;
The King of kings himself maintains
  The expenses of his heavenly birth.

The noblest creature seen below,
  Ordain'd to fill a throne above;
God gives him all he can bestow,
  His kingdom of eternal love!

My soul is ravish'd at the thought!
  Methinks from earth I see him rise!
Angels congratulate his lot,
  And shout him welcome to the skies!

LI. LIVELY HOPE AND GRACIOUS FEAR.

I WAS a groveling creature once,
  And basely cleaved to earth;
I wanted spirit to renounce
  The clod that gave me birth.

But God has breath'd upon a worm,
  And sent me from above
Wings such as clothe an angel's form,
  The wings of joy and love.

With these to Pisgah's top I fly,
  And there delighted stand,
To view beneath a shining sky
  The spacious promised land.

The Lord of all the vast domain
  Has promised it to me;
The length and breadth of all the plain
  As far as faith can see

How glorious is my privilege!
  To thee for help I call;
I stand upon a mountain's edge,
  Oh save me, lest I fall!

Though much exalted in the Lord,
  My strength is not my own;
Then let me tremble at his word,
  And none shall cast me down.

LII. FOR THE POOR.

When Hagar found the bottle spent
  And wept o'er Ishmael,
A message from the Lord was sent
  To guide her to a well.*

Should not Elijah's cake and cruse†
  Convince us at this day,
A gracious God will not refuse
  Provisions by the way?

His saints and servants shall be fed,
  The promise is secure;
'Bread shall be given them,' as he said,
  'Their water shall be sure.'‡

Repasts far richer they shall prove,
  Than all earth's dainties are;
'Tis sweet to taste a Saviour's love,
  Though in the meanest fare.

To Jesus then your trouble bring,
  Nor murmur at your lot;
While you are poor and he is King,
  You shall not be forgot.

* Gen. xxi. 19. † 1 Kings xvii. 14. ‡ Isa. xxxiii. 16.

LIII. MY SOUL THIRSTETH FOR GOD.

I THIRST, but not as once I did
  The vain delights of earth to share;
Thy wounds, Emmanuel, all forbid
  That I should seek my pleasures there.

It was the sight of thy dear cross
  First wean'd my soul from earthly things;
And taught me to esteem as dross
  The mirth of fools and pomp of kings.

I want that grace that springs from thee,
  That quickens all things where it flows,
And makes a wretched thorn like me
  Bloom as the myrtle, or the rose.

Dear fountain of delight unknown!
  No longer sink below the brim;
But overflow, and pour me down
  A living, and life-giving stream!

For sure, of all the plants that share
  The notice of thy Father's eye,
None proves less grateful to his care
  Or yields him meaner fruit than I.

LIV. LOVE CONSTRAINING TO OBEDIENCE.

No strength of nature can suffice
  To serve the Lord aright:
And what she has she misapplies,
  For want of clearer light.

How long beneath the law I lay
  In bondage and distress;
I toil'd the precept to obey,
  But toil'd without success.

Then, to abstain from outward sin
  Was more than I could do;
Now, if I feel its power within,
  I feel I hate it too.

Then all my servile works were done
  A righteousness to raise;
Now, freely chosen in the Son,
  I freely choose his ways.

'What shall I do,' was then the word,
  'That I may worthier grow?'
'What shall I render to the Lord?'
  Is my inquiry now.

To see the law by Christ fulfill'd,
  And hear his pardoning voice,
Changes a slave into a child,*
  And duty into choice.

---

17. THE HEART HEALED AND CHANGED BY MERCY.

Sin enslaved me many years,
  And led me bound and blind;
Till at length a thousand fears
  Came swarming o'er my mind.
'Where,' said I, in deep distress,
  'Will these sinful pleasures end?
How shall I secure my peace,
  And make the Lord my friend?

Friends and ministers said much
  The gospel to enforce;
But my blindness still was such,
  I chose a legal course:
Much I fasted, watch'd, and strove,
  Scarce would show my face abroad,
Fear'd almost to speak or move,
  A stranger still to God.

* Romans iii. 31.

Thus afraid to trust his grace,
  Long time did I rebel;
Till despairing of my case,
  Down at his feet I fell:
Then my stubborn heart he broke
  And subdued me to his sway;
By a simple word he spoke,
  'Thy sins are done away.'

LVI. HATRED OF SIN.

Holy Lord God! I love thy truth,
  Nor dare thy least commandment slight;
Yet pierced by sin, the serpent's tooth,
  I mourn the anguish of the bite.

But though the poison lurks within,
  Hope bids me still with patience wait;
Till death shall set me free from sin,
  Free from the only thing I hate.

Had I a throne above the rest,
  Where angels and archangels dwell,
One sin, unslain, within my breast,
  Would make that heaven as dark as hell.

The prisoner sent to breathe fresh air,
  And bless'd with liberty again,
Would mourn, were he condemn'd to wear
  One link of all his former chain.

But, oh, no foe invades the bliss,
  When glory crowns the Christian's head;
One view of Jesus as he is
  Will strike all sin for ever dead.

LVII. THE NEW CONVERT.

The new-born child of gospel grace,
  Like some fair tree when summer's nigh,
Beneath Emmanuel's shining face
  Lifts up his blooming branch on high.

No fears he feels, he sees no foes,
  No conflict yet his faith employs,
Nor has he learnt to whom he owes
  The strength and peace his soul enjoys.

But sin soon darts its cruel sting,
  And comforts sinking day by day:
What seem'd his own, a self-fed spring,
  Proves but a brook that glides away.

When Gideon arm'd his numerous host,
  The Lord soon made his numbers less,
And said, 'Lest Israel vainly boast,*
  "My arm procured me this success."'

Thus will he bring our spirits down
  And draw our ebbing comforts low,
That saved by grace, but not our own,
  We may not claim the praise we owe.

LVIII. TRUE AND FALSE COMFORTS

O God, whose favourable eye
  The sin sick soul revives,
Holy and heavenly is the joy
  Thy shining presence gives.

Not such as hypocrites suppose,
  Who with a graceless heart
Taste not of thee, but drink a dose,
  Prepared by Satan's art.

Intoxicating joys are theirs,
  Who, while they boast their light,
And seem to soar above the stars,
  Are plunging into night.

Lull'd in a soft and fatal sleep,
  They sin and yet rejoice;
Were they indeed the Saviour's sheep
  Would they not hear his voice?

* Judges vii. 2.

Be mine the comforts that reclaim
The soul from Satan's power;
That make me blush for what I am,
And hate my sin the more.

'Tis joy enough, my All in All,
At thy dear feet to lie;
Thou wilt not let me lower fall,
And none can higher fly.

LIX. A LIVING AND A DEAD FAITH.

The Lord receives his highest praise
From humble minds and hearts sincere;
While all the loud professor says
Offends the righteous Judge's ear.

To walk as children of the day,
To mark the precepts' holy light,
To wage the warfare, watch, and pray,
Show who are pleasing in his sight.

Not words alone it cost the Lord,
To purchase pardon for his own;
Nor will a soul by grace restored
Return the Saviour words alone.

With golden bells, the priestly vest,
And rich pomegranates border'd round,*
The need of holiness express'd,
And call'd for fruit as well as sound.

Easy, indeed, it were to reach
A mansion in the courts above,
If swelling words and fluent speech
Might serve instead of faith and love

But none shall gain the blissful place,
Or God's unclouded glory see,
Who talks of free and sovereign grace,
Unless that grace has made him free!

* Exod. xxviii. 33.

LX. ABUSE OF THE GOSPEL.

Too many, Lord, abuse thy grace
  In this licentious day;
And while they boast they see thy face,
  They turn their own away.

Thy book displays a gracious light
  That can the blind restore;
But these are dazzled by the sight,
  And blinded still the more.

The pardon such presume upon,
  They do not beg, but steal;
And when they plead it at thy throne,
  Oh! where's the Spirit's seal?

Was it for this, ye lawless tribe,
  The dear Redeemer bled?
Is this the grace the saints imbibe
  From Christ the living head?

Ah, Lord, we know thy chosen few
  Are fed with heavenly fare;
But these, the wretched husks they chew
  Proclaim them what they are.

The liberty our hearts implore
  Is not to live in sin;
But still to wait at wisdom's door,
  Till mercy calls us in.

LXI. THE NARROW WAY.

What thousands never knew the road!
  What thousands hate it when 'tis known!
None but the chosen tribes of God
  Will seek or choose it for their own.

A thousand ways in ruin end,
  One only leads to joys on high;
By that my willing steps ascend,
  Pleased with a journey to the sky.

No more I ask or hope to find
  Delight or happiness below;
Sorrow may well possess the mind
  That feeds where thorns and thistles grow.

The joy that fades is not for me,
  I seek immortal joys above;
There glory without end shall be
  The bright reward of faith and love.

Cleave to the world, ye sordid worms,
  Contented lick your native dust;
But God shall fight, with all his storms,
  Against the idol of your trust.

LXII. DEPENDENCE.

To keep the lamp alive,
  With oil we fill the bowl;
'Tis water makes the willow thrive,
  And grace that feeds the soul.

The Lord's unsparing hand
  Supplies the living stream;
It is not at our own command,
  But still derived from him.

Beware of Peter's word,*
  Nor confidently say,
'I never will deny thee, Lord,'
  But, 'Grant I never may.'

Man's wisdom is to seek
  His strength in God alone;
And e'en an angel would be weak,
  Who trusted in his own.

Retreat beneath his wings,
  And in his grace confide;
This more exalts the King of kings†
  Than all your works beside.

In Jesus is our store,
  Grace issues from his throne;
Whoever says, 'I want no more,'
  Confesses he has none.

* Matthew xxvi. 33. † John vi. 29.

LXIII. NOT OF WORKS.

GRACE, triumphant in the throne,
Scorns a rival, reigns alone;
Come and bow beneath her sway,
Cast your idol works away.
Works of man, when made his plea,
Never shall accepted be;
Fruits of pride (vain-glorious worm!)
Are the best he can perform.

Self, the god his soul adores,
Influences all his powers;
Jesus is a slighted name,
Self-advancement all his aim:
But when God the Judge shall come,
To pronounce the final doom,
Then for rocks and hills to hide
All his works and all his pride!

Still the boasting heart replies,
What! the worthy and the wise,
Friends to temperance and peace,
Have not these a righteousness?
Banish every vain pretence
Built on human excellence;
Perish every thing in man,
But the grace that never can.

LXIV. PRAISE FOR FAITH.

OF all the gifts thine hand bestows,
Thou Giver of all good!
Not heaven itself a richer knows
Than my Redeemer's blood.

Faith too, the blood-receiving grace,
From the same hand we gain;
Else, sweetly as it suits our case,
That gift had been in vain.

Till thou thy teaching power apply,
Our hearts refuse to see,
And weak, as a distemper'd eye,
Shut out the view of thee.

Blind to the merits of thy Son,
What misery we endure!
Yet fly that hand from which alone
We could expect a cure.

We praise thee, and would praise thee more,
  To thee our all we owe;
The precious Saviour, and the power
  That makes him precious too.

LXV. GRACE AND PROVIDENCE.

Almighty King! whose wondrous hand
Supports the weight of sea and land,
Whose grace is such a boundless store,
No heart shall break that sighs for more

Thy providence supplies my food,
And 'tis thy blessing makes it good;
My soul is nourish'd by thy word,
Let soul and body praise the Lord.

My streams of outward comfort came
From him who built this earthly frame;
Whate'er I want his bounty gives,
By whom my soul for ever lives.

Either his hand preserves from pain,
Or, if I feel it, heals again;
From Satan's malice shields my breast,
Or overrules it for the best.

Forgive the song that falls so low,
Beneath the gratitude I owe;
It means thy praise, however poor,
An angel's song can do no more.

LXVI. I WILL PRAISE THE LORD AT ALL TIMES.

Winter has a joy for me,
  While the Saviour's charms I read,
Lowly, meek, from blemish free,
  In the snowdrop's pensive head.

Spring returns, and brings alone
  Life-invigorating suns:
Hark! the turtle's plaintive song
  Seems to speak his dying groans!

Summer has a thousand charms,
  All expressive of his worth;
'Tis his sun that lights and warms,
  His the air that cools the earth.

What! has Autumn left to say
  Nothing of a Saviour's grace?
Yes, the beams of milder day
  Tell me of his smiling face.

Light appears with early dawn,
  While the sun makes haste to rise;
See his bleeding beauties drawn
  On the blushes of the skies.

Evening with a silent pace,
  Slowly moving in the west,
Shows an emblem of his grace—
  Points to an eternal rest.

LXVII. THE WAITING SOUL.

Breathe from the gentle south, O Lord,
  And cheer me from the north;
Blow on the treasures of thy word,
  And call the spices forth!

I wish, thou know'st, to be resign'd,
  And wait with patient hope;
But hope delay'd fatigues the mind,
  And drinks the spirits up.

Help me to reach the distant goal,
  Confirm my feeble knee,
Pity the sickness of a soul
  That faints for love of thee.

Cold as I feel this heart of mine,
  Yet since I *feel* it so,
It yields some hope of life divine
  Within, however low.

I seem forsaken and alone;
  I hear the lion roar;
And every door is shut but one,
  And that is mercy's door.

There, till the dear Deliv'rer come,
  I'll wait with humble pray'r;
And when he calls his exile home,
  The Lord shall find him there.

FRAGMENT OF A HYMN.

To Jesus, the Crown of my Hope,
  My soul is in haste to begone;
O bear me, ye cherubims, up,
  And waft me away to his throne!

My Saviour, whom absent I love,
  Whom not having seen I adore;
Whose name is exalted above
  All glory dominion, and power—

TRANSLATIONS FROM THE FRENCH

OF

MADAME DE LA MOTHE GUION.

THE NATIVITY

'Tis folly all—let me no more be told
Of Parian porticos, and roofs of gold;
Delightful views of nature, dress'd by art,
Enchant no longer this indifferent heart;
The Lord of all things, in his humble birth,
Makes mean the proud magnificence of earth;
The straw, the manger, and the mouldering wall,
Eclipse its lustre; and I scorn it all.
  Canals, and fountains, and delicious vales,
Green slopes and plains, whose plenty never fails;
Deep-rooted groves, whose heads sublimely rise,
Earth-born, and yet ambitious of the skies;
The abundant foliage of whose gloomy shades,
Vainly the sun in all its power invades;
Where warbled airs of sprightly birds resound,
Whose verdure lives while Winter scowls around;
Rocks, lofty mountains, caverns dark and deep,
And torrents raving down the rugged steep;
Smooth downs, whose fragrant herbs the spirits cheer;
Meads crown'd with flowers; streams musical and clear
Whose silver waters, and whose murmurs, join
Their artless charms, to make the scene divine;
The fruitful vineyard, and the furrow'd plain,
That seems a rolling sea of golden grain:
All, all have lost the charms they once possess'd;
An infant God reigns sovereign in my breast;
From Bethlehem's bosom I no more will rove;
There dwells the Saviour, and there rests my love.
  Ye mightier rivers, that, with sounding force,
Urge down the valleys your impetuous course!

Winds, clouds and lightnings! and, ye waves whose
heads,
Curl'd into monstrous forms, the seaman dreads!
Horrid abyss, where all experience fails,
Spread with the wreck of planks and shatter'd sails;
On whose broad back grim Death triumphant rides,
While havoc floats on all thy swelling tides,
Thy shores a scene of ruin, strew'd around
With vessels bulged, and bodies of the drown'd!
Ye fish, that sport beneath the boundless waves,
And rest, secure from man, in rocky caves;
Swift-darting sharks, and whales of hideous size,
Whom all the aquatic world with terror eyes!
Had I but faith immoveable and true,
I might defy the fiercest storm, like you:
The world, a more disturb'd and boisterous sea
When Jesus shows a smile, affrights not me;
He hides me, and in vain the billows roar,
Break harmless at my feet, and leave the shore.
Thou azure vault, where through the gloom of
night,
Thick sown, we see such countless worlds of light!
Thou moon, whose car, encompassing the skies,
Restores lost nature to our wondering eyes;
Again retiring, when the brighter sun
Begins the course he seems in haste to run!
Behold him where he shines! His rapid rays,
Themselves unmeasured, measure all our days·
Nothing impedes the race he would pursue,
Nothing escapes his penetrating view,
A thousand lands confess his quickening heat
And all he cheers are fruitful, fair, and sweet.
Far from enjoying what these scenes disclose,
I feel the thorn, alas! but miss the rose:
Too well I know this aching heart requires
More solid good to fill its vast desires;
In vain they represent his matchless might,
Who call'd them out of deep primeval night;
Their form and beauty but augment my woe:
I seek the Giver of those charms they show:
Nor, Him beside, throughout the world he made,
Lives there in whom I trust for cure or aid.

Infinite God, thou great unrival'd ONE!
Whose glory makes a blot of yonder sun;
Compared with thine, how dim his beauty seems,
How quench'd the radiance of his golden beams!
Thou art my bliss, the light by which I move;
In thee alone dwells all that I can love;
All darkness flies when thou art pleased to appear,
A sudden spring renews the fading year;
Where'er I turn I see thy power and grace,
The watchful guardians of our heedless race;
Thy various creatures in one strain agree,
All, in all times and places, speak of thee;
E'en I, with trembling heart and stammering tongue
Attempt thy praise, and join the general song.
Almighty Former of this wondrous plan,
Faintly reflected in thine image, man—
Holy and just—the greatness of whose name
Fills and supports this universal frame,
Diffused throughout the infinitude of space,
Who art thyself thine own vast dwelling-place:
Soul of our soul, whom yet no sense of ours
Discerns, eluding our most active powers;
Encircling shades attend thine awful throne,
That veil thy face, and keep thee still unknown
Unknown though dwelling in our inmost part,
Lord of the thoughts, and Sovereign of the heart!
Repeat the charming truth, that never tires,
No God is like the God my soul desires;
He at whose voice heaven trembles, even He,
Great as he is, knows how to stoop to me—
Lo! there he lies—that smiling infant said,
'Heaven, earth, and sea, exist!'—and they obey'd.
E'en He, whose being swells beyond the skies,
Is born of woman, lives, and mourns, and dies;
Eternal and immortal, seems to cast
That glory from his brows, and breathes his last.
Trivial and vain the works that man has wrought,
How do they shrink and vanish at the thought!
Sweet solitude, and scene of my repose!
This rustic sight assuages all my woes—
That crib contains the Lord, whom I adore;
And earth's a shade, that I pursue no more.

He is my firm support, my rock, my tower,
I dwell secure beneath his sheltering power,
And hold this mean retreat for ever dear
For all I love, my soul's delight, is here.
I see the Almighty swath'd in infant bands,
Tied helpless down the thunder-bearer's hands!
And, in this shed, that mystery discern,
Which faith and love, and they alone, can learn.
Ye tempests, spare the slumbers of your Lord!
Ye zephyrs, all your whisper'd sweets afford!
Confess the God, that guides the rolling year;
Heaven do him homage; and thou, earth, revere!
Ye shepherds, monarchs, sages, hither bring
Your hearts an offering, and adore your King!
Pure be those hearts, and rich in faith and love
Join in his praise, the harmonious world above;
To Bethlehem haste, rejoice in his repose,
And praise him there for all that he bestows!
Man, busy man, alas! can ill afford
To obey the summons, and attend the Lord;
Perverted reason revels and runs wild,
By glittering shows of pomp and wealth beguiled;
And, blind to genuine excellence and grace,
Finds not her author in so mean a place.
Ye unbelieving! learn a wiser part,
Distrust your erring sense, and search your heart;
There, soon ye shall perceive a kindling flame
Glow for that infant God, from whom it came;
Resist not, quench not, that divine desire
Melt all your adamant in heavenly fire!
Not so will I requite thee, gentle love!
Yielding and soft this heart shall ever prove;
And every heart beneath thy power should fall,
Glad to submit could mine contain them all.
But I am poor, oblation I have none,
None for a Saviour, but himself alone:
Whate'er I render thee, from thee it came;
And, if I give my body to the flame,
My patience, love, and energy divine
Of heart, and soul, and spirit, all are thine.
Ah, vain attempt to expunge the mighty score!
The more I pay, I owe thee still the more.

Upon my meanness, poverty, and guilt,
The trophy of thy glory shall be built;
My self-disdain shall be the unshaken base,
And my deformity its fairest grace;
For destitute of good, and rich in ill,
Must be my state and my description still.
And do I grieve at such an humbling lot?
Nay, but I cherish and enjoy the thought—
Vain pageantry and pomp of earth, adieu!
I have no wish, no memory for you;
The more I feel my misery, I adore
The sacred inmate of my soul the more;
Rich in his love, I feel my noblest pride
Spring from the sense of having nought beside.
In Thee I find wealth, comfort, virtue, might;
My wanderings prove thy wisdom infinite;
All that I have I give thee; and then see
All contrarieties unite in thee;
For thou hast join'd them, taking up our woe,
And pouring out thy bliss on worms below
By filling with thy grace and love divine
A gulf of evil in this heart of mine.
This is, indeed, to bid the valleys rise,
And the hills sink—'tis matching earth and skies,
I feel my weakness, thank thee, and deplore
An aching heart, that throbs to thank thee more;
The more I love thee, I the more reprove
A soul so lifeless, and so slow to love;
Till, on a deluge of thy mercy toss'd,
I plunge into that sea, and there am lost.

GOD NEITHER KNOWN NOR LOVED BY THE WORLD.

Ye linnets, let us try, beneath this grove,
Which shall be loudest in our Maker's praise!
In quest of some forlorn retreat I rove,
For all the world is blind and wanders from his ways.

That God alone should prop the sinking soul,
Fills them with rage against his empire now:
I traverse earth in vain from pole to pole,
To seek one simple heart set free from all below.

They speak of love, yet little feel its sway,
While in their bosoms many an idol lurks;
Their base desires, well satisfied, obey,
Leave the Creator's hand, and lean upon his works.

'Tis therefore I can dwell with man no more;
Your fellowship, ye warblers! suits me best:
Pure love has lost its price, though prized of yore,
Profaned by modern tongues, and slighted as a jest.

My God, who form'd you for his praise alone,
Beholds his purpose well fulfill'd in you;
Come, let us join the choir before his throne,
Partaking in his praise with spirits just and true!

Yes, I will always love; and, as I ought,
Tune to the praise of love my ceaseless voice;
Preferring love too vast for human thought,
In spite of erring men, who cavil at my choice.

Why have I not a thousand thousand hearts,
Lord of my soul! that they might all be thine?
If thou approve—the zeal thy smile imparts,
How should it ever fail! can such a fire decline?

Love, pure and holy, is a deathless fire;
Its object heavenly, it must ever blaze
Eternal love a God must needs inspire,
When once he wins the heart, and fits it for his praise.

Self-love dismiss'd—'tis then we live indeed—
In her embrace, death, only death is found:
Come, then, one noble effort, and succeed,
Cast off the chain of self with which thy soul is bound!

Oh! I could cry, that all the world might hear,
Ye self-tormentors, love your God alone:
Let his unequal'd excellence be dear,
Dear to your inmost souls, and make him all your own!

They hear me not—alas! how fond to rove
In endless chase of folly's specious lure!
'Tis here alone, beneath this shady grove,
I taste the sweets of truth—here only am secure

THE SWALLOW.

I AM fond of the swallow—I learn from her flight,
Had I skill to improve it, a lesson of love:
How seldom on earth do we see her alight!
She dwells in the skies, she is ever above.

It is on the wing that she takes her repose,
Suspended and poised in the regions of air,
'Tis not in our fields that her sustenance grows,
It is wing'd like herself, 'tis ethereal fare.

She comes in the spring, all the summer she stays,
And, dreading the cold, still follows the sun—
So, true to our love, we should covet his rays,
And the place where he shines not, immediately shun

Our light should be love, and our nourishment prayer;
It is dangerous food that we find upon earth;
The fruit of this world is beset with a snare,
In itself it is hurtful, as vile in its birth.

'Tis rarely, if ever, she settles below,
And only when building a nest for her young;
Were it not for her brood, she would never bestow
A thought upon any thing filthy as dung.

Let us leave it ourselves ('tis a mortal abode),
To bask every moment in infinite love;
Let us fly the dark winter, and follow the road
That leads to the dayspring appearing above.

THE TRIUMPH OF HEAVENLY LOVE DESIRED.

Ah! reign, wherever man is found,
  My spouse, beloved and divine!
Then I am rich, and I abound,
  When every human heart is thine.

A thousand sorrows pierce my soul,
  To think that all are not thine own:
Ah! be adored from pole to pole;
  Where is thy zeal? arise; be known!

All hearts are cold, in every place,
  Yet earthly good with warmth pursue;
Dissolve them with a flash of grace,
  Thaw these of ice, and give us new!

A FIGURATIVE DESCRIPTION OF THE PROCEDURE OF DIVINE LOVE,

IN BRINGING A SOUL TO THE POINT OF SELF-RENUNCIATION AND ABSOLUTE ACQUIESCENCE.

'Twas my purpose, on a day,
To embark, and sail away;
As I climb'd the vessel's side,
Love was sporting in the tide;
'Come,' he said,—'ascend—make haste,
Launch into the boundless waste.'

Many mariners were there,
Having each his separate care;
They that row'd us held their eyes
Fix'd upon the starry skies;
Others steer'd, or turn'd the sails
To receive the shifting gales.

Love, with power divine supplied,
Suddenly my courage tried;
In a moment it was night,
Ship and skies were out of sight;
On the briny wave I lay,
Floating rushes all my stay.

Did I with resentment burn
At this unexpected turn?
Did I wish myself on shore,
Never to forsake it more?
No—'My soul,' I cried, 'be still;
If I must be lost, I will.'

Next he hasten'd to convey
Both my frail supports away;
Seized my rushes; bade the waves
Yawn into a thousand graves:
Down I went, and sunk as lead,
Ocean closing o'er my head.

Still, however, life was safe;
And I saw him turn and laugh:
'Friend,' he cried, 'adieu! lie low,
While the wintry storms shall blow;
When the spring has calm'd the main,
You shall rise and float again.'

Soon I saw him, with dismay,
Spread his plumes, and soar away;
Now I mark his rapid flight;
Now he leaves my aching sight;
He is gone whom I adore,
'Tis in vain to seek him more.

How I trembled then and fear'd,
When my love had disappear'd!
'Wilt thou leave me thus,' I cried,
'Whelm'd beneath the rolling tide?'
Vain attempt to reach his ear!
Love was gone, and would not hear.

Ah! return, and love me still;
See me subject to thy will;
Frown with wrath, or smile with grace,
Only let me see thy face!
Evil I have none to fear,
All is good, if thou art near.

Yet he leaves me—cruel fate!
Leaves me in my lost estate—
Have I sinn'd? Oh say wherein;
Tell me, and forgive my sin!
King, and Lord, whom I adore,
Shall I see thy face no more?

Be not angry; I resign,
Henceforth, all my will to thine:
I consent that thou depart,
Though thine absence breaks my heart
Go, then, and for ever too;
All is right that thou wilt do.

This was just what love intended,
He was now no more offended;
Soon as I became a child,
Love return'd to me and smiled:
Never strife shall more betide
'Twixt the bridegroom and his bride.

A CHILD OF GOD LONGING TO SEE HIM BELOVED.

There's not an echo round me,
  But I am glad should learn,
How pure a fire has found me—,
  The love with which I burn.
For none attends with pleasure
  To what I would reveal;
They slight me out of measure,
  And laugh at all I feel.

The rocks receive less proudly
  The story of my flame;
When I approach, they loudly
  Reverberate his name.
I speak to them of sadness,
  And comforts at a stand;
They bid me look for gladness,
  And better days at hand

Far from all habitation,
  I heard a happy sound;
Big with the consolation,
  That I have often found;
I said, 'My lot is sorrow,
  My grief has no alloy;'
The rocks replied—'To-morrow,
  To-morrow brings thee joy.'

These sweet and secret tidings
  What bliss it is to hear!
For, spite of all my chidings,
  My weakness and my fear,
No sooner I receive them,
  Than I forget my pain,
And, happy to believe them,
  I love as much again.

I fly to scenes romantic,
  Where never men resort;
For in an age so frantic
  Impiety is sport.
For riot and confusion
  They barter things above;
Condemning, as delusion,
  The joy of perfect love.

In this sequester'd corner,
  None hears what I express;
Deliver'd from the scorner,
  What peace do I possess!
Beneath the boughs reclining,
  Or roving o'er the wild,
I live, as undesigning,
  And harmless as a child.

No troubles here surprise me,
  I innocently play,
While Providence supplies me,
  And guards me all the day:
My dear and kind defender
  Preserves me safely here,
From men of pomp and splendour,
  Who fill a child with fear.

ASPIRATIONS OF THE SOUL AFTER GOD

My Spouse! in whose presence I live,
  Sole object of all my desires,
Who know'st what a flame I conceive,
  And can'st easily double its fires;
How pleasant is all that I meet!
  From fear of adversity free,
I find even sorrow made sweet;
  Because 'tis assign'd me by thee.

Transported I see thee display
  Thy riches and glory divine;
I have only my life to repay,
  Take what I would gladly resign.
Thy will is the treasure I seek,
  For thou art as faithful as strong;
There let me, obedient and meek,
  Repose myself all the day long.

My spirit and faculties fail;
  Oh finish what love has begun!
Destroy what is sinful and frail,
  And dwell in the soul thou hast won!
Dear theme of my wonder and praise,
  I cry, who is worthy as thou!
I can only be silent and gaze:
  'Tis all that is left to me now.

Oh glory in which I am lost,
  Too deep for the plummet of thought;
On an ocean of deity toss'd,
  I am swallow'd, I sink into nought.
Yet, lost and absorb'd as I seem,
  I chant to the praise of my King;
And, though overwhelm'd by the theme
  Am happy whenever I sing.

GRATITUDE AND LOVE TO GOD.

All are indebted much to thee,
  But I far more than all,
From many a deadly snare set free,
  And raised from many a fall.
Overwhelm me, from above,
Daily, with thy boundless love.

What bonds of gratitude I feel
  No language can declare;
Beneath the oppressive weight I reel,
  'Tis more than I can bear:
When shall I that blessing prove,
To return thee love for love?

Spirit of charity, dispense
  Thy grace to every heart;
Expel all other spirits thence,
  Drive self from every part;
Charity divine, draw nigh,
Break the chains in which we lie!

All selfish souls, whate'er they feign,
  Have still a slavish lot;
They boast of liberty in vain,
  Of love, and feel it not.
He whose bosom glows with thee
He, and he alone, is free.

Oh blessedness, all bliss above
  When thy pure fires prevail!
Love only teaches what is love;
  All other lessons fail:
We learn its name, but not its powers,
Experience only makes it ours.

HAPPY SOLITUDE—UNHAPPY MEN.

My heart is easy, and my burden light;
I smile, though sad, when thou art in my sight:
The more my woes in secret I deplore,
I taste thy goodness, and I love the more.

There, while a solemn stillness reigns around,
Faith, love, and hope within my soul abound;
And, while the world suppose me lost in care,
The joys of angels, unperceived, I share.

Thy creatures wrong thee, O thou sovereign good
Thou art not loved, because not understood;
This grieves me most, that vain pursuits beguile
Ungrateful men, regardless of thy smile.

Frail beauty and false honour are adored;
While Thee they scorn, and trifle with thy word;
Pass, unconcern'd, a Saviour's sorrows by;
And hunt their ruin with a zeal to die.

LIVING WATER.

The fountain in its source
  No drought of summer fears;
The farther it pursues its course,
  The nobler it appears.

But shallow cisterns yield
  A scanty short supply;
The morning sees them amply fill'd,
  At evening they are dry.

TRUTH AND DIVINE LOVE REJECTED BY THE WORLD.

O LOVE, of pure and heavenly birth!
O simple truth, scarce known on earth!
Whom men resist with stubborn will;
And, more perverse and daring still,
Smother and quench, with reasonings vain,
While error and deception reign.

Whence comes it, that, your power the same
As His on high, from whence you came,
Ye rarely find a listening ear,
Or heart that makes you welcome here?—
Because ye bring reproach and pain,
Where'er ye visit, in your train.

The world is proud, and cannot bear
The scorn and calumny ye share;
The praise of men the mark they mean,
They fly the place where ye are seen;
Pure love, with scandal in the rear,
Suits not the vain; it costs too dear

Then, let the price be what it may,
Though poor, I am prepared to pay;
Come shame, come sorrow; spite of tears,
Weakness, and heart-oppressing fears;
One soul, at least, shall not repine,
To give you room; come, reign in mine!

DIVINE JUSTICE AMIABLE.

THOU hast no lightnings, O thou Just!
Or I their force should know;
And, if thou strike me into dust,
My soul approves the blow.

The heart, that values less its ease
  Than it adores thy ways,
In thine avenging anger sees
  A subject of its praise.

Pleased I could lie, conceal'd and lost,
  In shades of central night;
Not to avoid thy wrath, thou know'st,
  But lest I grieve thy sight.

Smite me, O thou, whom I provoke!
  And I will love thee still:
The well deserved, and righteous stroke,
  Shall please me, though it kill.

Am I not worthy to sustain
  The worst thou canst devise;
And dare I seek thy throne again,
  And meet thy sacred eyes?

Far from afflicting, thou art kind;
  And, in my saddest hours,
An unction of thy grace I find,
  Pervading all my powers.

Alas! thou sparest me yet again;
  And, when thy wrath should move,
Too gentle to endure my pain,
  Thou sooth'st me with thy love.

I have no punishment to fear;
  But, ah! that smile from thee
Imparts a pang far more severe
  Than woe itself would be.

THE SOUL THAT LOVES GOD FINDS HIM EVERY WHERE.

OH thou, by long experience tried,
Near whom no grief can long abide;
My love! how full of sweet content
I pass my years of banishment!

All scenes alike engaging prove
To souls impress'd with sacred love!
Where'er they dwell, they dwell in thee;
In heaven, in earth, or on the sea.

To me remains nor place nor time
My country is in every clime;
I can be calm and free from care
On any shore, since God is there.

While place we seek, or place we shun,
The soul finds happiness in none;
But with a God to guide our way,
'Tis equal joy to go or stay.

Could I be cast where thou art not,
That were indeed a dreadful lot;
But regions none remote I call,
Secure of finding God in all.

My country, Lord, art thou alone;
Nor other can I claim or own;
The point where all my wishes meet;
My law, my love; life's only sweet!

I hold by nothing here below;
Appoint my journey, and I go;
Though pierced by scorn, oppress'd by pride,
I feel thee good—feel nought beside.

No frowns of men can hurtful prove
To souls on fire with heavenly love;
Though men and devils both condemn,
No gloomy days arise from them.

Ah then! to his embrace repair;
My soul, thou art no stranger there;
There love divine shall be thy guard,
And peace and safety thy reward.

THE TESTIMONY OF DIVINE ADOPTION.

How happy are the new-born race,
Partakers of adopting grace;
How pure the bliss they share!
Hid from the world and all its eyes,
Within their heart the blessing lies
And conscience feels it there.

The moment we believe, 'tis ours;
And if we love with all our powers
The God from whom it came;
And if we serve with hearts sincere,
'Tis still discernible and clear,
An undisputed claim.

But, ah! if foul and wilful sin
Stain and dishonour us within,
Farewell the joy we knew;
Again the slaves of nature's sway,
In labyrinths of our own we stray,
Without a guide or clue.

The chaste and pure, who fear to grieve
The gracious spirit they receive,
His work distinctly trace:
And, strong in undissembling love,
Boldly assert and clearly prove
Their hearts his dwelling-place.

Oh messenger of dear delight,
Whose voice dispels the deepest night,
Sweet peace-proclaiming dove!
With thee at hand, to sooth our pains,
No wish unsatisfied remains
No task but that of love.

'Tis love unites what sin divides;
The centre, where all bliss resides
To which the soul once brought,
Reclining on the first great cause,
From his abounding sweetness draws
Peace passing human thought.

Sorrow foregoes its nature there,
And life assumes a tranquil air,
  Divested of its woes;
There sovereign goodness soothes the breast,
Till then incapable of rest,
  In sacred sure repose.

DIVINE LOVE ENDURES NO RIVAL.

Love is the Lord whom I obey,
Whose will transported I perform;
The centre of my rest, my stay,
Love's all in all to me, myself a worm.

For uncreated charms I burn,
Oppress'd by slavish fear no more;
For one in whom I may discern,
E'en when he frowns, a sweetness I adore.

He little loves him who complains,
And finds him rigorous and severe;
His heart is sordid, and he feigns,
Though loud in boasting of a soul sincere.

Love causes grief, but 'tis to move
And stimulate the slumbering mind;
And he has never tasted love,
Who shuns a pang so graciously design'd.

Sweet is the cross, above all sweet
To souls enamour'd with thy smiles;
The keenest woe life ever meets,
Love strips of all its terrors, and beguiles.

'Tis just that God should not be dear
Where self engrosses all the thought,
And groans and murmurs make it clear,
Whatever else is loved, the Lord is not.

The love of thee flows just as much
As that of ebbing self subsides;
Our hearts, their scantiness is such,
Bear not the conflict of two rival tides.

Both cannot govern in one soul;
Then let self-love be dispossess'd;
The love of God deserves the whole,
And will not dwell with so despised a guest.

SELF-DIFFIDENCE.

Source of love, and light of day,
Tear me from myself away;
Every view and thought of mine
Cast into the mould of thine;
Teach, O teach this faithless heart,
A consistent constant part;
Or, if it must live to grow
More rebellious, break it now!

Is it thus that I requite
Grace and goodness infinite?
Every trace of every boon,
Cancel'd and erased so soon!
Can I grieve thee, whom I love;
Thee, in whom I live and move?
If my sorrow touch thee still,
Save me from so great an ill!

Oh! the oppressive, irksome weight,
Felt in an uncertain state;
Comfort, peace, and rest, adieu,
Should I prove at last untrue!
Still I choose thee, follow still
Every notice of thy will;
But, unstable, strangely weak,
Still let slip the good I seek.

Self-confiding wretch, I thought
I could serve thee as I ought,
Win thee, and deserve to feel
All the love thou canst reveal;
Trusting self, a bruised reed,
Is to be deceived indeed:
Save me from this harm and loss,
Lest my gold turn all to dross!

Self is earthly—faith alone
Makes an unseen world our own;
Faith relinquish'd, how we roam,
Feel our way, and leave our home!
Spurious gems our hopes entice,
While we scorn the pearl of price;
And, preferring servants' pay,
Cast the children's bread away.

THE ACQUIESCENCE OF PURE LOVE.

Love! if thy destined sacrifice am I,
Come, slay thy victim, and prepare thy fires;
Plunged in thy depths of mercy, let me die
The death which every soul that lives desires

I watch my hours, and see them fleet away;
The time is long that I have languish'd here,
Yet all my thoughts thy purposes obey,
With no reluctance, cheerful and sincere.

To me 'tis equal, whether love ordain
My life or death, appoint me pain or ease;
My soul perceives no real ill in pain;
In ease or health no real good she sees.

One good she covets, and that good alone,
To choose thy will, from selfish bias free;
And to prefer a cottage to a throne,
And grief to comfort, if it pleases thee.

That we should bear the cross is thy command,
Die to the world, and live to self no more;
Suffer, unmov'd, beneath the rudest hand,
As pleased when shipwreck'd as when safe on shore.

REPOSE IN GOD.

Blest! who, far from all mankind
This world's shadows left behind,
Hears from heaven a gentle strain
Whispering love, and loves again.

Blest! who, free from self-esteem,
Dives into the great Supreme,
All desire beside discards,
Joys inferior none regards.

Blest! who in thy bosom seeks
Rest that nothing earthly breaks,
Dead to self and worldly things,
Lost in thee, thou King of kings!

Ye that know my secret fire,
Softly speak and soon retire;
Favour my divine repose,
Spare the sleep a God bestows.

GLORY TO GOD ALONE.

Oh loved! but not enough—though dearer far
Than self and its most loved enjoyments are;
None duly loves thee, but who, nobly free
From sensual objects, finds his all in thee.

Glory of God! thou stranger here below,
Whom man nor knows, nor feels a wish to know
Our faith and reason are both shock'd to find
Man in the post of honour—Thee behind.

Reason exclaims—'Let every creature fall,
Ashamed, abased, before the Lord of all;'
And faith, o'erwhelm'd with such a dazzling blaze,
Feebly describes the beauty she surveys.

Yet man, dim-sighted man, and rash as blind,
Deaf to the dictates of his better mind,
In frantic competition dares the skies,
And claims precedence of the Only Wise.

Oh lost in vanity, till once self-known!
Nothing is great, or good, but God alone;
When thou shalt stand before his awful face,
Then, at the last, thy pride shall know his place.

Glorious, Almighty, First, and without end!
When wilt thou melt the mountains and descend?
When wilt thou shoot abroad thy conquering rays,
And teach these atoms, thou hast made, thy praise?

Thy glory is the sweetest heaven I feel;
And, if I seek it with too fierce a zeal,
Thy love, triumphant o'er a selfish will,
Taught me the passion, and inspires it still.

My reason, all my faculties, unite,
To make thy glory their supreme delight;
Forbid it, fountain of my brightest days,
That I should rob thee, and usurp thy praise!

My soul! rest happy in thy low estate,
Nor hope, nor wish, to be esteem'd or great.
To take the impression of a will divine,
Be that thy glory, and those riches thine.

Confess him righteous in his just decrees,
Love what he loves, and let his pleasure please;
Die daily; from the touch of sin recede;
Then thou hast crown'd him, and he reigns indeed

SELF-LOVE AND TRUTH INCOMPATIBLE.

From thorny wilds a monster came,
That fill'd my soul with fear and shame;
The birds, forgetful of their mirth,
Droop'd at the sight, and fell to earth;
When thus a sage address'd mine ear,
Himself unconscious of a fear.
'Whence all this terror and surprise,
Distracted looks, and streaming eyes?
Far from the world and its affairs,
The joy it boasts, the pain it shares,
Surrender, without guile or art,
To God, an undivided heart;
The savage form, so fear'd before,
Shall scare your trembling soul no more;
For loathsome as the sight may be,
'Tis but the love of self you see.
Fix all your love on God alone,
Choose but his will, and hate your own:
No fear shall in your path be found,
The dreary waste shall bloom around,
And you, through all your happy days,
Shall bless his name, and sing his praise."
Oh lovely solitude, how sweet
The silence of this calm retreat!
Here truth, the fair whom I pursue,
Gives all her beauty to my view;
The simple, unadorn'd display
Charms every pain and fear away.
O truth, whom millions proudly slight;
O truth, my treasure and delight;
Accept this tribute to thy name,
And this poor heart from which it came!

THE LOVE OF GOD, THE END OF LIFE.

SINCE life in sorrow must be spent,
So be it—I am well content,
And meekly wait my last remove,
Seeking only growth in love

No bliss I seek, but to fulfill
In life, in death, thy lovely will;
No succours in my woes I want,
Save what thou art pleased to grant.

Our days are number'd, let us spare
Our anxious hearts a needless care:
'Tis thine to number out our days;
Ours to give them to thy praise.

Love is our only business here,
Love, simple, constant, and sincere
O blessed days, thy servants see!
Spent, O Lord! in pleasing thee.

LOVE FAITHFUL IN THE ABSENCE OF THE BELOVED.

IN vain ye woo me to your harmless joys,
Ye pleasant bowers, remote from strife and noise;
Your shades, the witnesses of many a vow,
Breath'd forth in happier days, are irksome now;
Denied that smile 'twas once my heaven to see,
Such scenes, such pleasures, are all past with me.

In vain he leaves me, I shall love him still;
And though I mourn, not murmur at his will;
I have no cause—an object all divine
Might well grow weary of a soul like mine;
Yet pity me, great God! forlorn, alone,
Heartless and hopeless, life and love all gone.

LOVE PURE AND FERVENT.

JEALOUS, and with love o'erflowing,
God demands a fervent heart;
Grace and bounty still bestowing,
Calls us to a grateful part.

Oh, then, with supreme affection
His paternal will regard!
If it cost us some dejection,
Every sigh has its reward.

Perfect love has power to soften
Cares that might our peace destroy,
Nay, does more—transforms them often,
Changing sorrow into joy.

Sovereign love appoints the measure,
And the number of our pains;
And is pleased when we find pleasure
In the trials he ordains.

THE ENTIRE SURRENDER.

PEACE has unveil'd her smiling face,
And woos thy soul to her embrace,
Enjoy'd with ease, if thou refrain
From earthly love, else sought in vain;
She dwells with all who truth prefer,
But seeks not them who seek not her.

Yield to the Lord, with simple heart,
All that thou hast, and all thou art;
Renounce all strength but strength divine;
And peace shall be for ever thine:
Behold the path which I have trod,
My path, till I go home to God.

THE PERFECT SACRIFICE.

I PLACE an offering at thy shrine,
From taint and blemish clear,
Simple and pure in its design,
Of all that I hold dear.

I yield thee back thy gifts again,
Thy gifts which most I prize;
Desirous only to retain
The notice of thine eyes.

But if, by thine adored decree,
That blessing be denied;
Resign'd, and unreluctant, see
My every wish subside.

Thy will in all things I approve,
Exalted or cast down!
Thy will in every state I love,
And even in thy frown.

GOD HIDES HIS PEOPLE.

To lay the soul that loves him low,
Becomes the Only Wise:
To hide, beneath a veil of woe,
The children of the skies.

Man, though a worm, would yet be great;
Though feeble, would seem strong:
Assumes an independent state,
By sacrilege and wrong.

Strange the reverse, which, once abased,
The haughty creature proves!
He feels his soul a barren waste,
Nor dares affirm he loves.

Scorn'd by the thoughtless and the vain,
  To God he presses near;
Superior to the world's disdain,
  And happy in its sneer.

Oh welcome, in his heart he says,
  Humility and shame!
Farewell the wish for human praise,
  The music of a name!

But will not scandal mar the good
  That I might else perform?
And can God work it, if he would,
  By so despised a worm?

Ah, vainly anxious!—leave the Lord
  To rule thee, and dispose;
Sweet is the mandate of his word,
  And gracious all he does.

He draws from human littleness
  His grandeur and renown;
And gen'rous hearts with joy confess
  The triumph all his own.

Down then with self-exalting thoughts;
  Thy faith and hope employ,
To welcome all that he allots,
  And suffer shame with joy.

No longer, then, thou wilt encroach
  On his eternal right;
And he shall smile at thy approach,
  And make thee his delight.

THE SECRETS OF DIVINE LOVE ARE TO BE KEPT.

Sun! stay thy course, this moment stay
Suspend the o'erflowing tide of day,
Divulge not such a love as mine,
Ah! hide the mystery divine;
Lest man, who deems my glory shame,
Should learn the secret of my flame.

O night! propitious to my views,
Thy sable awning wide diffuse;
Conceal alike my joy and pain,
Nor draw thy curtain back again,
Though morning, by the tears she shows,
Seems to participate my woes.

Ye stars! whose faint and feeble fires
Express my languishing desires,
Whose slender beams pervade the skies
As silent as my secret sighs,
Those emanations of a soul,
That darts her fires beyond the Pole;

Your rays, that scarce assist the sight,
That pierce, but not displace the night,
That shine indeed, but nothing show
Of all those various scenes below,
Bring no disturbance, rather prove
Incentives to a sacred love.

Thou moon! whose never-failing course
Bespeaks a providential force,
Go, tell the tidings of my flame
To Him who calls the stars by name;
Whose absence kills, whose presence cheers;
Who blots, or brightens, all my years.

While, in the blue abyss of space,
Thine orb performs its rapid race;
Still whisper in his listening ears
The language of my sighs and tears;
Tell him, I seek him, far below,
Lost in a wilderness of woe.

Ye thought-composing, silent hours,
Diffusing peace o'er all my powers;
Friends of the pensive! who conceal,
In darkest shades, the flames I feel;
To you I trust, and safely may,
The love that wastes my strength away.

In sylvan scenes, and caverns rude
I taste the sweets of solitude;
Retired indeed, but not alone,
I share them with a spouse unknown,
Who hides me here, from envious eyes,
From all intrusion and surprise.

Imbowering shades, and dens profound!
Where echo rolls the voice around;
Mountains! whose elevated heads,
A moist and misty veil o'erspreads;
Disclose a solitary bride
To him I love—to none beside.

Ye rills! that, murmuring all the way,
Among the polish'd pebbles stray;
Creep silently along the ground,
Lest, drawn by that harmonious sound,
Some wanderer, whom I would not meet,
Should stumble on my loved retreat.

Enamel'd meads, and hillocks green,
And streams that water all the scene!
Ye torrents, loud in distant ears!
Ye fountains, that receive my tears!
Ah! still conceal, with caution due,
A charge I trust with none but you.

If, when my pain and grief increase,
I seem to enjoy the sweetest peace,
It is because I find so fair
The charming object of my care,
That I can sport and pleasure make
Of torment suffer'd for his sake.

Ye meads and groves, unconscious things!
Ye know not whence my pleasure springs;
Ye know not, and ye cannot know,
The source from which my sorrows flow:
The dear sole cause of all I feel,—
He knows and understands them well.

Ye deserts! where the wild beasts rove,
Scenes sacred to my hours of love;
Ye forests! in whose shades I stray
Benighted under burning day;
Ah! whisper not how blest am I,
Nor while I live, nor when I die.

Ye lambs! who sport beneath these shades
And bound along the mossy glades;
Be taught a salutary fear,
And cease to bleat when I am near:
The wolf may hear your harmless cry,
Whom ye should dread as much as I.

How calm, amid these scenes, my mind
How perfect is the peace I find!
Oh hush, be still, my every part,
My tongue, my pulse, my beating heart!
That love, aspiring to its cause,
May suffer not a moment's pause.

Ye swift-finn'd nations, that abide
In seas, as fathomless as wide;
And, unsuspicious of a snare,
Pursue at large your pleasures there:
Poor sportive fools! how soon does man
Your heedless ignorance trepan!

Away! dive deep into the brine,
Where never yet sunk plummet line
Trust me, the vast leviathan
Is merciful, compared with man;
Avoid his arts, forsake the beach,
And never play within his reach.

My soul her bondage ill endures;
I pant for liberty like yours;
I long for that immense profound,
That knows no bottom, and no bound;
Lost in infinity, to prove
The incomprehensible of love.

Ye birds! that lessen as ye fly,
And vanish in the distant sky;
To whom yon airy waste belongs,
Resounding with your cheerful songs;
Haste to escape from human sight;
Fear less, the vulture and the kite.

How blest, and how secure am I,
When quitting earth, I soar on high;
When lost, like you I disappear,
And float in a sublimer sphere!
Whence falling, within human view,
I am ensnared, and caught like you.

Omniscient God, whose notice deigns
To try the heart and search the reins;
Compassionate the numerous woes,
I dare not, e'en to thee, disclose;
Oh save me from the cruel hands
Of men, who fear not thy commands!

Love, all-subduing and divine,
Care for a creature truly thine;
Reign in a heart, disposed to own
No sovereign but thyself alone;
Cherish a bride who cannot rove,
Nor quit thee for a meaner love!

THE VICISSITUDES EXPERIENCED IN THE CHRISTIAN LIFE.

I suffer fruitless anguish day by day,
Each moment, as it passes, marks my pain;
Scarce knowing whither, doubtfully I stray,
And see no end of all that I sustain.

The more I strive the more I am withstood;
Anxiety increasing every hour,
My spirit finds no rest, performs no good,
And nought remains of all my former power.

My peace of heart is fled, I know not where;
My happy hours, like shadows, pass'd away;
Their sweet remembrance doubles all my care,
Night darker seems, succeeding such a day.

Dear faded joys and impotent regret,
What profit is there in incessant tears?
Oh Thou, whom once beheld, we ne'er forget,
Reveal thy love, and banish all my fears!

Alas! he flies me—treats me as his foe,
Views not my sorrows, hears not when I plead;
Woe such as mine, despised, neglected woe,
Unless it shortens life, is vain indeed.

Pierced with a thousand wounds, I yet survive;
My pangs are keen, but no complaint transpires,
And, while in terrors of thy wrath I live,
Hell seems to loose its less tremendous fires.

Has hell a pain I would not gladly bear,
So thy severe displeasure might subside?
Hopeless of ease, I seem already there,
My life extinguish'd, and yet death denied.

Is this the joy so promised—this the love,
The unchanging love, so sworn in better days?
Ah! dangerous glories! shown me, but to prove
How lovely thou, and I how rash to gaze.

Why did I see them? had I still remain'd
Untaught, still ignorant how fair thou art,
My humbler wishes I had soon obtain'd,
Nor known the torments of a doubting heart.

Deprived of all, yet feeling no desires,
Whence then, I cry, the pangs that I sustain?
Dubious and uninform'd, my soul inquires,
Ought she to cherish, or shake off her pain?

Suffering, I suffer not—sincerely love,
Yet feel no touch of that enlivening flame;
As chance inclines me, unconcern'd I move,
All times, and all events to me the same.

I search my heart, and not a wish is there,
But burns with zeal that hated self may fall;
Such is the sad disquietude I share,
A sea of doubts, and self the source of all.

I ask not life, nor do I wish to die;
And, if thine hand accomplish not my cure,
I would not purchase, with a single sigh,
A free discharge from all that I endure.

I groan in chains, yet want not a release;
Am sick, and know not the distemper'd part;
Am just as void of purpose as of peace;
Have neither plan, nor fear, nor hope, nor heart.

My claim to life, though sought with earnest care,
No light within me, or without me, shows;
Once I had faith, but now, in self-despair
Find my chief cordial and my best repose.

My soul is a forgotten thing; she sinks,
Sinks and is lost, without a wish to rise;
Feels an indifference she abhors, and thinks
Her name erased for ever from the skies.

Language affords not my distress a name,—
Yet is it real, and no sickly dream;
'Tis love inflicts it; though to feel that flame
Is all I know of happiness supreme.

When love departs, a chaos wide and vast,
And dark as hell, is open'd in the soul;
When love returns, the gloomy scene is past,
No tempests shake her, and no fears control.

Then tell me why these ages of delay?
Oh love, all excellent, once more appear;
Disperse the shades, and snatch me into day,
From this abyss of night, these floods of fear!

No—love is angry, will not now endure
A sigh of mine, or suffer a complaint;
He smites me, wounds me, and withholds the cure;
Exhausts my powers, and leaves me sick and faint.

He wounds, and hides the hand that gave the blow
He flies, he reappears, and wounds again—
Was ever heart that loved thee treated so?
Yet I adore thee, though it seem in vain.

And wilt thou leave me, whom, when lost and blind,
Thou didst distinguish, and vouchsafe to choose.
Before thy laws were written in my mind,
While yet the world had all my thoughts and views?

Now leave me? when, enamour'd of thy laws,
I make thy glory my supreme delight;
Now blot me from thy register, and cause
A faithful soul to perish from thy sight?

What can have caused the change which I deplore
Is it to prove me, if my heart be true?
Permit me then, while prostrate I adore,
To draw, and place its picture in thy view

'Tis thine without reserve, most simply thine;
So given to thee, that it is not my own;
A willing captive of thy grace divine;
And loves and seeks thee, for thyself alone.

Pain cannot move it, danger cannot scare;
Pleasure and wealth, in its esteem, are dust;
It loves thee, e'en when least inclined to spare
Its tenderest feelings, and avows thee just.

'Tis all thine own; my spirit is so too,
An undivided offering at thy shrine;
It seeks thy glory with no double view,
Thy glory, with no secret bent to mine.

Love, holy love! and art thou not severe,
To slight me, thus devoted, and thus fix'd?
Mine is an everlasting ardour, clear
From all self-bias, generous and unmix'd.

But I am silent, seeing what I see—
And fear, with cause, that I am self-deceived;
Not e'en my faith is from suspicion free,
And, that I love, seems not to be believed.

Live thou, and reign for ever, glorious Lord!
My last, least offering, I present thee now—
Renounce me, leave me, and be still adored!
Slay me, my God, and I applaud the blow.

WATCHING UNTO GOD IN THE NIGHT SEASON.

Sleep at last has fled these eyes,
Nor do I regret his flight,
More alert my spirits rise,
And my heart is free and light.

Nature silent all around,
Not a single witness near;
God as soon as sought is found;
And the flame of love burns clear.

Interruption, all day long,
Checks the current of my joys;
Creatures press me with a throng,
And perplex me with their noise.

Undisturb'd I muse all night,
On the first Eternal Fair;
Nothing there obstructs delight,
Love is renovated there.

Life, with its perpetual stir,
Proves a foe to love and me;
Fresh entanglements occur—
Comes the night, and sets me free

Never more, sweet sleep, suspend
My enjoyments, always new:
Leave me to possess my friend;
)ther eyes and hearts subdue.

Hush the world, that I may wake
To the taste of pure delights;
Oh the pleasures I partake—
God, the partner of my nights!

David, for the selfsame cause,
Night preferr'd to busy day:
Hearts whom heavenly beauty draws
Wish the glaring sun away.

Sleep, self-lovers, is for you—
Souls that love celestial know,
Fairer scenes by night can view
Than the sun could ever show.

ON THE SAME.

Season of my purest pleasure,
  Sealer of observing eyes!
When, in larger, freer measure,
  I can commune with the skies;
While, beneath thy shade extended,
  Weary man forgets his woes;
I, my daily trouble ended,
  Find, in watching, my repose.

Silence all around prevailing,
  Nature hush'd in slumber sweet,
No rude noise mine ears assailing,
  Now my God and I can meet:
Universal nature slumbers,
  And my soul partakes the calm,
Breathes her ardour out in numbers,
  Plaintive song or lofty psalm.

Now my passion, pure and holy,
  Shines and burns without restraint;
Which the day's fatigue and folly
  Cause to languish, dim and faint:
Charming hours of relaxation!
  How I dread the ascending sun!
Surely, idle conversation
  Is an evil, match'd by none.

Worldly prate and babble hurt me;
  Unintelligible prove;
Neither teach me nor divert me;
  I have ears for none but love.
Me they rude esteem, and foolish,
  Hearing my absurd replies;
I have neither art's fine polish,
  Nor the knowledge of the wise.

Simple souls, and unpolluted,
  By conversing with the great,
Have a mind and taste, ill suited
  To their dignity and state;
All their talking, reading, writing,
  Are but talents misapplied;
Infants' prattle I delight in,
  Nothing human choose beside.

'Tis the secret fear of sinning
  Checks my tongue, or I should say,
When I see the night beginning,
  I am glad of parting day:
Love this gentle admonition
  Whispers soft within my breast;
'Choice befits not thy condition,
  Acquiescence suits thee best.'

Henceforth, the repose and pleasure
  Night affords me I resign;
And thy will shall be the measure,
  Wisdom infinite! of mine:
Wishing is but inclination
  Quarreling with thy decrees;
Wayward nature finds the occasion--
  'Tis her folly and disease.

Night, with its sublime enjoyments
  Now no longer will I choose;
Nor the day, with its employments,
  Irksome as they seem, refuse;
Lessons of a God's inspiring
  Neither time nor place impedes;
From our wishing and desiring
  Our unhappiness proceeds.

ON THE SAME.

NIGHT! how I love thy silent shades,
  My spirits they compose;
The bliss of heaven my soul pervades,
  In spite of all my woes.

While sleep instils her poppy dews
  In every slumbering eye,
I watch, to meditate and muse,
  In blest tranquillity.

And when I feel a God immense
  Familiarly impart,
With every proof he can dispense,
  His favour to my heart;

My native meanness I lament,
  Though most divinely fill'd
With all the ineffable content
  That Deity can yield.

His purpose and his course he keeps;
  Treads all my reasonings down;
Commands me out of nature's deeps,
  And hides me in his own.

When in the dust, its proper place,
  Our pride of heart we lay;
'Tis then a deluge of his grace
  Bears all our sins away.

Thou whom I serve, and whose I am,
  Whose influence from on high
Refines, and still refines my flame,
  And makes my fetters fly.—

How wretched is the creature's state
  Who thwarts thy gracious power;
Crush'd under sin's enormous weight,
  Increasing every hour!

The night, when pass'd entire with thee,
  How luminous and clear!
Then sleep has no delights for me,
  Lest thou shouldst disappear.

My Saviour! occupy me still
  In this secure recess;
Let reason slumber if she will,
  My joy shall not be less:

Let reason slumber out the night;
  But if thou deign to make
My soul the abode of truth and light,
  Ah, keep my heart awake!

THE JOY OF THE CROSS.

Long plunged in sorrow, I resign
My soul to that dear hand of thine,
  Without reserve or fear;
That hand shall wipe my streaming eyes;
Or into smiles of glad surprise
  Transform the falling tear.

My sole possession is thy love;
In earth beneath, or heaven above,
  I have no other store;
And though with fervent suit I pray,
And importune thee night and day,
  I ask thee nothing more.

My rapid hours pursue the course
Prescribed them by love's sweetest force,
  And I thy sovereign will,
Without a wish to escape my doom;
Though still a sufferer from the womb,
  And doom'd to suffer still.

By thy command, where'er I stray,
Sorrow attends me all my way,
  A never-failing friend;
And if my sufferings may augment
Thy praise, behold me well content—
  Let sorrow still attend!

It costs me no regret, that she,
Who follow'd Christ, should follow me;
  And though, where'er she goes,
Thorns spring spontaneous at her feet,
I love her, and extract a sweet
  From all my bitter woes.

Adieu! ye vain delights of earth;
Insipid sports, and childish mirth,
  I taste no sweets in you;
Unknown delights are in the cross
All joy beside to me is dross;
  And Jesus thought so too.

The cross! Oh ravishment and bliss—
How grateful e'en its anguish is·
  Its bitterness how sweet!
There every sense, and all the mind,
In all her faculties refined,
  Tastes happiness complete.

Souls once enabled to disdain
Base sublunary joys, maintain
  Their dignity secure;
The fever of desire is pass'd,
And love has all its genuine taste,
  Is delicate and pure.

Self-love no grace in sorrow sees,
Consults her own peculiar ease:
  'Tis all the bliss she knows:
But nobler aims true love employ;
In self-denial is her joy
  In suffering her repose.

Sorrow and love go side by side;
Nor height nor depth can e'er divide
  Their heaven-appointed bands;
Those dear associates still are one,
Nor till the race of life is run
  Disjoin their wedded hands.

Jesus, avenger of our fall,
Thou faithful lover, above all
  The cross has ever borne!
Oh tell me,—life is in thy voice—
How much afflictions were thy choice,
  And sloth and ease thy scorn!

Thy choice and mine shall be the same
Inspirer of that holy flame,
  Which must for ever blaze!
To take the cross and follow thee,
Where love and duty lead, shall be
  My portion and my praise.

JOY IN MARTYRDOM.

Sweet tenants of this grove!
  Who sing without design,
A song of artless love,
  In unison with mine:
These echoing shades return
  Full many a note of ours,
That wise ones cannot learn,
  With all their boasted powers.

O Thou! whose sacred charms
  These hearts so seldom love,
Although thy beauty warms
  And blesses all above;
How slow are human things,
  To choose their happiest lot!
All-glorious King of kings,
  Say why we love thee not?

This heart, that cannot rest,
Shall thine for ever prove;
Though bleeding and distress'd,
Yet joyful in thy love:
'Tis happy, though it breaks
Beneath thy chastening hand;
And speechless, yet it speaks
What thou canst understand.

SIMPLE TRUST.

Still, still, without ceasing,
I feel it increasing,
This fervour of holy desire;
And often exclaim,
Let me die in the flame
Of a love that can never expire!

Had I words to explain
What she must sustain
Who dies to the world and its ways;
How joy and affright,
Distress and delight,
Alternately chequer her days.

Thou, sweetly severe!
I would make thee appear,
In all thou art pleased to award,
Not more in the sweet,
Than the bitter I meet,
My tender and merciful Lord.

This faith, in the dark
Pursuing its mark,
Through many sharp trials of love;
Is the sorrowful waste
That is to be pass'd
In the way to the Canaan above.

THE NECESSITY OF SELF-ABASEMENT.

Source of love, my brighter sun,
Thou alone my comfort art;
See, my race is almost run;
Hast thou left this trembling heart?

In my youth thy charming eyes
Drew me from the ways of men;
Then I drank unmingled joys;
Frown of thine saw never then.

Spouse of Christ was then my name;
And devoted all to thee.
Strangely jealous, I became
Jealous of this self in me.

Thee to love, and none beside,
Was my darling, sole employ;
While alternately I died,
Now of grief, and now of joy.

Through the dark and silent night
On thy radiant smiles I dwelt;
And to see the dawning light
Was the keenest pain I felt.

Thou my gracious teacher wert;
And thine eye, so close applied,
While it watch'd thy pupil's heart,
Seem'd to look at none beside.

Conscious of no evil drift,
This, I cried, is love indeed—
'Tis the giver, not the gift,
Whence the joys I feel proceed

But soon humbled, and laid low,
Stript of all thou hast conferr'd,
Nothing left but sin and woe,
I perceived how I had err'd.

Oh, the vain conceit of man,
Dreaming of a good his own,
Arrogating all he can,
Though the Lord is good alone!

He the graces thou hast wrough
Makes subservient to his pride;
Ignorant, that one such thought
Passes all his sin beside.

Such his folly—proved, at last,
By the loss of that repose
Self-complacence cannot taste,
Only love divine bestows.

'Tis by this reproof severe,
And by this reproof alone,
His defects at last appear,
Man is to himself made known.

Learn, all earth! that feeble man,
Sprung from this terrestrial clod,
Nothing is, and nothing can;
Life and power are all in God.

LOVE INCREASED BY SUFFERING.

'I LOVE the Lord,' is still the strain
This heart delights to sing;
But I reply—your thoughts are vain,
Perhaps 'tis no such thing.

Before the power of love divine
Creation fades away;
Till only God is seen to shine
In all that we survey.

In gulfs of awful night we find
The God of our desires;
'Tis there he stamps the yielding mind,
And doubles all its fires.

Flames of encircling love invest,
  And pierce it sweetly through;
'Tis fill'd with sacred joy, yet press'd
  With sacred sorrow too.

Ah love! my heart is in the right—
  Amidst a thousand woes,
To thee, its ever new delight,
  And all its peace it owes.

Fresh causes of distress occur
  Where'er I look or move;
The comforts I to all prefer
  Are solitude and love.

Nor exile I nor prison fear;
  Love makes my courage great;
I find a Saviour every where,
  His grace in every state.

Nor castle walls, nor dungeons deep,
  Exclude his quickening beams;
There I can sit, and sing, and weep,
  And dwell on heavenly themes.

There sorrow, for his sake, is found
  A joy beyond compare;
There no presumptuous thoughts abound,
  No pride can enter there.

A Saviour doubles all my joys,
  And sweetens all my pains,
His strength in my defence employs,
  Consoles me and sustains.

I fear no ill, resent no wrong;
  Nor feel a passion move,
When malice whets her slanderous tongue;
  Such patience is in love.

SCENES FAVOURABLE TO MEDITATION.

Wilds horrid and dark with o'ershadowing trees
  Rocks that ivy and briars infold,
Scenes nature with dread and astonishment sees,
  But I with a pleasure untold.

Though awfully silent, and shaggy, and rude,
  I am charm'd with the peace ye afford,
Your shades are a temple where none will intrude
  The abode of my lover and Lord.

I am sick of thy splendour, O fountain of day,
  And here I am hid from its beams,
Here safely contemplate a brighter display
  Of the noblest and holiest of themes.

Ye forests, that yield me my sweetest repose,
  Where stillness and solitude reign,
To you I securely and boldly disclose
  The dear anguish of which I complain.

Here, sweetly forgetting and wholly forgot
  By the world and its turbulent throng,
The birds and the streams lend me many a note
  That aids meditation and song.

Here, wandering in scenes that are sacred to night,
  Love wears me and wastes me away,
And often the sun has spent much of his light
  Ere yet I perceive it is day.

While a mantle of darkness envelopes the sphere,
  My sorrows are sadly rehearsed,
To me the dark hours are all equally dear,
  And the last is as sweet as the first.

Here I and the beasts of the deserts agree,
  Mankind are the wolves that I fear,
They grudge me my natural right to be free,
  But nobody questions it here.

Though little is found in this dreary abode
  That appetite wishes to find,
My spirit is sooth'd by the presence of God,
  And appetite wholly resign'd.

Ye desolate scenes, to your solitude led,
  My life I in praises employ,
And scarce know the source of the tears that I shed
  Proceed they from sorrow or joy.

There's nothing I seem to have skill to discern,
  I feel out my way in the dark,
Love reigns in my bosom, I constantly burn,
  Yet hardly distinguish the spark.

I live, yet I seem to myself to be dead,
  Such a riddle is not to be found,
I am nourish'd without knowing how I am fed
  I have nothing, and yet I abound.

Oh love! who in darkness art pleased to abide,
  Though dimly, yet surely I see
That these contrarieties only reside
  In the soul that is chosen of thee.

Ah send me not back to the race of mankind,
  Perversely by folly beguiled,
For where, in the crowds I have left, shall I find
  The spirit and heart of a child?

Here let me, though fix'd in a desert, be free;
  A little one whom they despise,
Though lost to the world, if in union with thee,
  Shall be holy and happy and wise.

TRANSLATIONS

OF THE

LATIN AND ITALIAN POEMS OF MILTON.

ELEGY I.

TO CHARLES DEODATI.

At length, my friend, the far sent letters come,
Charged with thy kindness, to their destined home;
They come, at length, from Deva's Western side,
Where prone she seeks the salt Vergivian tide.
Trust me, my joy is great that thou shouldst be,
Though born of foreign race, yet born for me,
And that my sprightly friend, now free to roam,
Must seek again so soon his wonted home.
I well content, where Thames with influent tide
My native city laves, meantime reside,
Nor zeal nor duty now my steps impel
To reedy Cam, and my forbidden cell.
Nor aught of pleasure in those fields have I,
That to the musing bard all shade deny.
'Tis time that I a pedant's threats disdain,
And fly from wrongs my soul will ne'er sustain.
If peaceful days, in letter'd leisure spent
Beneath my father's roof, be banishment,
Then call me banish'd, I will ne'er refuse
A name expressive of the lot I choose.
I would that, exiled to the Pontic shore,
Rome's hapless bard had suffer'd nothing more.
He then had equall'd even Homer's lays,
And, Virgil! thou hadst won but second praise:
For here I woo the muse, with no control,
And here my books—my life—absorb me whole.
Here too I visit, or to smile or weep,
The winding theatre's majestic sweep;

The grave or gay colloquial scene recruits
My spirits, spent in learning's long pursuits;
Whether some senior shrewd, or spendthrift heir,
Suitor, or soldier, now unarm'd, be there,
Or some coif'd brooder o'er a ten years' cause,
Thunder the Norman gibberish of the laws.
The lacquey, there, oft dupes the wary sire,
And, artful, speeds the enamour'd son's desire.
There, virgins oft, unconscious what they prove,
What love is know not, yet, unknowing, love.
Or, if impassion'd tragedy wield high
The bloody sceptre, give her locks to fly,
Wild as the winds, and roll her haggard eye,
I gaze, and grieve, still cherishing my grief.
At times, e'en bitter tears yield sweet relief,
As, when from bliss untasted torn away,
Some youth dies, hapless, on his bridal day;
Or when the ghost, sent back from shades below,
Fills the assassin's heart with vengeful woe;
When Troy, or Argos, the dire scene affords
Or Creon's hall laments its guilty lords.
Nor always city-pent, or pent at home,
I dwell; but, when spring calls me forth to roam,
Expatiate in our proud suburban shades
Of branching elm that never sun pervades.
Here many a virgin troop I may descry,
Like stars of mildest influence, gliding by.
Oh forms divine! Oh looks that might inspire
E'en Jove himself, grown old, with young desire.
Oft have I gazed on gem-surpassing eyes,
Out-sparkling every star that gilds the skies;
Necks whiter than the ivory arm bestow'd
By Jove on Pelops, or the milky road!
Bright locks, love's golden snare! these falling low,
Those playing wanton o'er the graceful brow!
Cheeks, too, more winning sweet than after-shower
Adonis turn'd to Flora's favourite flower!
Yield, heroines, yield, and ye who shared the embrace
Of Jupiter in ancient times, give place!
Give place, ye turban'd fair of Persia's coast!
And ye, not less renown'd, Assyria's boast!

Submit, ye nymphs of Greece! ye, once the bloom
Of Ilion! and all ye, of haughty Rome,
Who swept, of old, her theatres with trains
Redundant, and still live in classic strains!
To British damsels beauty's palm is due;
Aliens! to follow them is fame for you.
Oh city, founded by Dardanian hands,
Whose towering front the circling realm comma·
Too blest abode! no loveliness we see
In all the earth, but it abounds in thee.
The virgin multitude that daily meets,
Radiant with gold and beauty, in thy streets
Outnumbers all her train of starry fires
With which Diana gilds thy lofty spires.
Fame says that, wafted hither by her doves,
With all her host of quiver-bearing loves,
Venus, preferring Paphian scenes no more
Has fix'd her empire on thy nobler shore.
But, lest the sightless boy enforce my stay,
I leave these happy walls while yet I may.
Immortal Moly shall secure my heart
From all the sorcery of Circæan art,
And I will e'en repass Cam's reedy pools
To face once more the warfare of the schools.
Meantime accept this trifle! rhymes though few,
Yet such as prove thy friend's remembrance true!

ELEGY II.

ON THE

DEATH OF THE UNIVERSITY BEADLE AT CAMBRIDGE.

Thee, whose refulgent staff and summons clear
  Minerva's flock long time was wont to obey,
Although thyself a herald, famous here,
  The last of heralds, death, has snatch'd away.
He calls on all alike, nor even deigns
To spare the office that himself sustains.

Thy locks were whiter than the plumes display'd
  By Leda's paramour in ancient time;
But thou wast worthy ne'er to have decay'd
  Or, Æson-like, to know a second prime,
Worthy, for whom some goddess should have won
New life, oft kneeling to Apollo's son.

Commission'd to converse with hasty call [stand!
  The gowned tribes, how graceful wouldst thou
So stood Cyllenius erst in Priam's hall,
  Wing-footed messenger of Jove's command!
And so Eurybates, when he address'd
To Peleus' son, Atrides' proud behest.

Dread queen of sepulchres! whose rigorous laws
  And watchful eyes run through the realms below,
Oh, oft too adverse to Minerva's cause!
  Too often to the muse not less a foe!
Choose meaner marks, and with more equal aim
Pierce useless drones, earth's burthen, and its shame

Flow, therefore, tears for him from every eye,
  All ye disciples of the muses, weep!
Assembling all in robes of sable dye,
  Around his bier lament his endless sleep!
And let complaining Elegy rehearse
In every school her sweetest, saddest verse.

ELEGY III.

ON THE

DEATH OF THE BISHOP OF WINCHESTER.

Silent I sat, dejected, and alone,
Making, in thought, the public woes my own,
When first arose the image in my breast
Of England's suffering by that scourge, the pest!
How Death, his funeral torch and scythe in hand,
Entering the lordliest mansions of the land,

Has laid the gem-illumined palace low,
And levell'd tribes of nobles at a blow.
I next deplored the famed paternal pair,
Too soon to ashes turn'd and empty air!
The heroes next, whom snatch'd into the skies
All Belgia saw, and follow'd with her sighs;
But thee far most I mourn'd, regretted most,
Winton's chief shepherd, and her worthiest boast!
Pour'd out in tears I thus complaining said:
'Death, next in power to him who rules the dead!
Is it not enough that all the woodlands yield
To thy fell force, and every verdant field;
That lilies, at one noisome blast of thine,
And e'en the Cyprian queen's own roses pine;
That oaks themselves, although the running rill
Suckle their roots, must wither at thy will;
That all the winged nations, even those
Whose heaven-directed flight the future shows,
And all the beasts that in dark forests stray,
And all the herds of Proteus are thy prey.
Ah envious! arm'd with powers so unconfined!
Why stain thy hands with blood of human kind?
Why take delight, with darts that never roam,
To chase a heaven-born spirit from her home?'
  While thus I mourn'd, the star of evening stood,
Now newly risen above the western flood,
And Phœbus from his morning goal again
Had reach'd the gulfs of the Iberian main.
I wish'd repose, and, on my couch reclined,
Took early rest, to night and sleep resign'd:
When—Oh for words to paint what I beheld!
I seem'd to wander in a spacious field,
Where all the champaign glow'd with purple light,
Like that of sunrise on the mountain height;
Flowers over all the field, of every hue
That ever Iris wore, luxuriant grew.
Nor Chloris, with whom amorous zephyrs play,
E'er dress'd Alcinous' garden half so gay.
A silver current, like the Tagus, roll'd
O'er golden sands, but sands of purer gold;
With dewy airs Favonius fann'd the flowers,
With airs awaken'd under rosy bowers.

Such, poets feign, irradiated all o'er
The sun's abode on India's utmost shore.
While I that splendour, and the mingled shade
Of fruitful vines, with wonder fix'd survey'd,
At once, with looks that beam'd celestial grace,
The seer of Winton stood before my face.
His snowy vesture's hem descending low
His golden sandals swept, and pure as snow
New fallen shone the mitre on his brow.
Where'er he trod, a tremulous sweet sound
Of gladness shook the flowery scene around:
Attendant angels clap their starry wings,
The trumpet shakes the sky, all ether rings;
Each chants his welcome, folds him to his breast
And thus a sweeter voice than all the rest:
'Ascend, my son! thy Father's kingdom share!
My son! henceforth be freed from every care!'
So spake the voice, and at its tender close
With psaltery's sound the angelic band arose;
Then night retired, and, chased by dawning day
The visionary bliss pass'd all away.
I mourn'd my banish'd sleep with fond concern;
Frequent to me may dreams like this return!

ELEGY IV.

TO HIS TUTOR THOMAS YOUNG,

CHAPLAIN TO THE ENGLISH FACTORY AT HAMBURGH

Hence my epistle—skim the deep—fly o'er
Yon smooth expanse to the Teutonic shore!
Haste—lest a friend should grieve for thy delay—
And the gods grant that nothing thwart thy way
I will myself invoke the king who binds
In his Sicanian echoing vault the winds
With Doris and her nymphs, and all the throng
Of azure gods, to speed thee safe along.

But rather, to insure thy happier haste
Ascend Medea's chariot, if thou mayst;
Or that whence young Triptolemus of yore
Descended, welcome on the Scythian shore.
The sands that line the German coast descried,
To opulent Hamburga turn aside!
So call'd, if legendary fame be true,
From Hama, whom a club-arm'd Cimbrian slew!
There lives, deep learn'd and primitively just,
A faithful steward of his Christian trust,
My friend, and favourite inmate of my heart
That now is forced to want its better part!
What mountains now, and seas, alas! how wide!
From me this other, dearer self divide,
Dear as the sage renown'd for moral truth
To the prime spirit of the Attic youth!
Dear as the Stagyrite to Ammon's son,
His pupil, who disdain'd the world he won;
Nor so did Chiron, or so Phœnix shine
In young Achilles' eyes, as he in mine.
First led by him through sweet Aonian shade,
Each sacred haunt of Pindus I survey'd;
And favour'd by the muse, whom I implored,
Thrice on my lip the hallow'd stream I pour'd.
But thrice the sun's resplendent chariot roll'd
To Aries, has new tinged his fleece with gold,
And Chloris twice has dress'd the meadows gay,
And twice has summer parch'd their bloom away,
Since last delighted on his looks I hung,
Or my ear drank the music of his tongue:
Fly, therefore, and surpass the tempest's speed;
Aware thyself that there is urgent need!
Him, entering, thou shalt haply seated see
Beside his spouse, his infants on his knee;
Or turning, page by page, with studious look,
Some bulky father, or God's holy book;
Or ministering (which is his weightiest care)
To Christ's assembled flock their heavenly fare.
Give him, whatever his employment be,
Such gratulation as he claims from me!
And, with a downcast eye, and carriage meek,
Addressing him, forget not thus to speak:

'If compass'd round with arms thou canst attend
To verse, verse greets thee from a distant friend.
Long due, and late, I left the English shore;
But make me welcome for that cause the more!
Such from Ulysses, his chaste wife to cheer
The slow epistle came, though late, sincere.
But wherefore this? why palliate I the deed
For which the culprit's self could hardly plead?
Self-charged, and self-condemn'd, his proper part
He feels neglected, with an aching heart;
But thou forgive—delinquents, who confess,
And pray forgiveness, merit anger less
From timid foes the lion turns away,
Nor yawns upon or rends a crouching prey,
E'en pike-wielding Thracians learn to spare,
Won by soft influence of a suppliant prayer;
And Heaven's dread thunderbolt arrested stands
By a cheap victim and uplifted hands.
Long had he wish'd to write, but was withheld,
And writes at last, by love alone compell'd,
For fame, too often true, when she alarms,
Reports thy neighbouring fields a scene of arms;
Thy city against fierce besiegers barr'd,
And all the Saxon chiefs for fight prepared.
Enyo wastes thy country wide around,
And saturates with blood the tainted ground;
Mars rests contented in his Thrace no more,
But goads his steeds to fields of German gore;
The ever-verdant olive fades and dies,
And peace, the trumpet-hating goddess, flies,
Flies from that earth which justice long had left,
And leaves the world of its last guard bereft.'
  Thus horror girds thee round. Meantime alone
Thou dwell'st, and helpless, in a soil unknown;
Poor, and receiving from a foreign hand
The aid denied thee in thy nat ve land.
Oh, ruthless country, and unfeeling more
Than thy own billow-beaten chalky shore!
Leavest thou to foreign care the worthies given
By providence to guide thy steps to heaven?
His ministers, commission'd to proclaim
Eternal blessings in a Saviour's name!

Ah then most worthy, with a soul unfed,
In Stygian night to lie for ever dead!
So once the venerable Tishbite stray'd
An exiled fugitive from shade to shade,
When, flying Ahab and his fury wife,
In lone Arabian wilds he shelter'd life;
So from Philippa wander'd forth forlorn
Cilician Paul, with sounding scourges torn;
And Christ himself, so left, and trod no more
The thankless Gergesene's forbidden shore.
  But thou take courage! strive against despair:
Quake not with dread, nor nourish anxious care!
Grim war, indeed, on every side appears,
And thou art menaced by a thousand spears;
Yet none shall drink thy blood, or shall offend
E'en the defenceless bosom of my friend.
For thee the Ægis of thy God shall hide,
Jehovah's self shall combat on thy side.
The same who vanquish'd under Sion's towers
At silent midnight all Assyria's powers,
The same who overthrew in ages past
Damascus' sons that laid Samaria waste!
Their king he fill'd and them with fatal fears
By mimic sounds of clarions in their ears,
Of hoofs, and wheels, and neighings from afar,
Of clashing armour, and the din of war.
  Thou, there (as the most afflicted may),
Still hope, and triumph o'er thy evil day!
Look forth, expecting happier times to come,
And to enjoy, once more, thy native home!

ELEGY V.

ON THE APPROACH OF SPRING.

Time, never wandering from his annual round,
Bids zephyr breathe the spring, and thaw the ground;
Bleak winter flies, new verdure clothes the plain,
And earth assumes her transient youth again.

Dream I, or also to the spring belong
Increase of genius, and new powers of song?
Spring gives them, and, how strange soe'er it seems,
Impels me now to some harmonious themes.
Castalia's fountain, and the forked hill
By day, by night, my raptured fancy fill;
My bosom burns and heaves, I hear within
A sacred sound that prompts me to begin.
Lo! Phœbus comes, with his bright hair he blends
The radiant laurel wreath; Phœbus descends!
I mount, and undepress'd by cumbrous clay,
Through cloudy regions win my easy way;
Rapt through poetic shadowy haunts I fly:
The shrines all open to my dauntless eye,
My spirit searches all the realms of light,
And no Tartarean gulfs elude my sight.
But this ecstatic trance—this glorious storm
Of inspiration—what will it perform?
Spring claims the verse that with his influence glows,
And shall be paid with what himself bestows.
  Thou, veil'd with opening foliage, lead'st the throng
Of feather'd minstrels, Philomel! in song;
Let us, in concert, to the season sing,
Civic and sylvan heralds of the spring!
  With notes triumphant spring's approach declare!
To spring, ye muses, annual tribute bear!
The orient left, and Ethiopia's plains,
The sun now northward turns his golden reins;
Night creeps not now; yet rules with gentle sway,
And drives her dusky horrors swift away
Now less fatigued, on this ethereal plain
Boötes follows his celestial wain;
And now the radiant centinels above,
Less numerous, watch around the courts of Jove,
For, with the night, force, ambush, slaughter fly,
And no gigantic guilt alarms the sky.
Now, haply says some shepherd, while he views,
Recumbent on a rock, the reddening dews,
This night, this, surely, Phœbus miss'd the fair,
Who stops his chariot by her amorous care.
Cynthia, delighted by the morning's glow,
Speeds to the woodland and resumes her bow;

Resigns her beams, and, glad to disappear,
Blesses his aid, who shortens her career.
Come—Phœbus cries—Aurora, come—too late
Thou lingerest, slumbering, with thy wither'd mate;
Leave him, and to Hymettus' top repair!
Thy darling Cephalus expects thee there.
The goddess with a blush her love betrays,
But mounts, and, driving rapidly, obeys.
Earth now desires thee, Phœbus! and, to engage
Thy warm embrace, casts off the guise of age;
Desires thee, and deserves; for who so sweet
When her rich bosom courts thy genial heat?
Her breath imparts to every breeze that blows
Arabia's harvest and the Paphian rose.
Her lofty front she diadems around
With sacred pines, like Ops on Ida crown'd;
Her dewy locks, with various flowers new blown,
She interweaves, various, and all her own;
For Proserpine, in such a wreath attired,
Tænarian Dis himself with love inspired.
Fear not, lest, cold and coy, the nymph refuse!
Herself, with all her sighing zephyrs, sues;
Each courts thee, fanning soft his scented wing,
And all her groves with warbled wishes ring.
Nor, unendow'd and indigent, aspires
The amorous earth to engage thy warm desires.
But, rich in balmy drugs, assists thy claim,
Divine Physician! to that glorious name.
If splendid recompense, if gifts can move
Desire in thee (gifts often purchase love),
She offers all the wealth her mountains hide,
And all that rests beneath the boundless tide.
How oft, when headlong from the heavenly steep
She sees thee playing in the western deep,
How oft she cries—'Ah Phœbus, why repair
Thy wasted force, why seek refreshment there?
Can Tethys win thee? wherefore shouldst thou lave
A face so fair in her unpleasant wave?
Come, seek my green retreats, and rather choose
To cool thy tresses in my crystal dews.
The grassy turf shall yield thee sweeter rest;
Come, lay thy evening glories on my breast,

And breathing fresh, through many a humid rose,
Soft whispering airs shall lull thee to repose!
No fears I feel like Semele to die,
Nor let thy burning wheels approach too nigh,
For thou canst govern them, here therefore rest,
And lay thy evening glories on my breast!'
  Thus breathes the wanton Earth her amorous flame,
And all her countless offspring feel the same;
For Cupid now through every region strays,
Brightening his faded fires with solar rays;
His new-strung bow sends forth a deadlier sound,
And his new-pointed shafts more deeply wound;
Nor Dian's self escapes him now untried,
Nor even Vesta at her altar side;
His mother too repairs her beauty's wane,
And seems sprung newly from the deep again.
Exulting youths the hymeneal sing,
With Hymen's name roofs, rocks, and valleys ring;
He, new attired, and by the season drest,
Proceeds, all fragrant, in his saffron vest.
Now many a golden-cinctured virgin roves
To taste the pleasures of the fields and groves,
All wish, and each alike, some favourite youth
Hers, in the bonds of hymeneal truth.
Now pipes the shepherd through his reeds again,
Nor Phillis wants a song that suits the strain;
With songs the seaman hails the starry sphere,
And dolphins rise from the abyss to hear:
Jove feels himself the season, sports again
With his fair spouse, and banquets all his train.
Now too the satyrs, in the dusk of eve,
Their mazy dance through flowery meadows weave
And neither god nor goat, but both in kind,
Silvanus, wreath'd with cypress, skips behind.
The dryads leave their hollow sylvan cells
To roam the banks and solitary dells;
Pan riots now; and from his amorous chafe
Ceres and Cybele seem hardly safe,
And Faunus, all on fire to reach the prize,
In chase of some enticing oread flies;
She bounds before, but fears too swift a bound,
And hidden lies, but wishes to be found.

Our shades entice the immortals from above,
And some kind power presides o'er every grove;
And long, ye powers, o'er every grove preside,
For all is safe, and blest, where ye abide!
Return, O Jove! the age of gold restore—
Why choose to dwell where storms and thunder roar?
At least thou, Phœbus! moderate thy speed!
Let not the vernal hours too swift proceed,
Command rough winter back, nor yield the pole
Too soon to night's encroaching, long control!

ELEGY VI.

TO CHARLES DEODATI,

Who, while he spent his Christmas in the country, sent the Author a poetical epistle, in which he requested that his verses, if not so good as usual, might be excused on account of the many feasts to which his friends invited him, and which would not allow him leisure to finish them as he wished.

With no rich viands overcharged, I send
Health, which perchance you want, my pamper'd friend.
But wherefore should thy muse tempt mine away
From what she loves, from darkness into day?
Art thou desirous to be told how well
I love thee, and in verse? verse cannot tell.
For verse has bounds, and must in measure move;
But neither bounds nor measure knows my love.
How pleasant, in thy lines described, appear
December's harmless sports, and rural cheer!
French spirits kindling with cærulean fires,
And all such gambols as the time inspires!
Think not that wine against good verse offends,
The muse and Bacchus have been always friends;
Nor Phœbus blushes sometimes to be found
With ivy, rather than with laurel, crown'd.
The Nine themselves ofttimes have join'd the song,
And revels of the Bacchanalian throng;
Not even Ovid could in Scythian air
Sing sweetly—why? no vine would flourish there.

What in brief numbers sung Anacreon's muse?
Wine, and the rose that sparkling wine bedews.
Pindar with Bacchus glows—his every line
Breathes the rich fragrance of inspiring wine,
While, with loud crash o'erturn'd, the chariot lies,
And brown with dust the fiery courser flies.
The Roman lyrist steep'd in wine his lays
So sweet in Glycera's and Chloe's praise.
Now too the plenteous feast and mantling bowl
Nourish the vigour of thy sprightly soul;
The flowing goblet makes thy numbers flow,
And casks not wine alone, but verse bestow.
Thus Phœbus favours, and the arts attend,
Whom Bacchus and whom Ceres both befriend.
What wonder, then, thy verses are so sweet
In which these triple powers so kindly meet!
The lute now also sounds, with gold inwrought,
And, touch'd with flying fingers nicely taught,
In tapestried halls, high roof'd, the sprightly lyre
Directs the dancers of the virgin choir.
If dull repletion fright the muse away,
Sights gay as these may more invite her stay;
And, trust me, while the ivory keys resound,
Fair damsels sport, and perfumes steam around,
Apollo's influence, like ethereal flame,
Shall animate, at once thy glowing frame,
And all the muse shall rush into thy breast,
By love and music's blended powers possest.
For numerous powers light elegy befriend,
Hear her sweet voice, and at her call attend;
Her, Bacchus, Ceres, Venus, all approve,
And, with his blushing mother, gentle Love.
Hence to such bards we grant the copious use
Of banquets, and the vine's delicious juice.
But they who demigods and heroes praise,
And feats perform'd in Jove's more youthful days,
Who now the counsels of high heaven explore,
Now shades that echo the Cerberean roar,
Simply let these, like him of Samos, live,
Let herbs to them a bloodless banquet give;
In beechen goblets let their beverage shine,
Cool from the crystal spring, their sober wine!

Their youth should pass in innocence secure
From stain licentious, and in manners pure,
Pure as the priest, when robed in white he stands,
The fresh lustration ready in his hands.
Thus Linus lived, and thus, as poets write,
Tiresias, wiser for his loss of sight;
Thus exiled Chalcas, thus the Bard of Thrace,
Melodious Tamar of the savage race;
Thus train'd by temperance, Homer led, of yore,
His chief of Ithaca from shore to shore,
Through magic Circe's monster-peopled reign,
And shoals insidious with the syren train;
And through the realms where grizzly spectres dwell,
Whose tribes he fetter'd in a gory spell;
For these are sacred bards, and from above
Drink large infusions from the mind of Jove.
Wouldst thou (perhaps 'tis hardly worth thine ear)
Wouldst thou be told my occupation here?
The promised King of peace employs my pen,
The eternal covenant made for guilty men,
The new-born Deity with infant cries
Filling the sordid hovel where he lies;
The hymning angels, and the herald star,
That led the wise, who sought him from afar,
And idols on their own unhallow'd shore
Dash'd, at his birth, to be revered no more.
This theme on reeds of Albion I rehearse:
The dawn of that blest day inspired the verse,
Verse that, reserved in secret, shall attend
Thy candid voice, my critic, and my friend!

ELEGY VII.

As yet a stranger to the gentle fires
That Amathusia's smiling queen inspires,
Not seldom I derided Cupid's darts,
And scorn'd his claim to rule all human hearts.
'Go, child,' I said, 'transfix the timorous dove!
An easy conquest suits an infant love;

Enslave the sparrow, for such prize shall be
Sufficient triumph to a chief like thee!
Why aim thy idle arms at human kind?
Thy shafts prevail not 'gainst the noble mind.'
 The Cyprian heard, and, kindling into ire,
(None kindles sooner) burn'd with double fire.
 It was the spring, and newly-risen day
Peep'd o'er the hamlets on the first of May;
My eyes, too tender for the blaze of light,
Still sought the shelter of retiring night,
When love approach'd, in painted plumes array'd,
The insidious god his rattling darts betray'd,
Nor less his infant features, and the sly,
Sweet intimations of his threatening eye.
 Such the Sigeian boy is seen above
Filling the goblet for imperial Jove;
Such he, on whom the nymphs bestow'd their charms,
Hylas, who perish'd in a naiad's arms.
Angry he seem'd, yet graceful in his ire,
And added threats not destitute of fire.
'My power,' he said, 'by others' pain alone,
'Twere best to learn; now learn it by thy own!
With those that feel my power, that power attest!
And in thy anguish be my sway confest!
I vanquish'd Phœbus, though returning vain
From his new triumph o'er the Python slain,
And, when he thinks on Daphne, even he
Will yield the prize of archery to me.
A dart less true the Parthian horseman sped,
Behind him kill'd, and conquer'd as he fled:
Less true the expert Cydonian, and less true
The youth whose shaft his latent Procris slew.
Vanquish'd by me see huge Orion bend,
By me Alcides, and Alcides' friend.
At me should Jove himself a bolt design,
His bosom first should bleed transfix'd by mine.
But all thy doubts this shaft will best explain,
Nor shall it reach thee with a trivial pain.
Thy muse, vain youth! shall not thy peace ensure,
Nor Phœbus' serpent yield thy wound a cure.'
 He spoke, and, waving a bright shaft in air,
Sought the warm bosom of the Cyprian fair.

That thus a child should bluster in my ear,
Provoked my laughter more than moved my fear.
I shunn'd not, therefore, public haunts, but stray'd
Careless in city or suburban shade,
And, passing and repassing nymphs that moved
With grace divine, beheld where'er I roved.
Bright shone the vernal day with double blaze
As beauty gave new force to Phœbus' rays.
By no grave scruples check'd, I freely eyed
The dangerous show, rash youth my only guide,
And many a look of many a fair unknown
Met full, unable to control my own.
But one I mark'd (then peace forsook my breast),
One—Oh how far superior to the rest!
What lovely features! such the Cyprian queen
Herself might wish, and Juno wish her mien.
The very nymph was she, whom, when I dared
His arrows, Love had even then prepared!
Nor was himself remote, nor unsupplied
With torch well trimm'd and quiver at his side;
Now to her lips he clung, her eyelids now,
Then settled on her cheeks, or on her brow;
And with a thousand wounds from every part
Pierced and transpierced my undefended heart.
A fever, new to me, of fierce desire
Now seized my soul, and I was all on fire;
But she, the while, whom only I adore,
Was gone, and vanish'd, to appear no more.
In silent sadness I pursue my way;
I pause, I turn, proceed, yet wish to stay,
And, while I follow her in thought, bemoan
With tears my soul's delight so quickly flown.
When Jove had hurl'd him to the Lemnian coast,
So Vulcan sorrow'd for Olympus lost,
And so Œclides, sinking into night,
From the deep gulf look'd up to distant light.
Wretch that I am, what hopes for me remain,
Who cannot cease to love, yet love in vain?
Oh could I once, once more behold the fair,
Speak to her, tell her of the pangs I bear;
Perhaps she is not adamant; would show,
Perhaps, some pity at my tale of woe.

Oh inauspicious flame—'tis mine to prove
A matchless instance of disastrous love.
Ah, spare me, gentle power!—If such thou be,
Let not thy deeds and nature disagree.
Spare me, and I will worship at no shrine
With vow and sacrifice save only thine.
Now I revere thy fires, thy bow, thy darts:
Now own thee sovereign of all human hearts.
Remove! no—grant me still this raging woe!
Sweet is the wretchedness that lovers know:
But pierce hereafter (should I chance to see
One destined mine) at once both her and me.
Such were the trophies that, in earlier days,
By vanity seduced, I toil'd to raise;
Studious, yet indolent, and urged by youth,
That worst of teachers! from the ways of truth;
Till learning taught me in his shady bower
To quit love's servile yoke, and spurn his power.
Then, on a sudden, the fierce flame suppress,
A frost continual settled on my breast,
Whence Cupid fears his flames extinct to see,
And Venus dreads a Diomede in me.

EPIGRAMS.

ON THE INVENTOR OF GUNS.

Praise in old time the sage Prometheus won,
Who stole ethereal radiance from the sun;
But greater he, whose bold invention strove
To emulate the fiery bolts of Jove.

[The Poems on the subject of the Gunpowder Treason I have not translated, both because the matter of them is unpleasant, and because they are written with an asperity, which, however it might be warranted in Milton's day, would be extremely unseasonable now.]

TO LEONORA SINGING AT ROME.*

Another Leonora once inspired
Tasso, with fatal love to phrensy fired;
But how much happier, lived he now, were he,
Pierced with whatever pangs for love of thee!
Since could he hear that heavenly voice of thine,
With Adriana's lute of sound divine,
Fiercer than Pentheus' though his eye might roll,
Or idiot apathy benumb his soul,
You still, with medicinal sounds might cheer
His senses wandering in a blind career;
And, sweetly breathing through his wounded breast,
Charm, with soul-soothing song, his thoughts to rest.

TO THE SAME.

Naples, too creaulous, ah! boast no more
The sweet-voiced syren buried on thy shore,
That, when Parthenope deceased, she gave
Her sacred dust to a Chalcidic grave,
For still she lives, but has exchanged the hoarse
Pausilipo for Tiber's placid course,
Where, idol of all Rome, she now in chains
Of magic song both gods and men detains.

THE COTTAGER AND HIS LANDLORD.

A FABLE

A peasant to his lord paid yearly court,
Presenting pippins of so rich a sort

* I have translated only two of the three poetical compliments addressed to Leonora, as they appear to me far superior to what I have omitted.

That he, displeased to have a part alone,
Removed the tree, that all might be his own.
The tree, too old to travel, though before
So fruitful, wither'd, and would yield no more.
The squire, perceiving all his labour void,
Cursed his own pains, so foolishly employ'd,
And, 'Oh,' he cried, 'that I had lived content
With tribute, small indeed, but kindly meant!
My avarice has expensive proved to me,
Has cost me both my pippins and my tree.'

TO CHRISTINA, QUEEN OF SWEDEN, WITH CROMWELL'S PICTURE.

Christina, maiden of heroic mien!
Star of the North! of northern stars the queen!
Behold what wrinkles I have earn'd, and how
The iron casque still chafes my veteran brow,
While following Fate's dark footsteps, I fulfil
The dictates of a hardy people's will.
But soften'd in thy sight my looks appear,
Not to all queens or kings alike severe.

ON THE DEATH OF THE VICE-CHANCELLOR,

A PHYSICIAN.

Learn, ye nations of the earth,
The condition of your birth,
Now be taught your feeble state!
Know, that all must yield to fate!

If the mournful rover, Death,
Say but once—'Resign your breath!'
Vainly of escape you dream,
You must pass the Stygian stream.

Could the stoutest overcome
Death's assault, and baffle doom,
Hercules had both withstood,
Undiseased by Nessus' blood

Ne'er had Hector press'd the plain
By a trick of Pallas slain,
Nor the chief to Jove allied
By Achilles' phantom died.

Could enchantments life prolong,
Circe, saved by magic song,
Still had lived, and equal skill
Had preserved Medea still.

Dwelt in herbs and drugs a power
To avert man's destined hour,
Learn'd Machaon should have known
Doubtless to avert his own.

Chiron had survived the smart
Of the hydra-tainted dart,
And Jove's bolt had been, with ease
Foil'd by Asclepiades.

Thou too, sage! of whom forlorn
Helicon and Cirrha mourn,
Still hadst fill'd thy princely place
Regent of the gowned race:

Hadst advanced to higher fame
Still thy much-ennobled name,
Nor in Charon's skiff explored
The Tartarean gulf abhorr'd.

But resentful Proserpine,
Jealous of thy skill divine,
Snapping short thy vital thread,
Thee too number'd with the dead.

Wise and good! untroubled be
The green turf that covers thee!
Thence, in gay profusion, grow
All the sweetest flowers that blow

Pluto's consort bid thee rest!
Æacus pronounce thee blest!
To her home thy shade consign
Make Elysium ever thine!

ON THE DEATH OF THE BISHOP OF ELY.

My lids with grief were tumid yet,
And still my sullied cheek was wet
With briny dews, profusely shed
For venerable Winton dead;
When fame, whose tales of saddest sound,
Alas! are ever truest found,
The news through all our cities spread
Of yet another mitred head
By ruthless fate to death consign'd,
Ely, the honour of his kind!
At once a storm of passion heaved
My boiling bosom, much I grieved;
But more I raged, at every breath
Devoting Death himself to death.
With less revenge did Naso teem
When hated Ibis was his theme;
With less Archilochus denied
The lovely Greek his promised bride.
But lo! while thus I execrate
Incensed the minister of fate,
Wondrous accents, soft, yet clear,
Wafted on the gale I hear.
'Ah, much deluded! lay aside
Thy threats, and anger misapplied!
Art not afraid with sounds like these
To offend, where thou canst not appease?
Death is not (wherefore dream'st thou thus?)
The son of night and Erebus:
Nor was of fell Erynnis born
On gulfs where Chaos rules forlorn.
But sent from God, his presence leaves,
To gather home his ripen'd sheaves,
To call encumber'd souls away
From fleshly bonds to boundless day,
(As when the winged hours excite,
And summon forth the morning light)
And each to convoy to her place
Before the Eternal Father's face.

But not the wicked—them, severe
Yet just, from all their pleasures here
He hurries to the realms below,
Terrific realms of penal woe!
Myself no sooner heard his call,
Than, 'scaping through my prison wall,
I bade adieu to bolts and bars,
And soar'd, with angels, to the stars,
Like him of old, to whom 'twas given
To mount on fiery wheels to heaven.
Boöte's waggon, slow with cold,
Appall'd me not; nor to behold
The sword that vast Orion draws,
Or e'en the scorpion's horrid claws.
Beyond the sun's bright orb I fly,
And far beneath my feet descry
Night's dread goddess, seen with awe,
Whom her winged dragons draw.
Thus, ever wondering at my speed,
Augmented still as I proceed,
I pass the planetary sphere,
The milky way—and now appear
Heaven's crystal battlements, her door
Of massy pearl, and emerald floor.
  But here I cease. For never can
The tongue of once a mortal man
In suitable description trace
The pleasures of that happy place;
Suffice it, that those joys divine
Are all, and all for ever mine!'

NATURE UNIMPAIRED BY TIME.

Ah, how the human mind wearies herself
With her own wanderings, and, involved in gloom
Impenetrable, speculates amiss!
Measuring in her folly things divine
By human; laws inscribed on adamant

By laws of man's device, and counsels fix'd
For ever, by the hours that pass and die.
How?—shall the face of nature then be plough'd
Into deep wrinkles, and shall years at last
On the great parent fix a sterile curse?
Shall even she confess old age, and halt,
And, palsy-smitten, shake her starry brows?
Shall foul antiquity with rust, and drought,
And famine, vex the radiant worlds above?
Shall time's unsated maw crave and ingulf
The very heavens, that regulate his flight?
And was the sire of all able to fence
His works, and to uphold the circling worlds,
But, through improvident and heedless haste
Let slip the occasion?—so then—all is lost—
And in some future evil hour, yon arch
Shall crumble, and come thundering down, the poles
Jar in collision, the Olympian king
Fall with his throne, and Pallas, holding forth
The terrors of the Gorgon shield in vain,
Shall rush to the abyss, like Vulcan hurl'd
Down into Lemnos, through the gate of heaven.
Thou also, with precipitated wheels,
Phœbus! thy own son's fall shall imitate,
With hideous ruin shalt impress the deep
Suddenly, and the flood shall reek, and hiss,
At the extinction of the lamp of day.
Then too shall Hæmus, cloven to his base,
Be shatter'd, and the huge Ceraunian hills,
Once weapons of Tartarean Dis, immersed
In Erebus, shall fill himself with fear.
No. The Almighty Father surer laid
His deep foundations, and, providing well
For the event of all, the scales of fate
Suspended in just equipoise, and bade
His universal works, from age to age,
One tenour hold, perpetual, undisturb'd.
Hence the prime mover wheels itself about
Continual, day by day, and with it bears
In social measure swift the heavens around.
Not tardier now is Saturn than of old,
Nor radiant less the burning casque of Mars.

Phœbus, his vigour unimpair'd, still shows
The effulgence of his youth, nor needs the god
A downward course, that he may warm the vales;
But, ever rich in influence, runs his road,
Sign after sign, through all the heavenly zone
Beautiful, as at first, ascends the star
From odoriferous Ind, whose office is
To gather home betimes the ethereal flock,
To pour them o'er the skies again at eve,
And to discriminate the night and day.
Still Cynthia's changeful horn waxes and wan
Alternate, and with arms extended still
She welcomes to her breast her brother's beams.
Nor have the elements deserted yet
Their functions; thunder with as loud a stroke
As erst smites through the rocks and scatters them.
The east still howls; still the relentless north
Invades the shuddering Scythian, still he breathes
The winter, and still rolls the storms along.
The king of ocean, with his wonted force,
Beats on Pelorus; o'er the deep is heard
The hoarse alarm of Triton's sounding shell;
Nor swim the monsters of the Ægean sea
In shallows, or beneath diminish'd waves.
Thou too, thy ancient vegetative power
Enjoy'st, O earth! Narcissus still is sweet
And Phœbus! still thy favourite, and still
Thy favourite Cytherea! both retain
Their beauty; nor the mountains, ore-enrich'd
For punishment of man, with purer gold
Teem'd ever, or with brighter gems the deep.
 Thus in unbroken series all proceeds;
And shall, till wide involving either pole,
And the immensity of yonder heaven,
The final flames of destiny absorb
The world, consumed in one enormous pyre

ON THE PLATONIC IDEA,

AS IT WAS UNDERSTOOD BY ARISTOTLE.

Ye sister powers, who o'er the sacred groves
Preside, and thou, fair mother of them all,
Mnemosyne! and thou who, in thy grot
Immense, reclined at leisure, hast in charge
The archives and the ordinances of Jove,
And dost record the festivals of heaven,
Eternity!—inform us who is He,
That great original by nature chosen
To be the archetype of human kind,
Unchangeable, immortal, with the poles
Themselves coeval, one, yet every where
An image of the God who gave him being?
Twin-brother of the goddess born from Jove,
He dwells not in his father's mind, but, though
Of common nature with ourselves, exists
Apart, and occupies a local home.
Whether, companion of the stars, he spend
Eternal ages, roaming at his will
From sphere to sphere the tenfold heavens, or dwell
On the moon's side that nearest neighbours earth,
Or torpid on the banks of Lethe sit,
Among the multitude of souls ordain'd
To flesh and blood; or whether (as may chance)
That vast and giant model of our kind
In some far distant region of this globe
Sequester'd stalk, with lifted head on high
O'ertowering Atlas, on whose shoulders rest
The stars, terrific even to the gods.
Never the Theban seer, whose blindness proved
His best illumination, him beheld
In secret vision; never him the son
Of Pleione, amid the noiseless night
Descending, to the prophet-choir reveal'd;
Him never knew the Assyrian priest, who yet
The ancestry of Ninus' chronicles,
And Belus, and Osiris, far renown'd,
Nor even thrice great Hermes, although skill'd

So deep in mystery, to the worshippers
Of Isis show'd a prodigy like him.
  And thou, who hast immortalized the shades
Of Academus, if the schools received
This monster of the fancy first from thee
Either recall at once the banish'd bards
To thy republic, or thyself, evinced
A wilder fabulist, go also forth.

TO HIS FATHER.

Oh that Pieria's spring would through my breast
Pour its inspiring influence, and rush
No rill, but rather an o'erflowing flood
That, for my venerable father's sake
All meaner themes renounced, my muse, on wings
Of duty borne, might reach a loftier strain.
For thee, my father! howsoe'er it please,
She frames this slender work; nor know I aught
That may thy gifts more suitably requite;
Though to requite them suitably would ask
Returns much nobler, and surpassing far
The meagre stores of verbal gratitude:
But, such as I possess, I send thee all.
This page presents thee in their full amount
With thy son's treasures, and the sum is nought;
Nought, save the riches that from airy dream
In secret grottos and in laurel bowers,
I have, by golden Clio's gift, acquired.
  Verse is a work divine; despise not thou
Verse therefore, which evinces (nothing more)
Man's heavenly source, and which, retaining still
Some scintillations of Promethean fire,
Bespeaks him animated from above.
The gods love verse; the infernal powers themselves
Confess the influence of verse, which stirs
The lowest deep, and binds in triple chains
Of adamant both Pluto and the shades.

In verse the Delphic priestess and the pale
Tremulous sybil make the future known;
And he who sacrifices, on the shrine [bull
Hangs verse, both when he smites the threatening
And when he spreads his reeking entrails wide
To scrutinize the fates enveloped there.
We too, ourselves, what time we seek again
Our native skies, and one eternal now
Shall be the only measure of our being,
Crown'd all with gold, and chanting to the lyre
Harmonious verse, shall range the courts above,
And make the starry firmament resound.
And, even now, the fiery spirit pure
That wheels yon circling orbs, directs himself
Their mazy dance with melody of verse
Unutterable, immortal, hearing which
Huge Ophiuchus holds his hiss suppress'd;
Orion, soften'd, drops his ardent blade,
And Atlas stands unconscious of his load.
Verse graced of old the feasts of kings, ere yet
Luxurious dainties, destined to the gulf
Immense of gluttony, were known, and ere
Lyæus deluged yet the temperate board.
Then sat the bard a customary guest
To share the banquet, and, his length of locks
With beechen honours bound, proposed in verse
The characters of heroes and their deeds,
To imitation, sang of chaos old,
Of nature's birth, of gods that crept in search
Of acorns fallen, and of the thunderbolt
Not yet produced from Ætna's fiery cave.
And what avails, at last, tune without voice,
Devoid of matter? Such may suit perhaps
The rural dance, but such was ne'er the song
Of Orpheus, whom the streams stood still to hear
And the oaks follow'd. Not by chords alone
Well touch'd, but by resistless accents more
To sympathetic tears the ghosts themselves
He moved; these praises to his verse he owes.
  Nor thou persist, I pray thee, still to slight
The sacred Nine, and to imagine vain
And useless powers, by whom inspired, thyself

Art skilful to associate verse with airs
Harmonious, and to give the human voice
A thousand modulations, heir by right
Indisputable of Arion's fame.
Now say, what wonder is it, if a son
Of thine delight in verse, if, so conjoin'd
In close affinity, we sympathize
In social arts and kindred studies sweet?
Such distribution of himself to us
Was Phœbus' choice; thou hast thy gift, and I
Mine also, and between us we receive,
Father and son, the whole inspiring god.
 No! howsoe'er the semblance thou assume
Of hate, thou hatest not the gentle muse,
My father! for thou never badest me tread
The beaten path, and broad, that leads right on
To opulence, nor didst condemn thy son
To the insipid clamours of the bar,
To laws voluminous, and ill observed;
But, wishing to enrich me more, to fill
My mind with treasure, ledst me far away
From city din to deep retreats, to banks
And streams Aonian, and, with free consent
Didst place me happy at Apollo's side.
I speak not now, on more important themes
Intent, of common benefits, and such
As nature bids, but of thy larger gifts,
My father! who, when I had open'd once
The stores of Roman rhetorick, and learn'd
The full-toned language of the eloquent Greeks,
Whose lofty music graced the lips of Jove,
Thyself didst counsel me to add the flowers
That Gallia boasts, those too, with which the smooth
Italian his degenerate speech adorns,
That witnesses his mixture with the Goth;
And Palestine's prophetic songs divine.
To sum the whole, whate'er the heaven contains,
The earth beneath it, and the air between,
The rivers and the restless deep, may all
Prove intellectual gain to me, my wish
Concurring with thy will; science herself,
All cloud removed, inclines her beauteous head,

And offers me the lip, if, dull of heart,
I shrink not, and decline her gracious boon.
Go now, and gather dross, ye sordid minds
That covet it; what could my father more?
What more could Jove himself, unless he gave
His own abode, the heaven, in which he reigns?
More eligible gifts than these were not
Apollo's to his son, had they been safe
As they were insecure, who made the boy
The world's vice-luminary, bade him rule
The radiant chariot of the day, and bind
To his young brows his own all-dazzling wreath.
I therefore, although last and least, my place
Among the learned in the laurel grove
Will hold, and where the conqueror's ivy twines,
Henceforth exempt from the unletter'd throng
Profane, nor even to be seen by such.
Away then, sleepless care, complaint, away,
And envy, with thy 'jealous leer malign!'
Nor let the monster calumny shoot forth
Her venom'd tongue at me. Detested foes!
Ye all are impotent against my peace,
For I am privileged, and bear my breast
Safe, and too high, for your viperean wound.
But thou, my father! since to render thanks
Equivalent, and to requite by deeds
Thy liberality, exceeds my power,
Suffice it, that I thus record thy gifts,
And bear them treasured in a grateful mind!
Ye, too, the favourite pastime of my youth,
My voluntary numbers, if ye dare
To hope longevity, and to survive
Your master's funeral, not soon absorb'd
In the oblivious Lethæan gulf,
Shall to futurity perhaps convey
This theme, and by these praises of my sire
Improve the fathers of a distant age!

TO SALSILLUS, A ROMAN POET, MUCH INDISPOSED.

The original is written in a measure called Scazon, which signifies limping, and the measure is so denominated, because, though in other respects Iambic, it terminates with a Spondee, and has, consequently, a more tardy movement.

The reader will immediately see that this property of the Latin verse cannot be imitated in English.

My halting muse, that dragg'st by choice along
Thy slow, slow step, in melancholy song,
And likest that pace, expressive of thy cares,
Not less than Diopeia's sprightlier airs,
When in the dance she beats with measured tread
Heaven's floor, in front of Juno's golden bed;
Salute Salsillus, who to verse divine
Prefers, with partial love, such lays as mine.
Thus writes that Milton, then, who, wafted o'er
From his own nest on Albion's stormy shore,
Where Eurus, fiercest of the Æolian band,
Sweeps with ungovern'd rage the blasted land,
Of late to more serene Ausonia came
To view her cities of illustrious name,
To prove, himself a witness of the truth,
How wise her elders, and how learn'd her youth.
Much good, Salsillus! and a body free
From all disease, that Milton asks for thee,
Who now endurest the languor and the pains
That bile inflicts, diffused through all thy veins;
Relentless malady! not moved to spare
By thy sweet Roman voice and Lesbian air!
  Health, Hebe's sister, sent us from the skies
And thou, Apollo, whom all sickness flies,
Pythius, or Pæan, or what name divine
Soe'er thou choose, haste, heal a priest of thine!
Ye groves of Faunus, and ye hills that melt
With vinous dews, where meek Evander dwelt!
If aught salubrious in your confines grow,
Strive which shall soonest heal your poet's woe,
That, render'd to the muse he loves, again
He may enchant the meadows with his strain.

Numa, reclined in everlasting ease
Amid the shade of dark embowering trees,
Viewing with eyes of unabated fire
His loved Ægeria, shall that strain admire
So sooth'd, the tumid Tiber shall revere
The tombs of kings, nor desolate the year,
Shall curb his waters with a friendly rein,
And guide them harmless, till they meet the main.

TO GIOVANNI BATTISTA MANSO

MARQUIS OF VILLA.

MILTON'S ACCOUNT OF MANSO.

Giovanni Battista Manso, Marquis of Villa, is an Italian nobleman of the highest estimation among his countrymen, for genius, literature, and military accomplishments. To him Torquato Tasso addressed his Dialogues on Friendship, for he was much the friend of Tasso, who has also celebrated him among the other princes of his country, in his poem entitled Gerusalemme Conquistata, book xx

Fra cavalier magnanimi, e cortesi,
Risplende il Manso.

During the Author's stay at Naples, he received at the hands of the Marquis a thousand kind offices and civilities, and, desirous not to appear ungrateful, sent him this poem a short time before his departure from that city.

These verses also to thy praise, the Nine,
O Manso! happy in that theme, design,
For, Gallus and Mæcenas gone, they see
None such besides, or whom they love as thee
And if my verse may give the meed of fame,
Thine too shall prove an everlasting name.
Already such, it shines in Tasso's page
(For thou wast Tasso's friend) from age to age,
And, next, the muse consign'd (not unaware
How high the charge) Marino to thy care,
Who, singing to the nymphs Adonis' praise,
Boasts thee the patron of his copious lays.
To thee alone the poet would entrust
His latest vows, to thee alone his dust;

And thou with punctual piety hast paid,
In labour'd brass, thy tribute to his shade.
Nor this contented thee—but lest the grave [save,
Should aught absorb of theirs which thou couldst
All future ages thou hast deign'd to teach
The life, lot, genius, character of each,
Eloquent as the Carian sage, who, true
To his great theme, the life of Homer drew.
I, therefore, though a stranger youth, who come
Chill'd by rude blasts that freeze my northern home.
Thee dear to Clio, confident proclaim,
And thine, for Phœbus' sake, a deathless name.
Nor thou, so kind, wilt view with scornful eye
A muse scarce rear'd beneath our sullen sky,
Who fears not, indiscreet as she is young,
To seek in Latium hearers of her song.
We too, where Thames with its unsullied waves
The tresses of the blue-hair'd Ocean laves,
Hear oft by night, or, slumbering, seem to hear,
O'er his wide stream, the swan's voice warbling
And we could boast a Tityrus of yore [clear;
Who trod, a welcome guest, your happy shore.
Yes—dreary as we own our northern clime,
E'en we to Phœbus raise the polish'd rhyme,
We too serve Phœbus; Phœbus has received
(If legends old may claim to be believed)
No sordid gifts from us, the golden ear,
The burnish'd apple, ruddiest of the year,
The fragrant crocus, and, to grace his fane,
Fair damsels chosen from the druid train
Druids, our native bards in ancient time,
Who gods and heroes praised in hallow'd rhyme!
Hence, often as the maids of Greece surround
Apollo's shrine with hymns of festive sound,
They name the virgins who arrived of yore
With British offerings on the Delian shore,
Loxo, from giant Corineus sprung,
Upis, on whose blest lips the future hung,
And Hacaerge, with the golden hair, [bare.
All deck'd with Pictish hues, and all with bosoms
Thou, therefore, happy sage, whatever clime
Shall ring with Tasso's praise in after time,

Or with Marino's, shalt be known their friend
And with an equal flight to fame ascend.
The world shall hear how Phœbus and the Nine
Were inmates once, and willing guests of thine.
Yet Phœbus, when of old constrain'd to roam
The earth, an exile from his heavenly home
Enter'd, no willing guest, Admetus' door,
Though Hercules had ventured there before.
But gentle Chiron's cave was near, a scene
Of rural peace, cloth'd with perpetual green,
And thither, oft as respite he required
From rustic clamours loud, the god retired.
There, many a time, on Peneus' bank reclined
At some oak's root, with ivy thick entwined,
Won by his hospitable friend's desire,
He sooth'd his pains of exile with the lyre.
Then shook the hills, then trembled Peneus' shore,
Nor Œta felt his load of forest more;
The upland elms descended to the plain,
And soften'd lynxes wonder'd at that strain.
Well may we think, Oh, dear to all above!
Thy birth distinguish'd by the smile of Jove,
And that Apollo shed his kindliest power,
And Maia's son, on that propitious hour,
Since only minds so born can comprehend
A poet's worth, or yield that worth a friend.
Hence on thy yet unfaded cheek appears
The lingering freshness of thy greener years,
Hence in thy front and features we admire
Nature unwither'd and a mind entire.
O might so true a friend to me belong,
So skill'd to grace the votaries of song,
Should I recall hereafter into rhyme
The kings and heroes of my native clime,
Arthur the chief, who even now prepares,
In subterraneous being, future wars,
With all his martial knights, to be restored
Each to his seat around the federal board;
And Oh, if spirit fail me not, disperse
Our Saxon plunderers in triumphant verse!
Then, after all, when, with the past content,
A life I finish, not in silence spent;

Should he, kind mourner, o'er my death-bed bend
I shall but need to say—'Be yet my friend!'
He, too, perhaps, shall bid the marble breathe
To honour me, and with the graceful wreath
Or of Parnassus or the Paphian isle
Shall bind my brows—but I shall rest the while
Then also, if the fruits of faith endure,
And virtue's promised recompense be sure,
Born to those seats to which the blest aspire
By purity of soul and virtuous fire,
These rites, as fate permits, I shall survey
With eyes illumined by celestial day,
And, every cloud from my pure spirit driven,
Joy in the bright beatitude of heaven!

ON THE DEATH OF DAMON.

THE ARGUMENT.

Thyrsis and Damon, shepherds and neighbours, had always pursued the same studies, and had, from their earliest days, been united in the closest friendship. Thyrsis, while travelling for improvement, received intelligence of the death of Damon, and, after a time, returning and finding it true, deplores himself, and his solitary condition, in this poem.

By Damon is to be understood Charles Deodati, connected with the Italian city of Lucca by his father's side, in other respects an Englishman; a youth of uncommon genius, erudition, and virtue.

Ye Nymphs of Himera, (for ye have shed
Erewhile for Daphnis, and for Hylas dead,
And over Bion's long-lamented bier,
The fruitless meed of many a sacred tear)
Now through the villas laved by Thames rehearse
The woes of Thyrsis in Sicilian verse,
What sighs he heaved, and how with groans profound
He made the woods and hollow rocks resound,
Young Damon dead; nor even ceased to pour
His lonely sorrows at the midnight hour.
The green wheat twice had nodded in the ear,
And golden harvest twice enrich'd the year,
Since Damon's lips had gasp'd for vital air
The last, last time, nor Thyrsis yet was there;

For he, enamour'd of the muse, remain'd
In Tuscan Fiorenza long detain'd,
But, stored at length with all he wish'd to learn,
For his flock's sake now hasted to return;
And when the shepherd had resumed his seat
At the elm's root, within his old retreat,
Then 'twas his lot, then all his loss to know,
And from his burthen'd heart he vented thus his woe:
'Go, seek your home, my lambs; my thoughts are
To other cares than those of feeding you. [due
Alas! what deities shall I suppose
In heaven, or earth, concern'd for human woes,
Since, Oh my Damon! their severe decree
So soon condemns me to regret of thee!
Depart'st thou thus, thy virtues unrepaid
With fame and honour, like a vulgar shade!
Let him forbid it whose bright rod controls,
And separates sordid from illustrious souls;
Drive far the rabble, and to thee assign
A happier lot with spirits worthy thine!
'Go, seek your home, my lambs; my thoughts are
To other cares than those of feeding you. [due
Whate'er befall, unless by cruel chance
The wolf first give me a forbidding glance,
Thou shalt not moulder undeplored, but long
Thy praise shall dwell on every shepherd's tongue.
To Daphnis first they shall delight to pay,
And, after him, to thee the votive lay,
While Pales shall the flocks and pastures love,
Or Faunus to frequent the field or grove;
At least, if ancient piety and truth,
With all the learned labours of thy youth,
May serve thee aught, or to have left behind
A sorrowing friend, and of the tuneful kind.
'Go, seek your home, my lambs; my thoughts are
To other cares than those of feeding you. [due
Who, now, my pains and perils shall divide,
As thou wast wont, for ever at my side,
Both when the rugged frost annoy'd our feet,
And when the herbage all was parch'd with heat;
Whether the grim wolf's ravage to prevent,
Or the huge lion's, arm'd with darts we went;

Whose converse now shall calm my stormy day,
With charming song who now beguile my way?
 'Go, seek your home, my lambs; my thoughts are
To other cares than those of feeding you. [due
In whom shall I confide? Whose counsel find
A balmy medicine for my troubled mind?
Or whose discourse with innocent delight
Shall fill me now, and cheat the wintry night,
While hisses on my hearth the pulpy pear,
And blackening chestnuts start and crackle there,
While storms abroad the dreary meadows whelm,
And the wind thunders through the neighbouring elm.
 'Go, seek your home, my lambs; my thoughts are
To other cares than those of feeding you. [due
Or who, when summer suns their summit reach,
And Pan sleeps hidden by the sheltering beech,
When shepherds disappear, nymphs seek the sedge,
And the stretch'd rustic snores beneath the hedge,
Who then shall render me thy pleasant vein
Of Attic wit, thy jests, thy smiles again?
 'Go, seek your home, my lambs; my thoughts are
To other cares than those of feeding you. [due
Where glens and vales are thickest overgrown
With tangled boughs, I wander now alone,
Till night descend, while blustering wind and shower
Beat on my temples through the shatter'd bower.
 'Go, seek your home, my lambs; my thoughts are
To other cares than those of feeding you. [due
Alas! what rampant weeds now shame my fields,
And what a mildew'd crop the furrow yields;
My rambling vines, unwedded to the trees,
Bear shrivel'd grapes; my myrtles fail to please;
Nor please me more my flocks: they, slighted, turn
Their unavailing looks on me, and mourn.
 'Go, seek your home, my lambs; my thoughts are
To other cares than those of feeding you. [due
Ægon invites me to the hazel grove,
Amyntas, on the river's bank to rove,
And young Alphesibœus to a seat
Where branching elms exclude the mid-day heat.
"Here fountains spring—here mossy hillocks rise;
Here zephyr whispers, and the stream replies."

Thus each persuades, but, deaf to every call,
I gain the thickets, and escape them all.
' Go, seek your home, my lambs; my thoughts are
To other cares than those of feeding you. [due
Then Mopsus said, (the same who reads so well
The voice of birds, and what the stars foretell,
For he by chance had noticed my return)
' What means thy sullen mood, this deep concern?
Ah, Thyrsis! thou art either crazed with love,
Or some sinister influence from above;
Dull Saturn's influence oft the shepherds rue;
His leaden shaft oblique has pierced thee through.'
' Go, go, my lambs, unpastured as ye are,
My thoughts are all now due to other care.
The nymphs amazed, my melancholy see,
And, " Thyrsis!" cry—" what will become of thee?
What wouldst thou, Thyrsis? such should not appear
The brow of youth, stern, gloomy, and severe;
Brisk youth should laugh, and love—ah, shun the fate
Of those, twice wretched mopes! who love too late!"
' Go, go, my lambs, unpastured as ye are;
My thoughts are all now due to other care.
Ægle with Hyas came, to soothe my pain,
And Baucis' daughter, Dryope, the vain,
Fair Dryope, for voice and finger neat
Known far and near, and for her self-conceit
Chloris too came, whose cottage on the lands
That skirt the Idumanian current stands;
But all in vain they came, and but to see
Kind words, and comfortable, lost on me.
' Go, go, my lambs, unpastured as ye are;
My thoughts are all now due to other care.
Ah blest indifference of the playful herd,
None by his fellow chosen, or preferr'd!
No bonds of amity the flocks inthral,
But each associates, and is pleased with all;
So graze the dappled deer in numerous droves,
And all his kind alike the zebra loves;
The same law governs, where the billows roar,
And Proteus' shoals o'erspread the desert shore;
The sparrow, meanest of the feather'd race,
His fit companion finds in every place,

With whom he picks the grain that suits him best,
Flirts here and there, and late returns to rest,
And whom, if chance the falcon make his prey
Or hedger with his well-aim'd arrow slay,
For no such loss the gay survivor grieves,
New love he seeks, and new delight receives.
We only, an obdurate kind, rejoice,
Scorning all others, in a single choice.
We scarce in thousands meet one kindred mind,
And if the long-sought good at last we find,
When least we fear it, Death our treasure steals,
And gives our heart a wound that nothing heals.
'Go, go, my lambs, unpastured as ye are;
My thoughts are all now due to other care.
Ah, what delusion lured me from my flocks,
To traverse Alpine snows and rugged rocks!
What need so great had I to visit Rome,
Now sunk in ruins, and herself a tomb?
Or, had she flourish'd still, as when, of old,
For her sake Tityrus forsook his fold,
What need so great had I to incur a pause
Of thy sweet intercourse for such a cause,
For such a cause to place the roaring sea,
Rocks, mountains, woods, between my friend and me?
Else, had I grasp'd thy feeble hand, composed
Thy decent limbs, thy drooping eyelids closed,
And, at the last, had said—"Farewell—ascend—
Nor even in the skies forget thy friend!"
'Go, go, my lambs, untended homeward fare;
My thoughts are all now due to other care.
Although well pleased, ye tuneful Tuscan swains!
My mind the memory of your worth retains,
Yet not your worth can teach me less to mourn
My Damon lost.—He too was Tuscan born,
Born in your Lucca, city of renown!
And wit possess'd, and genius, like your own
Oh how elate was I, when stretch'd beside
The murmuring course of Arno's breezy tide,
Beneath the poplar grove I pass'd my hours,
Now cropping myrtles, and now vernal flowers,
And hearing, as I lay at ease along,
Your swains contending for the prize of song!

I also dared attempt (and, as it seems,
Not much displeased attempting) various themes,
For even I can presents boast from you,
The shepherd's pipe, and ozier basket too,
And Dati, and Francini, both have made
My name familiar to the beechen shade,
And they are learn'd, and each in every place
Renown'd for song, and both of Lydian race.
'Go, go, my lambs, untended homeward fare;
My thoughts are all now due to other care.
While bright the dewy grass with moonbeams shone,
And I stood hurdling in my kids alone,
How often have I said (but thou hadst found
Ere then thy dark cold lodgment underground)
Now Damon sings, or springes sets for hares,
Or wickerwork for various use prepares!
How oft, indulging fancy, have I plann'd
New scenes of pleasure that I hoped at hand,
Call'd thee abroad as I was wont, and cried—
"What, hoa! my friend—come, lay thy task aside;
Haste, let us forth together, and beguile
The heat beneath yon whispering shades awhile,
Or on the margin stray of Colne's clear flood,
Or where Cassibelan's gray turrets stood!
There thou shalt cull me simples, and shalt teach
Thy friend the name and healing powers of each,
From the tall bluebell to the dwarfish weed,
What the dry land, and what the marshes breed,
For all their kinds alike to thee are known
And the whole art of Galen is thy own."
Ah, perish Galen's art, and wither'd be
The useless herbs that gave not health to thee!
Twelve evenings since, as in poetic dream
I meditating sat some statelier theme,
The reeds no sooner touch'd my lip, though new,
And unessay'd before, than wide they flew,
Bursting their waxen bands, nor could sustain
The deep-toned music of the solemn strain;
And I am vain, perhaps, but I will tell
How proud a theme I chose—ye groves, farewell!
'Go, go, my lambs, untended homeward fare;
My thoughts are all now due to other care.

Of Brutus, Dardan chief, my song shall be,
How with his barks he plough'd the British sea,
First from Rutupia's towering headland seen,
And of his consort's reign, fair Imogen;
Of Brennus, and Belinus, brothers bold,
And of Arviragus, and how of old
Our hardy sires th' Armorican control'd,
And of the wife of Gorloïs, who, surprised
By Uther, in her husband's form disguised,
(Such was the force of Merlin's art) became
Pregnant with Arthur of heroic fame.
These themes I now revolve—and Oh—if Fate
Proportion to these themes my lengthen'd date,
Adieu my shepherd's reed—yon pine tree bough
Shall be thy future home, there dangle thou
Forgotten and disused, unless ere long
Thou change thy Latian for a British song:
A British?—even so—the powers of man
Are bounded; little is the most he can;
And it shall well suffice me, and shall be
Fame and proud recompense enough for me,
If Usa, golden-hair'd, my verse may learn,
If Alain bending o'er his crystal urn,
Swift-whirling Abra, Trent's o'ershadow'd stream
Thames, lovelier far than all in my esteem,
Tamar's ore-tinctured flood, and, after these,
The wave-worn shores of utmost Orcades.
'Go, go, my lambs, untended homeward fare;
My thoughts are all now due to other care.
All this I kept in leaves of laurel rind
Enfolded safe, and for thy view design'd,
This—and a gift from Manso's hand beside,
(Manso, not least his native city's pride)
Two cups that radiant as their giver shone,
Adorn'd by sculpture with a double zone.
The spring was graven there; here slowly wind
The Red Sea shores with groves of spices lined,
Her plumes of various hues amid the boughs
The sacred, solitary phœnix shows,
And, watchful of the dawn, reverts her head
To see Aurora leave her watery bed.

—In other part, the expansive vault above
And there too, even there, the god of love;
With quiver arm'd he mounts, his torch displays
A vivid light, his gem-tipt arrows blaze,
Around his bright and fiery eyes he rolls,
Nor aims at vulgar minds or little souls,
Nor deigns one look below, but, aiming high,
Sends every arrow to the lofty sky;
Hence forms divine, and minds immortal, learn
The power of Cupid, and enamour'd burn.
'Thou also, Damon (neither need I fear
That hope delusive) thou art also there;
For whither should simplicity like thine
Retire, where else such spotless virtue shine?
Thou dwell'st not (thought profane) in shades below,
Nor tears suit thee—cease then, my tears, to flow.
Away with grief: on Damon ill bestow'd!
Who, pure himself, has found a pure abode,
Has pass'd the showery arch, henceforth resides
With saints and heroes, and from flowing tides
Quaffs copious immortality and joy
With hallow'd lips!—Oh! blest without alloy,
And now enrich'd with all that faith can claim,
Look down, entreated by whatever name,
If Damon please thee most (that rural sound
Shall oft with echoes fill the groves around),
Or if Deodatus, by which alone
In those ethereal mansions thou art known.
Thy blush was maiden, and thy youth the taste
Of wedded bliss knew never, pure and chaste,
The honours, therefore, by divine decree
The lot of virgin worth, are given to thee:
Thy brows encircled with a radiant band,
And the green palm-branch waving in thy hand,
Thou in immortal nuptials shalt rejoice,
And join with seraphs thy according voice,
Where rapture reigns, and the ecstatic lyre
Guides the blest orgies of the blazing quire.

AN ODE,

ADDRESSED TO MR. JOHN ROUSE,

LIBRARIAN OF THE UNIVERSITY OF OXFORD.

On a lost Volume of my Poems, which he desired me to replace, that he might add them to my other Works deposited in the Library.

This Ode is rendered without rhyme, that it might more adequately represent the original, which, as Milton himself informs us, is of no certain measure. It may possibly for this reason disappoint the reader, though it cost the writer more labour than the translation of any other piece in the whole collection.

STROPHE.

My twofold book! single in show,
But double in contents,
Neat, but not curiously adorn'd,
Which, in his early youth,
A poet gave, no lofty one in truth,
Although an earnest wooer of the muse—
Say while in cool Ausonian shades
Or British wilds he roam'd,
Striking by turns his native lyre,
By turns the Daunian lute,
And stepp'd almost in air—

ANTISTROPHE.

Say, little book, what furtive hand
Thee from thy fellow books convey'd,
What time, at the repeated suit
Of my most learned friend,
I sent thee forth, an honour'd traveller,
From our great city to the source of Thames,
Cærulean sire!
Where rise the fountains, and the raptures ring,
Of the Aonian choir,
Durable as yonder spheres,
And through the endless lapse of years
Secure to be admired?

STROPHE II.

Now what god, or demigod,
For Britain's ancient genius moved,
(If our afflicted land
Have expiated at length the guilty sloth
Of her degenerate sons)
Shall terminate our impious feuds,
And discipline with hallow'd voice recall?
Recall the muses too,
Driven from their ancient seats
In Albion, and well nigh from Albion's shore,
And with keen Phœbean shafts
Piercing the unseemly birds,
Whose talons menace us,
Shall drive the harpy race from Helicon afar?

ANTISTROPHE.

But thou, my book, though thou hast stray'd,
Whether by treachery lost,
Or indolent neglect, thy bearer's fault,
From all thy kindred books,
To some dark cell or cave forlorn,
Where thou endurest, perhaps,
The chafing of some hard untutor'd hand,
Be comforted—
For lo! again the splendid hope appears
That thou mayst yet escape
The gulfs of Lethe, and on oary wings
Mount to the everlasting courts of Jove!

STROPHE III.

Since Rouse desires thee, and complains
That, though by promise his,
Thou yet appear'st not in thy place
Among the literary noble stores
Given to his care,
But, absent, leavest his numbers incomplete.
He, therefore, guardian vigilant
Of that unperishing wealth,

Calls thee to the interior shrine, his charge,
Where he intends a richer treasure far
Than Iön kept (Iön, Erectheus' son
Illustrious, of the fair Creüsa born)
In the resplendent temple of his god,
Tripods of gold, and Delphic gifts divine.

ANTISTROPHE.

Haste, then, to the pleasant groves,
The muses' favourite haunt;
Resume thy station in Apollo's dome,
Dearer to him
Than Delos, or the fork'd Parnassian hill!
Exulting go,
Since now a splendid lot is also thine,
And thou art sought by my propitious friend;
For there thou shalt be read
With authors of exalted note,
The ancient glorious lights of Greece and Rome.

EPODE.

Ye, then, my works, no longer vain,
And worthless deem'd by me!
Whate'er this sterile genius has produced,
Expect, at last, the rage of envy spent,
An unmolested happy home,
Gift of kind Hermes, and my watchful friend,
Where never flippant tongue profane
Shall entrance find,
And whence the coarse unletter'd multitude
Shall babble far remote.
Perhaps some future distant age,
Less tinged with prejudice, and better taught
Shall furnish minds of power
To judge more equally.
Then, malice silenced in the tomb,
Cooler heads and sounder hearts,
Thanks to Rouse, if aught of praise
I merit, shall with candour weigh the claim.

TRANSLATIONS

OF

THE ITALIAN POEMS.

SONNET.

FAIR LADY! whose harmonious name the Rhine,
  Through all his grassy vale, delights to hear,
  Base were indeed the wretch who could forbear
To love a spirit elegant as thine,
That manifests a sweetness all divine,
  Nor knows a thousand winning acts to spare,
  And graces, which Love's bow and arrows are,
Tempering thy virtues to a softer shine.
When gracefully thou speak'st, or singest gay,
  Such strains as might the senseless forest move,
Ah then—turn each his eyes and ears away
  Who feels himself unworthy of thy love!
Grace can alone preserve him ere the dart
Of fond desire yet reach his inmost heart.

SONNET.

As on a hill-top rude, when closing day
  Imbrowns the scene, some pastoral maiden fair
  Waters a lovely foreign plant with care,
Borne from its native genial airs away,
That scarcely can its tender bud display,
  So, on my tongue these accents, new and rare,
  Are flowers exotic, which Love waters there.
While thus, O sweetly scornful! I essay
  Thy praise in verse to British ears unknown,
  And Thames exchange for Arno's fair domain;
  So Love has will'd, and ofttimes Love has shown
  That what he wills, he never wills in vain.
Oh that this hard and sterile breast might be
To Him, who plants from Heaven, a soil as free!

CANZONE.

They mock my toil—the nymphs and amorous
swains—
And whence this fond attempt to write, they cry,
Love-songs in language that thou little know'st?
How darest thou risk to sing these foreign strains?
Say truly. Find'st not oft thy purpose cross'd
And that thy fairest flowers here fade and die
Then with pretence of admiration high--
Thee other shores expect, and other tides,
Rivers, on whose grassy sides
Her deathless laurel leaf, with which to bind
Thy flowing locks, already Fame provides;
Why then this burthen, better far declined?
Speak, muse! for me—the fair one said, who guides
My willing heart, and all my fancy's flights,
'This is the language in which Love delights.

SONNET,

TO CHARLES DEODATI.

Charles—and I say it wondering—thou must know
That I, who once assumed a scornful air
And scoff'd at Love, am fallen in his snare,
(Full many an upright man has fallen so:)
Yet think me not thus dazzled by the flow
Of golden locks, or damask cheek; more rare
The heartfelt beauties of my foreign fair;
A mien majestic, with dark brows that show
The tranquil lustre of a lofty mind;
Words exquisite, of idioms more than one,
And song, whose fascinating power might bind,
And from her sphere draw down the labouring moon;
With such fire-darting eyes that, should I fill
My ears with wax, she would enchant me still.

SONNET.

Lady! It cannot be but that thine eyes
 Must be my sun, such radiance they display,
 And strike me e'en as Phœbus him whose way
Through horrid Libya's sandy desert lies.
Meantime, on that side steamy vapours rise
 Where most I suffer. Of what kind are they,
 New as to me they are, I cannot say,
But deem them, in the lover's language—sighs.
Some, though with pain, my bosom close conceals,
Which, if in part escaping thence, they tend
To soften thine, thy coldness soon congeals.
While others to my tearful eyes ascend,
Whence my sad nights in showers are ever drown'd
Till my Aurora comes, her brow with roses bound.

SONNET.

Enamour'd, artless, young, on foreign ground,
 Uncertain whither from myself to fly;
 To thee, dear Lady, with an humble sigh
Let me devote my heart, which I have found
By certain proofs, not few, intrepid, sound,
 Good, and addicted to conceptions high:
When tempests shake the world, and fire the sky,
It rests in adamant self-wrapt around,
As safe from envy, and from outrage rude,
From hopes and fears that vulgar minds abuse,
As fond of genius, and fix'd fortitude,
Of the resounding lyre, and every muse.
Weak you will find it in one only part,
Now pierced by love's immedicable dart.

SIMILE IN PARADISE LOST.

'So when, from mountain tops, the dusky clouds
Ascending,' &c.

Quales aërii montis de vertice nubes
Cum surgunt, et jam Boreæ tumida ora quièrunt,
Cælum hilares abdit, spissâ caligine, vultus:
Tum si jucundo tandem sol prodeat ore,
Et croceo montes et pascua lumine tingat,
Gaudent omnia, aves mulcent concentibus agros,
Balatuque ovium colles vallesque resultant.

TRANSLATION OF DRYDEN'S EPIGRAM ON MILTON.

Tres tria, sed longè distantia, sæcula vates
  Ostentant tribus è gentibus eximios.
Græcia sublimem, cùm majestate disertum
  Roma tulit, felix Anglia utrique parem.
Partubus ex binis Natura exhausta, coacta est,
  Tertius ut fieret, consociare duos.

July, 1780.

TRANSLATIONS

FROM

VINCENT BOURNE.

THE THRACIAN.

THRACIAN parents, at his birth,
  Mourn their babe with many a tear
But with undissembled mirth
  Place him breathless on his bier.

Greece and Rome with equal scorn,
  'O the savages!' exclaim,
'Whether they rejoice or mourn,
  Well entitled to the name!'

But the cause of this concern,
  And this pleasure, would they trace,
Even they might somewhat learn
  From the savages of Thrace.

RECIPROCAL KINDNESS THE PRIMARY LAW OF NATURE.

ANDROCLES, from his injured lord, in dread
Of instant death, to Libya's desert fled.
Tired with his toilsome flight, and parch'd with heat,
He spied at length a cavern's cool retreat;
But scarce had given to rest his weary frame,
When, hugest of his kind, a lion came:
He roar'd approaching: but the savage din
To plaintive murmurs changed—arrived within,
And with expressive looks, his lifted paw
Presenting, aid implored from whom he saw.

The fugitive, through terror at a stand,
Dared not awhile afford his trembling hand;
But bolder grown, at length inherent found
A pointed thorn, and drew it from the wound.
The cure was wrought; he wiped the sanious blood
And firm and free from pain the lion stood.
Again he seeks the wilds, and day by day
Regales his inmate with the parted prey.
Nor he disdains the dole, though unprepared,
Spread on the ground, and with a lion shared.
But thus to live—still lost—sequester'd still—
Scarce seem'd his lord's revenge a heavier ill.
Home! native home! O might he but repair!
He must—he will, though death attends him there.
He goes, and doom'd to perish on the sands
Of the full theatre unpitied stands:
When lo! the selfsame lion from his cage
Flies to devour him, famish'd into rage.
He flies, but viewing in his purposed prey
The man, his healer, pauses on his way,
And, soften'd by remembrance into sweet
And kind composure, crouches at his feet.
Mute with astonishment, the assembly gaze:
But why, ye Romans? Whence your mute amaze?
All this is natural: nature bade him rend
An enemy; she bids him spare a friend.

A MANUAL,

MORE ANCIENT THAN THE ART OF PRINTING, AND NOT TO BE FOUND IN ANY CATALOGUE.

There is a book, which we may call
(Its excellence is such)
Alone a library, though small;
The ladies thumb it much.

Words none, things numerous it contains:
And things with words compared,
Who needs be told, that has his brains,
Which merits most regard?

Ofttimes its leaves of scarlet hue
 A golden edging boast;
And open'd, it displays to view
 Twelve pages at the most.

Nor name nor title, stamp'd behind,
 Adorns its outer part;
But all within 'tis richly lined,
 A magazine of art.

The whitest hands that secret hoard
 Oft visit: and the fair
Preserve it in their bosoms stored
 As with a miser's care.

Thence implements of every size,
 And form'd for various use,
(They need but to consult their eyes)
 They readily produce.

The largest and the longest kind
 Possess the foremost page,
A sort most needed by the blind,
 Or nearly such from age.

The full-charged leaf, which next ensues,
 Presents in bright array
The smaller sort, which matrons use,
 Not quite so blind as they.

The third, the fourth, the fifth supply
 What their occasions ask,
Who with a more discerning eye
 Perform a nicer task.

But still with regular decrease
 From size to size they fall,
In every leaf grow less and less;
 The last are least of all.

O! what a fund of genius, pent
 In narrow space is here!
This volume's method and inten
 How luminous and clear.

It leaves no reader at a loss
    Or posed, whoever reads :
No commentator's tedious gloss,
    Nor even index needs.

Search Bodley's many thousands o'er!
    No book is treasured there,
Nor yet in Granta's numerous store,
    That may with this compare.

No !—rival none in either host
    Of this was ever seen,
Or that contents could justly boast
    So brilliant and so keen.

AN ENIGMA.

A NEEDLE, small as small can be,
In bulk and use surpasses me,
    Nor is my purchase dear;
For little, and almost for nought,
As many of my kind are bought
    As days are in the year.

Yet though but little use we boast,
And are procured at little cost,
    The labour is not light;
Nor few artificers it asks,
All skilful in their several tasks,
    To fashion us aright.

One fuses metal o'er the fire,
A second draws it into wire,
    The shears another plies ,
Who clips in length the brazen thread
For him who, chafing every shred
    Gives all an equal size.

A fifth prepares, exact and round,
The knob with which it must be crown'd
His follower makes it fast:
And with his mallet and his file
To shape the point, employs awhile
The seventh and the last.

Now therefore, Œdipus! declare
What creature, wonderful, and rare,
A process that obtains
Its purpose with so much ado
At last produces!—tell me true,
And take me for your pains!

SPARROWS SELF-DOMESTICATED IN TRINITY COLLEGE, CAMBRIDGE.

None ever shared the social feast,
Or as an inmate or a guest,
Beneath the celebrated dome
Where once Sir Isaac had his home,
Who saw not (and with some delight
Perhaps he view'd the novel sight)
How numerous, at the tables there,
The sparrows beg their daily fare.
For there, in every nook and cell
Where such a family may dwell,
Sure as the vernal season comes
Their nest they weave in hope of crumbs,
Which kindly given, may serve with food
Convenient their unfeather'd brood;
And oft as with its summons clear
The warning bell salutes their ear,
Sagacious listeners to the sound,
They flock from all the fields around,
To reach the hospitable hall,
None more attentive to the call.
Arrived, the pensionary band
Hopping and chirping, close at hand,

Solicit what they soon receive,
The sprinkled, plenteous donative.
Thus is a multitude, though large,
Supported at a trivial charge:
A single doit would overpay
The expenditure of every day,
And who can grudge so small a grace
To suppliants, natives of the place?

FAMILIARITY DANGEROUS.

As in her ancient mistress' lap
    The youthful tabby lay,
They gave each other many a tap,
    Alike disposed to play.

But strife ensues. Puss waxes warm,
    And with protruded claws
Ploughs all the length of Lydia's arm,
    Mere wantonness the cause.

At once, resentful of the deed,
    She shakes her to the ground
With many a threat that she shall bleed
    With still a deeper wound.

But, Lydia, bid thy fury rest:
    It was a venial stroke:
For she that will with kittens jest
    Should bear a kitten's joke.

INVITATION TO THE REDBREAST

Sweet bird, whom the winter constrains—
    And seldom another it can—
To seek a retreat while he reigns
    In the well-shelter'd dwellings of man

Who never can seem to intrude,
    Though in all places equally free,
Come, oft as the season is rude,
    Thou art sure to be welcome to me.

At sight of the first feeble ray
    That pierces the clouds of the east,
To inveigle thee every day
    My windows shall shew thee a feast.
For, taught by experience, I know
    Thee mindful of benefit long;
And that, thankful for all I bestow,
    Thou wilt pay me with many a song.

Then, soon as the swell of the buds
    Bespeaks the renewal of spring,
Fly hence, if thou wilt, to the woods,
    Or where it shall please thee to sing:
And shouldst thou, compell'd by a frost,
    Come again to my window or door,
Doubt not an affectionate host,
    Only pay as thou paid'st me before.

Thus music must needs be confess'd
    To flow from a fountain above;
Else how should it work in the breast
    Unchangeable friendship and love?
And who on the globe can be found,
    Save your generation and ours,
That can be delighted by sound,
    Or boasts any musical powers?

STRADA'S NIGHTINGALE.

The shepherd touch'd his reed; sweet Philomel
    Essay'd, and oft essay'd to catch the strain,
And treasuring, as on her ear they fell,
    The numbers, echo'd note for note again.

The peevish youth, who ne'er had found before
  A rival of his skill, indignant heard,
And soon (for various was his tuneful store)
  In loftier tones defied the simple bird.

She dared the task, and, rising as he rose,
  With all the force that passion gives inspired,
Return'd the sounds awhile, but in the close
  Exhausted fell, and at his feet expired.

Thus strength, not skill prevail'd. O fatal strife,
  By thee, poor songstress, playfully begun;
And, O sad victory, which cost thy life,
  And he may wish that he had never won!

ODE ON THE DEATH OF A LADY,

WHO LIVED ONE HUNDRED YEARS, AND DIED ON HER BIRTHDAY, 1728.

Ancient dame, how wide and vast
  To a race like ours appears,
Rounded to an orb at last,
  All thy multitude of years!

We, the herd of human kind,
  Frailer and of feebler powers;
We, to narrow bounds confined,
  Soon exhaust the sum of ours.

Death's delicious banquet—we
  Perish even from the womb,
Swifter than a shadow flee,
  Nourish'd but to feed the tomb.

Seeds of merciless disease
  Lurk in all that we enjoy;
Some that waste us by degrees,
  Some that suddenly destroy.

And, if life o'erleap the bourn
  Common to the sons of men,
What remains, but that we mourn,
  Dream, and dote, and drivel then?

Fast as moons can wax and wane
  Sorrow comes; and while we groan,
Pant with anguish, and complain,
  Half our years are fled and gone.

If a few (to few 'tis given),
  Lingering on this earthly stage,
Creep and halt with steps uneven
  To the period of an age,

Wherefore live they, but to see
  Cunning, arrogance, and force,
Sights lamented much by thee,
  Holding their accustom'd course?

Oft was seen, in ages past,
  All that we with wonder view;
Often shall be to the last;
  Earth produces nothing new.

Thee we gratulate, content
  Should propitious heaven design
Life for us as calmly spent,
  Though but half the length of thine.

THE CAUSE WON.

Two neighbours furiously dispute;
A field—the subject of the suit.
Trivial the spot, yet such the rage
With which the combatants engage,
'Twere hard to tell who covets most
The prize——at whatsoever cost.
The pleadings swell. Words still suffice:
No single word but has its price.

No term but yields some fair pretence
For novel and increased expense.
Defendant thus becomes a name,
Which he that bore it may disclaim,
Since both, in one description blended,
Are plaintiffs—when the suit is ended.

THE SILKWORM.

The beams of April, ere it goes,
A worm, scarce visible, disclose;
All winter long content to dwell
The tenant of his native shell.
The same prolific season gives
The sustenance by which he lives,
The mulberry leaf, a simple store,
That serves him—till he needs no more!
For, his dimensions once complete,
Thenceforth none ever sees him eat;
Though till his growing time be past
Scarce ever is he seen to fast.
That hour arrived, his work begins,
He spins and weaves, and weaves and spins;
Till circle upon circle wound
Careless around him and around,
Conceals him with a veil, though slight,
Impervious to the keenest sight.
Thus self-enclosed as in a cask,
At length he finishes his task;
And, though a worm when he was lost,
Or caterpillar at the most,
When next we see him, wings he wears,
And in papilio pomp appears;
Becomes oviparous; supplies
With future worms and future flies
The next ensuing year—and dies!
Well were it for the world, if all
Who creep about this earthly ball,
Though shorter lived than most he
Were useful in their kind as he.

THE INNOCENT THIEF.

Not a flower can be found in the fields,
Or the spot that we till for our pleasure,
From the largest to the least, but it yields
The bee, never wearied, a treasure.

Scarce any she quits unexplored
With a diligence truly exact;
Yet, steal what she may for her hoard,
Leaves evidence none of the fact.

Her lucrative task she pursues,
And pilfers with so much address,
That none of their odour they lose,
Nor charm by their beauty the less.

Not thus inoffensively preys
The cankerworm in-dwelling foe!
His voracity not thus allays
The sparrow, the finch, or the crow.

The worm, more expensively fed,
The pride of the garden devours;
And birds peck the seed from the bed,
Still less to be spared than the flowers.

But she with such delicate skill
Her pillage so fits for her use,
That the chemist in vain with his still
Would labour the like to produce.

Then grudge not her temperate meals,
Nor a benefit blame as a theft;
Since, stole she not all that she steals,
Neither honey nor wax would be left.

DENNER'S OLD WOMAN.

In this mimic form of a matron in years,
How plainly the pencil of Denner appears!
The matron herself, in whose old age we see
Not a trace of decline what a wonder is she!

No dimness of eye, and no cheek hanging low,
No wrinkle, or deep-furrow'd frown on the brow!
Her forehead indeed is here circled around
With locks like the ribbon with which they are bound;
While glossy and smooth, and as soft as the skin
Of a delicate peach, is the down of her chin;
But nothing unpleasant, or sad, or severe,
Or that indicates life in its winter—is here.
Yet all is express'd with fidelity due,
Nor a pimple or freckle conceal'd from the view.
Many fond of new sights, or who cherish a taste
For the labours of art, to the spectacle haste.
The youths all agree, that could old age inspire
The passion of love, her's would kindle the fire,
And the matrons with pleasure confess that they see
Ridiculous nothing or hideous in thee.
The nymphs for themselves scarcely hope a decline,
O wonderful woman! as placid as thine.
Strange magic of art! which the youth can engage
To peruse, half enamour'd, the features of age;
And force from the virgin a sigh of despair,
That she when as old shall be equally fair!
How great is the glory that Denner has gain'd,
Since Apelles not more for his Venus obtain'd.

THE TEARS OF A PAINTER.

Apelles, hearing that his boy
Had just expired—his only joy!
Although the sight with anguish tore him
Bade place his dear remains before him.
He seized his brush, his colours spread;
And—'Oh! my child, accept,'—he said,
'('Tis all that I can now bestow),
This tribute of a father's woe!'
Then, faithful to the twofold part,
Both of his feelings and his art,
He closed his eyes with tender care,
And form'd at once a fellow pair.
His brow with amber locks beset,
And lips he drew not livid yet;

And shaded all that he had done
To a just image of his son.
 Thus far is well. But view again
The cause of thy paternal pain!
Thy melancholy task fulfil!
It needs the last, last touches still.
Again his pencil's powers he tries,
For on his lips a smile he spies;
And still his cheek unfaded shows
The deepest damask of the rose.
Then, heedful to the finish'd whole,
With fondest eagerness he stole,
Till scarce himself distinctly knew
The cherub copied from the true.
 Now, painter, cease! Thy task is done.
Long lives this image of thy son;
Nor short-lived shall the glory prove
Or of thy labour or thy love.

THE MAZE.

From right to left, and to and fro,
Caught in a labyrinth you go,
And turn, and turn, and turn again,
To solve the mystery, but in vain;
Stand still, and breathe, and take from me
A clue, that soon shall set you free!
Not Ariadne, if you meet her,
Herself could serve you with a better.
You enter'd easily—find where—
And make with ease your exit there!

NO SORROW PECULIAR TO THE SUFFERER

The lover, in melodious verses,
His singular distress rehearses.
Still closing with a rueful cry,
'Was ever such a wretch as I!'

Yes! thousands have endured before
All thy distress; some, haply, more.
Unnumber'd Corydons complain,
And Strephons, of the like disdain;
And if thy Chloe be of steel,
Too deaf to hear, too hard to feel;
Not her alone that censure fits,
Nor thou alone hast lost thy wits.

THE SNAIL.

To grass, or leaf, or fruit, or wall,
The Snail sticks close, nor fears to fall,
As if he grew there, house and all
Together.

Within that house secure he hides,
When danger imminent betides
Of storm, or other harm besides
Of weather.

Give but his horns the slightest touch,
His self-collecting power is such,
He shrinks into his house, with much
Displeasure.

Where'er he dwells, he dwells alone,
Except himself has chattels none,
Well satisfied to be his own
Whole treasure

Thus, hermit-like, his life he leads,
Nor partner of his banquet needs,
And if he meets one, only feeds
The faster.

Who seeks him must be worse than blind
(He and his house are so combined)
If, finding it, he fails to find
Its master.

THE CANTAB.

WITH two spurs or one, and no great matter which,
Boots bought, or boots borrow'd, a whip or a switch,
Five shillings or less for the hire of his beast,
Paid part into hand; you must wait for the rest.
Thus equipt, Academicus climbs up his horse,
And out they both sally for better or worse;
His heart void of fear, and as light as a feather;
And in violent haste to go not knowing whither:
Through the fields and the towns; (see!) he scampers along,
And is look'd at and laugh'd at by old and by young.
Till at length overspent, and his sides smear'd with blood,
Down tumbles his horse, man and all in the mud.
In a waggon or chaise, shall he finish his route?
Oh! scandalous fate! he must do it on foot.
Young gentlemen, hear!—I am older than you!
The advice that I give I have proved to be true,
Wherever your journey may be, never doubt it,
The faster you ride, you're the longer about it.

ON THE PICTURE OF A SLEEPING CHILD.

SWEET babe! whose image here express'd
Does thy peaceful slumbers show;
Guilt or fear, to break thy rest,
Never did thy spirit know.

Soothing slumbers! soft repose!
Such as mock the painter's skill,
Such as innocence bestows,
Harmless infant! lull thee still!

MINOR POEMS

VERSES WRITTEN AT BATH, ON FINDING THE HEEL OF A SHOE.

Fortune! I thank thee: gentle goddess! thanks!
Not that my muse, though bashful, shall deny
She would have thank'd thee rather hadst thou cast
A treasure in her way; for neither meed
Of early breakfast, to dispel the fumes,
And bowel-racking pains of emptiness,
Nor noontide feast, nor evening's cool repast,
Hopes she from this—presumptuous, though, perhaps
The cobbler, leather-carving artist! might.
Nathless she thanks thee, and accepts thy boon,
Whatever; not as erst the fabled cock,
Vain-glorious fool! unknowing what he found,
Spurn'd the rich gem thou gavest him. Wherefore, ah!
Why not on me that favour, (worthier sure!)
Conferr'dst thou, goddess! Thou art blind, thou sayst:
Enough!—thy blindness shall excuse the deed.
  Nor does my muse no benefit exhale
From this thy scant indulgence!—even here
Hints worthy sage philosophy are found;
Illustrious hints, to moralize my song!
This ponderous heel of perforated hide
Compact, with pegs indented, many a row,
Haply (for such its massy form bespeaks)
The weighty tread of some rude peasant clown
Upbore: on this supported oft, he stretch'd,
With uncouth strides, along the furrow'd glebe,
Flattening the stubborn clod, till cruel time
(What will not cruel time) on a wry step
Severed the strict cohesion; when, alas!
He, who could erst, with even, equal pace,
Pursue his destined way with symmetry,
And some proportion form'd, now on one side,

Curtail'd and maim'd, the sport of vagrant boys,
Cursing his frail supporter, treacherous prop.
With toilsome steps, and difficult, moves on:
Thus fares it oft with other than the feet
Of humble villager—the statesman thus,
Up the steep road where proud ambition leads,
Aspiring, first, uninterrupted winds
His prosperous way; nor fears miscarriage foul,
While policy prevails, and friends prove true:
But that support soon failing, by him left,
On whom he most depended, basely left,
Betray'd, deserted; from his airy height
Headlong he falls; and through the rest of life
Drags the dull load of disappointment on.

1748.

AN ODE,

ON READING RICHARDSON'S HISTORY OF SIR CHARLES GRANDISON.

Say, ye apostate and profane,
Wretches, who blush not to disdain
    Allegiance to your God,—
Did e'er your idly wasted love
Of virtue for her sake remove,
    And lift you from the crowd?

Would you the race of glory run,
Know the devout, and they alone,
    Are equal to the task
The labours of the illustrious course
Far other than the unaided force
    Of human vigour ask.

To arm against reputed ill
The patient heart too brave to feel
    The tortures of despair
Nor safer yet high-crested pride,
When wealth flows in with every tide
    To gain admittance there.

To rescue from the tyrant's sword
The oppress'd;—unseen and unimplored,
To cheer the face of woe;
From lawless insult to defend
An orphan's right—a fallen friend,
And a forgiven foe;

These, these distinguish from the crowd,
And these alone, the great and good,
The guardians of mankind;
Whose bosoms with these virtues heave,
O, with what matchless speed they leave
The multitude behind!

Then ask ye, from what cause on earth
Virtues like these derive their birth.
Derived from Heaven alone;
Full on that favour'd breast they shine,
Where faith and resignation join
To call the blessing down.

Such is that heart:—but while the muse
Thy theme, O Richardson, pursues
Her feeble spirits faint:
She cannot reach, and would not wrong,
That subject for an angel's song,
The hero, and the saint!

1753.

AN EPISTLE TO ROBERT LLOYD, ESQ.

'Tis not that I design to rob
Thee of thy birthright, gentle Bob,
For thou art born sole heir, and single,
Of dear Mat Prior's easy jingle;
Not that I mean, while thus I knit
My threadbare sentiments together,

To show my genius or my wit,
When God and you know I have neither;
Or such as might be better shown
By letting poetry alone.
'Tis not with either of these views
That I presumed to address the muse:
But to divert a fierce banditti,
(Sworn foes to every thing that's witty!
That, with a black, infernal train,
Make cruel inroads in my brain,
And daily threaten to drive thence
My little garrison of sense;
The fierce banditti which I mean
Are gloomy thoughts, led on by spleen
Then there's another reason yet,
Which is, that I may fairly quit
The debt, which justly became due
The moment when I heard from you:
And you might grumble, crony mine,
If paid in any other coin;
Since twenty sheets of lead, God knows,
(I would say twenty sheets of prose)
Can ne'er be deem'd worth half so much
As one of gold, and your's was such.
Thus, the preliminaries settled,
I fairly find myself pitchkettled,
And cannot see, though few see better,
How I shall hammer out a letter.
  First, for a thought—since all agree—
A thought—I have it—let me see—
'Tis gone again—plague on't! I thought
I had it—but I have it not.
Dame Gurton thus, and Hodge her son,
That useful thing, her needle, gone!
Rake well the cinders, sweep the floor,
And sift the dust behind the door;
While eager Hodge beholds the prize
In old grimalkin's glaring eyes;

* Pitchkettled, a favourite phrase at the time when this Epistle was written, expressive of being puzzled, or what in the Spectator's time would have been called bamboozled.

And gammer finds it on her knees
In every shining straw she sees.
This simile were apt enough;
But I've another, critic proof
The virtuoso thus, at noon,
Broiling beneath a July sun,
The gilded butterfly pursues,
O'er hedge and ditch, through gaps and mews;
And, after many a vain essay,
To captivate the tempting prey,
Gives him at length the lucky pat,
And has him safe beneath his hat:
Then lifts it gently from the ground;
But ah! 'tis lost as soon as found;
Culprit his liberty regains,
Flits out of sight, and mocks his pains.
The sense was dark; 'twas therefore fit
With simile to illustrate it;
But as too much obscures the sight,
As often as too little light,
We have our similes cut short,
For matters of more grave import.
That Matthew's numbers run with ease,
Each man of common sense agrees!
All men of common sense allow
That Robert's lines are easy too:
Where then the preference shall we place,
Or how do justice in this case?
Matthew (says Fame) with endless pains
Smooth'd and refined the meanest strains;
Nor suffer'd one ill chosen rhyme
To escape him at the idlest time;
And thus o'er all a lustre cast,
That, while the language lives, shall last.
An't please your ladyship (quoth I),
For 'tis my business to reply;
Sure so much labour, so much toil,
Bespeak at least a stubborn soil:
Theirs be the laurel-wreath decreed,
Who both write well, and write full speed
Who throw their Helicon about
As freely as a conduit spout!

Friend Robert, thus like chien scavant,
Lets fall a poem en passant,
Nor needs his genuine ore refine!
'Tis ready polish'd from the mine.

1754

THE FIFTH SATIRE OF THE FIRST BOOK OF HORACE.

A HUMOROUS DESCRIPTION OF THE AUTHOR'S JOURNEY FROM ROME TO BRUNDUSIUM.

'TWAS a long journey lay before us,
When I and honest Heliodorus,
Who far in point of rhetoric
Surpasses every living Greek,
Each leaving our respective home,
Together sallied forth from Rome.
First at Aricia we alight,
And there refresh, and pass the night,
Our entertainment rather coarse
Than sumptuous, but I've met with worse.
Thence o'er the causeway soft and fair
To Appiiforum we repair.
But as this road is well supplied
(Temptation strong!) on either side
With inns commodious, snug, and warm,
We split the journey, and perform
In two days' time what's often done
By brisker travellers in one.
Here, rather choosing not to sup
Than with bad water mix my cup,
After a warm debate, in spite
Of a provoking appetite,
I sturdily resolved at last
To balk it, and pronounce a fast,
And in a moody humour wait,
While my less dainty comrades bait.
Now o'er the spangled hemisphere
Diffused the starry train appear,

When there arose a desperate brawl;
The slaves and bargemen, one and all,
Rending their throats (have mercy on us)
As if they were resolved to stun us.
'Steer the barge this way to the shore;
I tell you we'll admit no more;
Plague! will you never be content?'
Thus a whole hour at least is spent,
While they receive the several fares,
And kick the mule into his gears.
Happy, these difficulties past,
Could we have fallen asleep at last!
But, what with humming, croaking, biting,
Gnats, frogs, and all their plagues uniting,
These tuneful natives of the lake
Conspired to keep us broad awake.
Besides, to make the concert full,
Two maudlin wights, exceeding dull,
The bargeman and a passenger,
Each in his turn, essay'd an air
In honour of his absent fair.
At length the passenger, opprest
With wine, left off, and snored the rest.
The weary bargeman too gave o'er,
And hearing his companion snore,
Seized the occasion, fix'd the barge,
Turn'd out his mule to graze at large,
And slept forgetful of his charge.
And now the sun o'er eastern hill
Discover'd that our barge stood still;
When one, whose anger vex'd him sore,
With malice fraught, leaps quick on shore;
Plucks up a stake, with many a thwack
Assails the mule and driver's back.
  Then slowly moving on with pain,
At ten Feronia's stream we gain,
And in her pure and glassy wave
Our hands and faces gladly lave.
Climbing three miles, fair Anxur's height
We reach, with stony quarries white.
While here, as was agreed, we wait,
Till, charged with business of the state,

Mæcenas and Cocceius come,
The messengers of peace from Rome.
My eyes by watery humours blear
And sore I with black balsam smear.
At length they join us, and with them
Our worthy friend Fonteius came;
A man of such complete desert,
Antony loved him at his heart.
At Fundi we refused to bait,
And laugh'd at vain Aufidius' state,
A prætor now, a scribe before,
The purple-border'd robe he wore,
His slave the smoking censor bore.
Tired, at Muræna's we repose,
At Formia sup at Capito's.
With smiles the rising morn we greet,
At Sinuessa pleased to meet
With Plotius, Varius, and the bard
Whom Mantua first with wonder heard.
The world no purer spirits knows;
For none my heart more warmly glows.
O! what embraces we bestow'd,
And with what joy our breasts o'erflow'd
Sure, while my sense is sound and clear,
Long as I live, I shall prefer
A gay, good-natured, easy friend,
To every blessing Heaven can send.
At a small village the next night
Near the Vulturnus we alight;
Where, as employ'd on state affairs,
We were supplied by the purveyors
Frankly at once, and without hire,
With food for man and horse, and fire.
Capua next day betimes we reach,
Where Virgil and myself, who each
Labour'd with different maladies,
His such a stomach, mine such eyes,
As would not bear strong exercies,
In drowsy mood to sleep resort;
Mæcenas to the tennis-court.
Next at Cocceius' farm were treated,
Above the Caudian tavern seated;

His kind and hospitable board
With choice of wholesome food was stored
  Now, O ye Nine, inspire my lays!
To nobler themes my fancy raise!
Two combatants, who scorn to yield
The noisy, tongue-disputed field,
Sarmentus and Cicirrus, claim
A poet's tribute to their fame;
Cicirrus of true Oscian breed,
Sarmentus, who was never freed,
But ran away. We don't defame him;
His lady lives, and still may claim him.
Thus dignified, in harder fray
These champions their keen wit display,
And first Sarmentus led the way.
'Thy locks,' quoth he, 'so rough and coarse
Look like the mane of some wild horse.'
We laugh: Cicirrus undismay'd—
'Have at you!'—cries, and shakes his head
''Tis well,' Sarmentus says, 'you've lost
That horn your forehead once could boast;
Since, maim'd and mangled as you are,
You seem to butt.' A hideous scar
Improved, 'tis true, with double grace
The native horrors of his face.
Well. After much jocosely said
Of his grim front, so fiery red,
(For carbuncles had blotch'd it o'er,
As usual on Campania's shore)
'Give us,' he cried, 'since you're so big,
A sample of the Cyclops' jig!
Your shanks methinks no buskins ask,
Nor does your phiz require a mask.'
To this Cicirrus: 'In return
Of you, Sir, now I fain would learn,
When 'twas, no longer deem'd a slave,
Your chains you to the Lares gave.
For though a scrivener's right you claim
Your lady's title is the same.
But what could make you run away,
Since, pigmy as you are, each day

A single pound of bread would quite
O'erpower your puny appetite?'
Thus joked the champions, while we laugh'd
And many a cheerful bumper quaff'd.
  To Beneventum next we steer;
Where our good host by over care
In roasting thrushes lean as mice
Had almost fallen a sacrifice.
The kitchen soon was all on fire,
And to the roof the flames aspire;
There might you see each man and master
Striving, amidst this sad disaster,
To save the supper. .Then they came
With speed enough to quench the flame.
From hence we first at distance see
The Apulian hills, well known to me,
Parch'd by the sultry western blast;
And which we never should have past,
Had not Trivicius by the way
Received us at the close of day.
But each was forced at entering here
To pay the tribute of a tear,
For more of smoke than fire was seen—
The hearth was piled with logs so green
From hence in chaises we were carried
Miles twenty-four, and gladly tarried
At a small town, whose name my verse
(So barbarous is it) can't rehearse.
Know it you may by many a sign,
Water is dearer far han wine.
There bread is deem'd such dainty fare
That every prudent traveller
His wallet loads with many a crust;
For at Canusium you might just
As well attempt to gnaw a stone
As think to get a morsel down:
That too with scanty streams is fed;
Its founder was brave Diomed.
Good Varius (ah, that friends must part!
Here left us all with aching heart
At Rubi we arrived that day,
Well jaded by the length of way,

And sure poor mortals ne'er were wetter:
Next day no weather could be better;
No roads so bad; we scarce could crawl
Along to fishy Barium's wall.
The Egnatians next, who by the rules
Of common sense are knaves or fools,
Made all our sides with laughter heave,
Since we with them must needs believe
That incense in their temples burns,
And without fire to ashes turns.
To circumcision's bigots tell
Such tales! for me, I know full well
That in high heaven, unmoved by care,
The gods eternal quiet share:
Nor can I deem their spleen the cause,
While fickle Nature breaks her laws.
Brundusium last we reach: and there
Stop short the muse and traveller.
1759.

THE NINTH SATIRE OF THE FIRST BOOK OF HORACE.

DESCRIPTION OF AN IMPERTINENT. ADAPTED TO THE PRESENT TIMES, 1759.

SAUNTERING along the street one day,
On trifles musing by the way—
Up steps a free familiar wight,
(I scarcely knew the man by sight)
'Carlos,' he cried, 'your hand, my dear;
Gad, I rejoice to meet you here!
Pray heaven I see you well?' 'So so;
E'en well enough as times now go.
The same good wishes, Sir, to you.'
Finding he still pursued me close—
'Sir, you have business I suppose.'
'My business, Sir, is quickly done,
'Tis but to make my merit known.
Sir, I have read'—'O learned Sir,

You and your learning I revere.'
Then sweating with anxiety,
And sadly longing to get free,
Gods, how I scamper'd, scuffled for't,
Ran, halted, ran again, stopp'd short,
Beckon'd my boy, and pull'd him near,
And whisper'd nothing in his ear.
Teased with his loose unjointed chat—
'What street is this? What house is that?'
O Harlow, how I envied thee
Thy unabash'd effrontery,
Who darest a foe with freedom blame,
And call a coxcomb by his name!
When I return'd him answer none,
Obligingly the fool ran on,
'I see you're dismally distress'd,
Would give the world to be released.
But by your leave, Sir, I shall still
Stick to your skirts, do what you will.
Pray which way does your journey tend?'
O, 'tis a tedious way, my friend;
Across the Thames, the Lord knows where,
I would not trouble you so far.'
'Well, I'm at leisure to attend you.'
'Are you?' thought I, 'the de'il befriend you.'
No ass with double panniers rack'd,
Oppress'd, o'erladen, broken-back'd,
E'er look'd a thousandth part so dull
As I, nor half so like a fool.
'Sir, I know little of myself,
(Proceeds the pert conceited elf)
If Gray or Mason you will deem
Than me more worthy your esteem.
Poems I write by folios
As fast as other men write prose;
Then I can sing so loud, so clear,
That Beard cannot with me compare.
In dancing too I all surpass,
Not Cooke can move with such a grace.'
Here I made shift with much ado
To interpose a word or two.—
'Have you no parents, Sir, no friends,

Whose welfare on your own depends?'
'Parents, relations, say you? No.
They're all disposed of long ago.'—
Happy to be no more perplex'd!
My fate too threatens, I go next
Dispatch me, Sir, 'tis now too late,
Alas! to struggle with my fate!
Well, I'm convinced my time is come—
When young, a gipsy told my doom.
The beldame shook her palsied head,
As she perused my palm, and said:
Of poison, pestilence, or war,
Gout, stone, defluxion, or catarrh,
You have no reason to beware.
Beware the coxcomb's idle prate;
Chiefly, my son, beware of that.
Be sure, when you behold him, fly
Out of all earshot, or you die.'
To Rufus' Hall we now draw near;
Where he was summon'd to appear,
Refute the charge the plaintiff brought,
Or suffer judgment by default.
'For Heaven's sake, if you love me, wait
One moment! I'll be with you straight.'
Glad of a plausible pretence—
'Sir, I must beg you to dispense
With my attendance in the court.
My legs will surely suffer for't.'
'Nay, prithee, Carlos, stop awhile!'
'Faith, Sir, in law I have no skill.
Besides I have no time to spare,
I must be going you know where.
'Well, I protest I'm doubtful now
Whether to leave my suit or you!'
'Me without scruple!' I reply,
'Me by all means, Sir!'—'No, not I.
Allons, Monsieur!' 'Twere vain, you know,
To strive with a victorious foe.
So I reluctantly obey,
And follow where he leads the way.
'You and Newcastle are so close,
Still hand and glove, Sir—I suppose.—

'Newcastle, let me tell you, Sir,
Has not his equal every where.'
'Well. There indeed your fortune's made,
Faith, Sir, you understand your trade.
Would you but give me your good word;
Just introduce me to my lord,
I should serve charmingly by way
Of second fiddle as they say:
What think you, Sir? 'twere a good jest.
'Slife, we should quickly scout the rest.'
'Sir, you mistake the matter far,
We have no second fiddles there—
Richer than I some folks may be;
More learned, but it hurts not me.
Friends though he has of different kind,
Each has his proper place assign'd.'
'Strange matters these alleged by you!'—
'Strange they may be, but they are true.'—
'Well then, I vow, 'tis mighty clever,
Now I long ten times more than ever
To be advanced extremely near
One of his shining character.
Have but the will—there wants no more,
'Tis plain enough you have the power.
His easy temper (that's the worst)
He knows, and is so shy at first.—
But such a cavalier as you—
Lord, Sir, you'll quickly bring him to!—
Well; if I fail in my design,
Sir, it shall be no fault of mine.
If by the saucy servile tribe
Denied, what think you of a bribe?
Shut out to-day, not die with sorrow,
But try my luck again to-morrow.
Never attempt to visit him
But at the most convenient time,
Attend him on each levee day,
And there my humble duty pay,
Labour, like this, our want supplies;
And they must stoop who mean to rise.'
While thus he wittingly harangued,
For which you'll guess I wish'd him hang'd,

Campley, a friend of mine, came by,
Who knew his humour more than I;
We stop, salute, and—'Why so fast,
Friend Carlos? Whither all this haste?'—
Fired at the thoughts of a reprieve,
I pinch him, pull him, twitch his sleeve,
Nod, beckon, bite my lips, wink, pout,
Do every thing but speak plain out:
While he, sad dog, from the beginning
Determined to mistake my meaning,
Instead of pitying my curse,
By jeering made it ten times worse.
'Campley, what secret (pray!) was that
You wanted to communicate?'
'I recollect. But 'tis no matter.
Carlos, we'll talk of that hereafter.
E'en let the secret rest. 'Twill tell
Another time, Sir, just as well.'
Was ever such a dismal day?
Unlucky cur, he steals away,
And leaves me, half bereft of life,
At mercy of the butcher's knife;
When sudden, shouting from afar,
See his antagonist appear!
The bailiff seized him quick as thought,
'Ho, Mr. Scoundrel! Are you caught?
Sir, you are witness to the arrest.'
'Ay, marry, Sir, I'll do my best.'
The mob huzzas. Away they trudge,
Culprit and all, before the judge.
Meanwhile I luckily enough
(Thanks to Apollo) got clear off.

A TALE, FOUNDED ON A FACT,

WHICH HAPPENED IN JANUARY 1779.

Where Humber pours his rich commercial stream
There dwelt a wretch, who breath'd but to blaspheme
In subterraneous caves his life he led,
Black as the mine in which he wrought for bread.

When on a day, emerging from the deep,
A sabbath-day, (such sabbaths thousands keep!
The wages of his weekly toil he bore
To buy a cock—whose blood might win him more;
As if the noblest of the feather'd kind
Were but for battle and for death design'd;
As if the consecrated hours were meant
For sport, to minds on cruelty intent;
It chanced (such chances Providence obey)
He met a fellow-labourer on the way,
Whose heart the same desires had once inflamed;
But now the savage temper was reclaim'd,
Persuasion on his lips had taken place;
For all plead well who plead the cause of grace.
His iron heart with scripture he assail'd,
Woo'd him to hear a sermon, and prevail'd.
His faithful bow the mighty preacher drew,
Swift as the lightning-glimpse the arrow flew.
He wept; he trembled; cast his eyes around,
To find a worse than he; but none he found.
He felt his sins, and wonder'd he should feel.
Grace made the wound, and grace alone could heal.
Now farewell oaths, and blasphemies, and lies!
He quits the sinner's for the martyr's prize.
That holy day was wash'd with many a tear,
Gilded with hope, yet shaded too by fear.
The next, his swarthy brethren of the mine
Learn'd, by his alter'd speech, the change divine!
Laugh'd when they should have wept, and swore the day
Was nigh when he would swear as fast as they.
'No,' said the penitent, 'such words shall share
This breath no more; devoted now to prayer.
O! if Thou seest (thine eye the future sees)
That I shall yet again blaspheme, like these;
Now strike me to the ground on which I kneel,
Ere yet this heart relapses into steel;
Now take me to that Heaven I once defied,
Thy presence, thy embrace!'—He spoke, and died!

TO THE REV. MR. NEWTON, ON HIS RETURN FROM RAMSGATE.

That ocean you have late survey'd,
Those rocks I too have seen,
But I afflicted and dismay'd,
You tranquil and serene.

You from the flood-controlling steep
Saw stretch'd before your view,
With conscious joy, the threatening deep,
No longer such to you.

To me the waves, that ceaseless broke
Upon the dangerous coast,
Hoarsely and ominously spoke
Of all my treasure lost.

Your sea of troubles you have past,
And found the peaceful shore;
I, tempest-toss'd, and wreck'd at last,
Come home to port no more.

Oct. 1780.

LOVE ABUSED.

What is there in the vale of life
Half so delightful as a wife,
When friendship, love, and peace combine
To stamp the marriage-bond divine?
The stream of pure and genuine love
Derives its current from above;
And earth a second Eden shows,
Where'er the healing water flows:
But ah, if from the dykes and drains
Of sensual nature's feverish veins,
Lust, like a lawless headstrong flood,
Impregnated with ooze and mud,
Descending fast on every side,
Once mingles with the sacred tide,

Farewell the soul-enlivening scene!
The banks that wore a smiling green,
With rank defilement overspread,
Bewail their flowery beauties dead.
The stream polluted, dark, and dull,
Diffused into a Stygian pool,
Through life's last melancholy years
Is fed with ever-flowing tears:
  Complaints supply the zephyr's part,
And sighs that heave a breaking heart.

A POETICAL EPISTLE TO LADY AUSTEN.

Dear Anna—between friend and friend
Prose answers every common end;
Serves, in a plain and homely way,
To express the occurrence of the day;
Our health, the weather, and the news;
What walks we take, what books we choose;
And all the floating thoughts we find
Upon the surface of the mind.
  But when a poet takes the pen,
Far more alive than other men,
He feels a gentle tingling come
Down to his finger and his thumb,
Derived from nature's noblest part,
The centre of a glowing heart:
And this is what the world, who knows
No flights above the pitch of prose,
His more sublime vagaries slighting,
Denominates an itch for writing.
No wonder I, who scribble rhyme
To catch the triflers of the time,
And tell them truths divine and clear
Which, couch'd in prose, they will not hear;
Who labour hard to allure and draw
The loiterers I never saw,
Should feel that itching, and that tingling,
With all my purpose intermingling,

To your intrinsic merit true,
When call'd to address myself to you.
Mysterious are His ways whose power
Brings forth that unexpected hour,
When minds, that never met before,
Shall meet, unite, and part no more:
It is the allotment of the skies,
The hand of the Supremely Wise,
That guides and governs our affections,
And plans and orders our connexions:
Directs us in our distant road,
And marks the bounds of our abode.
Thus we were settled when you found us,
Peasants and children all around us,
Not dreaming of so dear a friend,
Deep in the abyss of Silver-End.*
Thus Martha, e'en against her will,
Perch'd on the top of yonder hill;
And you, though you must needs prefer
The fairer scenes of sweet Sancerre,†
Are come from distant Loire, to choose
A cottage on the banks of Ouse.
This page of providence quite new,
And now just opening to our view,
Employs our present thoughts and pains
To guess and spell what it contains:
But day by day, and year by year,
Will make the dark enigma clear;
And furnish us, perhaps, at last,
Like other scenes already past,
With proof, that we, and our affairs,
Are part of a Jehovah's cares:
For God unfolds by slow degrees
The purport of his deep decrees;
Sheds every hour a clearer light
In aid of our defective sight;
And spreads, at length, before the soul,
A beautiful and perfect whole,
Which busy man's inventive brain

* An obscure part of Olney, adjoining to the residence of Cowper, which faced the market-place.
† Lady Austen's residence in France.

Toils to anticipate in vain.
 Say, Anna, had you never known
The beauties of a rose full blown,
Could you, though luminous your eye,
By looking on the bud, descry,
Or guess, with a prophetic power,
The future splendour of the flower?
Just so the Omnipotent, who turns
The system of a world's concerns,
From mere minutiæ can educe
Events of most important use;
And bid a dawning sky display
The blaze of a meridian day.
The works of man tend, one and all,
As needs they must, from great to small;
And vanity absorbs at length
The monuments of human strength.
But who can tell how vast the plan
Which this day's incident began?
Too small, perhaps, the slight occasion
For our dim-sighted observation;
It pass'd unnoticed, as the bird
That cleaves the yielding air unheard,
And yet may prove, when understood,
A harbinger of endless good.
 Not that I deem, or mean to call
Friendship a blessing cheap or small:
But merely to remark, that ours,
Like some of nature's sweetest flowers,
Rose from a seed of tiny size,
That seem'd to promise no such prize;
A transient visit intervening,
And made almost without a meaning,
(Hardly the effect of inclination,
Much less of pleasing expectation)
Produced a friendship, then begun,
That has cemented us in one;
And placed it in our power to prove
By long fidelity and love,
That Solomon has wisely spoken;
'A threefold cord is not soon broken.

Dec. 1781.

THE COLUBRIAD.

CLOSE by the threshold of a door nail'd fast
Three kittens sat; each kitten look'd aghast.
I, passing swift and inattentive by,
At the three kittens cast a careless eye;
Not much concern'd to know what they did there;
Not deeming kittens worth a poet's care.
But presently a loud and furious hiss
Caused me to stop, and to exclaim, 'What's this?'
When lo! upon the threshold met my view,
With head erect, and eyes of fiery hue,
A viper, long as Count de Grasse's queue.
Forth from his head his forked tongue he throws,
Darting it full against a kitten's nose;
Who having never seen, in field or house,
The like, sat still and silent as a mouse;
Only projecting, with attention due,
Her whisker'd face, she ask'd him, 'Who are you?
On to the hall went I, with pace not slow,
But swift as lightning, for a long Dutch hoe:
With which well arm'd I hasten'd to the spot,
To find the viper, but I found him not.
And turning up the leaves and shrubs around,
Found only that he was not to be found.
But still the kittens, sitting as before,
Sat watching close the bottom of the door.
'I hope,' said I, 'the villain I would kill
Has slipp'd between the door and the door sill;
And if I make dispatch, and follow hard,
No doubt but I shall find him in the yard:'
For long ere now it should have been rehearsed,
'Twas in the garden that I found him first.
E'en there I found him, there the full grown cat
His head, with velvet paw, did gently pat;
As curious as the kittens erst had been
To learn what this phenomenon might mean.
Fill'd with heroic ardour at the sight,
And fearing every moment he would bite,

And rob our household of our only cat
That was of age to combat with a rat;
With outstretch'd hoe I slew him at the door,
And taught him NEVER TO COME THERE NO MORE

1782.

ON FRIENDSHIP.

Amicitia nisi inter bonos esse non potest.
Cicero.

WHAT virtue can we name, or grace,
But men unqualified and base
Will boast it their possession?
Profusion apes the noble part
Of liberality of heart,
And dulness of discretion.

But, as the gem of richest cost
Is ever counterfeited most,
So, always, imitation
Employs the utmost skill she can
To counterfeit the faithful man,
The friend of long duration.

Some will pronounce me too severe—
But long experience speaks me clear;
Therefore, that censure scorning,
I will proceed to mark the shelves
n which so many dash themselves,
And give the simple warning.

Youth, unadmonish'd by a guide,
Will trust to any fair outside;
An error soon corrected;
For who but learns with riper years,
That man, when smoothest he appears
Is most to be suspected?

But here again a danger lies;
Lest thus deluded by our eyes,
And taking trash for treasure,
We should, when undeceived, conclude
Friendship imaginary good,
A mere Utopian pleasure.

An acquisition, rather rare,
Is yet no subject of despair;
Nor should it seem distressful
If, either on forbidden ground,
Or where it was not to be found,
We sought it unsuccessful.

No friendship will abide the test
That stands on sordid interest
And mean self-love erected;
Nor such as may awhile subsist
'Twixt sensualist and sensualist
For vicious ends connected.

Who hopes a friend, should have a heart
Himself well furnish'd for the part,
And ready on occasion
To shew the virtue that he seeks;
For 'tis a union that bespeaks
A just reciprocation.

A fretful temper will divide
The closest knot that may be tied,
By ceaseless sharp corrosion:
A temper passionate and fierce
May suddenly your joys disperse
At one immense explosion.

In vain the talkative unite
With hope of permanent delight:
The secret just committed
They drop through mere desire to prate,
Forgetting its important weight,
And by themselves outwitted.

How bright soe'er the prospect seems,
All thoughts of friendship are but dreams,
If envy chance to creep in;
An envious man, if you succeed,
May prove a dangerous foe indeed,
But not a friend worth keeping.

As envy pines at good possess'd,
So jealousy looks forth distress'd
On good that seems approaching;
And, if success his steps attend,
Discerns a rival in a friend,
And hates him for encroaching.

Hence authors of illustrious name
(Unless belied by common fame)
Are sadly prone to quarrel;
To deem the wit a friend displays
So much of loss to their own praise,
And pluck each other's laurel.

A man renown'd for repartee
Will seldom scruple to make free
With friendship's finest feeling;
Will thrust a dagger at your breast,
And tell you 'twas a special jest,
By way of balm for healing.

Beware of tatlers; keep your ear
Close stopt against the tales they bear,
Fruits of their own invention;
The separation of chief friends
Is what their kindness most intends;
Their sport is your dissension.

Friendship that wantonly admits
A joco-serious play of wits
In brilliant altercation,
Is union such as indicates,
Like hand-in-hand insurance-plates,
Danger of conflagration

Some fickle creatures boast a soul
True as the needle to the pole;
Yet shifting like the weather,
The needle's constancy forego
For any novelty, and show
Its variations rather.

Insensibility makes some
Unseasonably deaf and dumb,
When most you need their pity;
'Tis waiting till the tears shall fall
From Gog and Magog in Guildhall,
Those playthings of the city.

The great and small but rarely meet
On terms of amity complete:
The attempt would scarce be madder,
Should any from the bottom hope,
At one huge stride to reach the top
Of an erected ladder.

Courtier and patriot cannot mix
Their heterogeneous politics
Without an effervescence,
Such as of salts with lemon juice,
But which is rarely known to induce,
Like that, a coalescence.

Religion should extinguish strife,
And make a calm of human life:
But even those, who differ
Only on topics left at large,
How fiercely will they meet and charge
No combatants are stiffer.

To prove, alas! my main intent,
Needs no great cost of argument,
No cutting and contriving;
Seeking a real friend, we seem
To adopt the chymist's golden dream
With still less hope of thriving.

Then judge, or ere you choose your man,
As circumspectly as you can,
    And, having made election,
See that no disrespect of yours,
Such as a friend but ill endures,
    Enfeeble his affection.

It is not timber, lead, and stone,
An architect requires alone,
    To finish a great building;
The palace were but half complete
Could he by any chance forget
    The carving and the gilding.

As similarity of mind,
Or something not to be defined,
    First rivets our attention;
So manners, decent and polite,
The same we practised at first sight,
    Must save it from declension.

The man who hails you Tom—or Jack,
And proves by thumping on your back
    His sense of your great merit,
Is such a friend, that one had need
Be very much his friend indeed,
    To pardon or to bear it.

Some friends make this their prudent plan—
'Say little, and hear all you can;'
    Safe policy, but hateful.
So barren sands imbibe the shower,
But render neither fruit nor flower,
    Unpleasant and ungrateful.

They whisper trivial things, and small;
But to communicate at all
    Things serious deem improper;
Their feculence and froth they show,
But keep the best contents below,
    Just like a simmering copper.

These samples (for, alas! at last
These are but samples, and a taste
Of evils yet unmention'd)
May prove the task a task indeed,
In which 'tis much if we succeed,
However well intention'd.

Pursue the theme, and you shall find
A disciplined and furnish'd mind
To be at least expedient,
And, after summing all the rest,
Religion ruling in the breast
A principal ingredient.

True friendship has, in short, a grace
More than terrestrial in its face;
That proves it heaven-descended:
Man's love of woman not so pure,
Nor, when sincerest, so secure
To last till life is ended.

1782

ON THE LOSS OF THE ROYAL GEORGE.

WRITTEN WHEN THE NEWS ARRIVED.

TO HE MARCH IN SCIPIO.

Toll for the brave!
The brave that are no more!
All sunk beneath the wave,
Fast by their native shore!

Eight hundred of the brave,
Whose courage well was tried,
Had made the vessel heel,
And laid her on her side.

A land breeze shook the shrouds,
And she was overset;
Down went the Royal George,
With all her crew complete.

Toll for the brave!
  Brave Kempenfelt is gone;
His last sea-fight is fought;
  His work of glory done.

It was not in the battle;
  No tempest gave the shock;
She sprang no fatal leak;
  She ran upon no rock.

His sword was in its sheath;
  His fingers held the pen,
When Kempenfelt went down
  With twice four hundred men.

Weigh the vessel up,
  Once dreaded by our foes!
And mingle with our cup
  The tear that England owes.

Her timbers yet are sound,
  And she may float again
Full charged with England's thunder,
  And plough the distant main.

But Kempenfelt is gone,
  His victories are o'er;
And he and his eight hundred
  Shall plough the wave no more.

Sept. 1782.

IN SUBMERSIONEM NAVIGII, CUI GEORGIUS REGALE NOMEN INDITUM.

Plangimus fortes. Periêre fortes,
Patrium propter periêre littus
Bis quatèr centum; subitò sub alto
    Æquore mersi.

Navis, innitens lateri, jacebat,
Malus ad summas trepidabat undas,
Cùm levis, funes quatiens ad imum
    Depulit aura.

Plangimus fortes. Nimis, heu, caducam
Fortibus vitem voluêre parcæ,
Nec sinunt ultrà tibi nos recentes
Nectere laurus,

Magne, qui nomen, licèt incanorum,
Traditum ex multis atavis tulisti!
At tuos olim memorabit ævum
Omne triumphos.

Non hyems illos furibunda mersit,
Non mari in clauso scopuli latentes,
Fissa non rimis abies, nec atrox
Abstulit ensis.

Navitæ sed tum nimium jocosi
Voce fallebant hilari laborem,
Et quiescebat, calamoque dextram im-
pleverat heros.

Vos, quibus cordi est grave opus piumque,
Humidum ex alto spolium levate,
Et putrescentes sub aquis amicos
Reddite amicis!

Hi quidem (sic dîs placuit) fuêre:
Sed ratis, nondùm putris, ire possit
Rursùs in bellum, Britonumque nomen
Tollere ad astra.

SONG. ON PEACE.

WRITTEN IN THE SUMMER OF 1783, AT THE REQUEST OF LADY AUSTEN, WHO GAVE THE SENTIMENT.

AIR—'MY FOND SHEPHERDS OF LATE.'

No longer I follow a sound;
No longer a dream I pursue:
O happiness! not to be found,
Unattainable treasure adieu!

I have sought thee in splendour and dress
    In the regions of pleasure and taste;
I have sought thee, and seem'd to possess,
    But have proved thee a vision at last.

An humble ambition and hope
    The voice of true wisdom inspires;
'Tis sufficient, if peace be the scope,
    And the summit of all our desires.

Peace may be the lot of the mind
    That seeks it in meekness and love;
But rapture and bliss are confined
    To the glorified spirits above.

SONG.

ALSO WRITTEN AT THE REQUEST OF LADY AUSTEN.

AIR—'THE LASS OF PATTIE'S MILL.'

When all within is peace
  How nature seems to smile!
Delights that never cease
  The livelong day beguile.
From morn to dewy eve
  With open hand she showers
Fresh blessings, to deceive
  And soothe the silent hours.

It is content of heart
  Gives nature power to please;
The mind that feels no smart
  Enlivens all it sees;
Can make a wintry sky
  Seem bright as smiling May,
And evening's closing eye
  As peep of early day.

The vast majestic globe,
  So beauteously array'd
In nature's various robe,
  With wondrous skill display'd,

Is to a mourner's heart
  A dreary wild at best;
It flutters to depart,
  And longs to be at rest.

VERSES SELECTED FROM AN OCCASIONAL POEM ENTITLED VALEDICTION.

Oh Friendship! cordial of the human breast!
So little felt, so fervently profess'd!
Thy blossoms deck our unsuspecting years;
The promise of delicious fruit appears:
We hug the hopes of constancy and truth,
Such is the folly of our dreaming youth;
But soon, alas! detect the rash mistake
That sanguine inexperience loves to make;
And view with tears the expected harvest lost,
Decay'd by time, or wither'd by a frost.
Whoever undertakes a friend's great part
Should be renew'd in nature, pure in heart,
Prepared for martyrdom, and strong to prove
A thousand ways the force of genuine love.
He may be call'd to give up health and gain,
To exchange content for trouble, ease for pain,
To echo sigh for sigh, and groan for groan,
And wet his cheeks with sorrows not his own.
The heart of man, for such a task too frail,
When most relied on is most sure to fail;
And, summon'd to partake its fellow's woe,
Starts from its office like a broken bow.
  Votaries of business and of pleasure prove
Faithless alike in friendship and in love.
Retired from all the circles of the gay,
And all the crowds that bustle life away,
To scenes where competition, envy, strife,
Beget no thunder-clouds to trouble life,
Let me, the charge of some good angel, find
One who has known, and has escaped mankind;

Polite, yet virtuous, who has brought away
The manners, not the morals, of the day:
With him, perhaps with her (for men have known
No firmer friendships than the fair have shown),
Let me enjoy, in some unthought-of spot,
All former friends forgiven, and forgot,
Down to the close of life's fast-fading scene,
Union of hearts without a flaw between.
'Tis grace, 'tis bounty, and it calls for praise,
If God give health, that sunshine of our days!
And if he add, a blessing shared by few,
Content of heart, more praises still are due—
But if he grant a friend, that boon possess'd
Indeed is treasure, and crowns all the rest;
And giving one, whose heart is in the skies,
Born from above and made divinely wise,
He gives, what bankrupt nature never can,
Whose noblest coin is light and brittle man,
Gold, purer far than Ophir ever knew,
A soul, an image of himself, and therefore true.

Nov. 1783.

IN BREVITATEM VITÆ SPATII HOMINIBUS CONCESSI.

BY DR. JORTIN.

Heu mihi! Lege ratâ sol occidit atque resurgit,
Lunaque mutatæ reparat dispendia formæ,
Astraque, purpurei telis extincta diei,
Rursus nocte vigent. Humiles telluris alumni,
Graminis herba virens, et florum picta propago,
Quos crudelis hyems lethali tabe peredit,
Cum Zephyri vox blanda vocat, rediitque sereni
Temperies anni, fœcundo è cespite surgunt.
Nos domini rerum, nos, magna et pulchra minati,
Cum breve ver vitæ robustaque transiit ætas,
Deficimus; nec nos ordo revolubilis auras
Reddit in æthereas, tumuli neque claustra resolvit.

ON THE SHORTNESS OF HUMAN LIFE.

TRANSLATION OF THE FOREGOING.

Suns that set, and moons that wane,
Rise and are restored again;
Stars that orient day subdues,
Night at her return renews.
Herbs and flowers, the beauteous birth
Of the genial womb of earth,
Suffer but a transient death
From the winter's cruel breath.
Zephyr speaks; serener skies
Warm the glebe, and they arise.
We, alas! earth's haughty kings,
We, that promise mighty things,
Losing soon life's happy prime,
Droop, and fade, in little time.
Spring returns, but not our bloom;
Still 'tis winter in the tomb.

Jan. 1784.

EPITAPH ON DR. JOHNSON.

Here Johnson lies—a sage by all allow'd,
Whom to have bred may well make England proud,
Whose prose was eloquence, by wisdom taught,
The graceful vehicle of virtuous thought;
Whose verse may claim—grave, masculine, and strong
Superior praise to the mere poet's song;
Who many a noble gift from heaven possess'd,
And faith at last, alone worth all the rest.
O man, immortal by a double prize,
By fame on earth—by glory in the skies!

Jan. 1785.

TO MISS C——, ON HER BIRTHDAY.

How many between east and west
  Disgrace their parent earth,
Whose deeds constrain us to detest
  The day that gave them birth!
Not so when Stella's natal morn
  Revolving months restore,
We can rejoice that she was born,
  And wish her born once more!

1766.

GRATITUDE.

ADDRESSED TO LADY HESKETH.

This cap, that so stately appears,
  With ribbon-bound tassel on high,
Which seems by the crest that it rears
  Ambitious of brushing the sky:
This cap to my cousin I owe,
  She gave it, and gave me beside,
Wreath'd into an elegant bow,
  The ribbon with which it is tied.

This wheel-footed studying chair,
  Contrived both for toil and repose,
Wide-elbow'd, and wadded with hair,
  In which I both scribble and dose
Bright-studded to dazzle the eyes,
  And rival in lustre of that
In which, or astronomy lies,
  Fair Cassiopeïa sat:

These carpets, so soft to the foot,
  Caledonia's traffic and pride!
Oh spare them, ye knights of the boot,
  Escaped from a cross-country ride!

This table and mirror within,
  Secure from collision and dust,
At which I oft shave cheek and chin,
  And periwig nicely adjust:

This movable structure of shelves,
  For its beauty admired and its use,
And charged with octavos and twelves
  The gayest I had to produce;
Where, flaming in scarlet and gold,
  My poems enchanted I view,
And hope, in due time, to behold
  My Iliad and Odyssey too:

This china, that decks the alcove,
  Which here people call a boufet,
But what the gods call it above
  Has ne'er been reveal'd to us yet:
These curtains, that keep the room warm
  Or cool, as the season demands,
Those stoves that for pattern and form
  Seem the labour of Mulciber's hands:

All these are not half that I owe
  To one, from our earliest youth
To me ever ready to show
  Benignity, friendship, and truth;
For Time, the destroyer declared
  And foe of our perishing kind,
If even her face he has spared,
  Much less could he alter her mind.

Thus compass'd about with the goods
  And chattels of leisure and ease,
I indulge my poetical moods
  In many such fancies as these;
And fancies I fear they will seem—
  Poets' goods are not often so fine;
The poets will swear that I dream
  When I sing of the splendour of mine

1786

LINES COMPOSED FOR A MEMORIAL OF ASHLEY COWPER ESQ.

IMMEDIATELY AFTER HIS DEATH, BY HIS NEPHEW WILLIAM OF WESTON.

Farewell! endued with all that could engage
All hearts to love thee, both in youth and age!
In prime of life, for sprightliness enroll'd
Among the gay, yet virtuous as the old;

In life's last stage, (O blessings rarely found!)
Pleasant as youth with all its blossoms crown'd;
Through every period of this changeful state
Unchanged thyself—wise, good, affectionate!

Marble may flatter, and lest this should seem
O'ercharged with praises on so dear a theme,
Although thy worth be more than half supprest,
Love shall be satisfied, and veil the rest.

June, 1788.

ON THE QUEEN'S VISIT TO LONDON,

THE NIGHT OF THE SEVENTEENTH OF MARCH, 1789.

When, long sequester'd from his throne,
George took his seat again,
By right of worth, not blood alone,
Entitled here to reign,

Then loyalty, with all his lamps
New trimm'd, a gallant show!
Chasing the darkness and the damps,
Set London in a glow.

'Twas hard to tell, of streets or squares,
Which form'd the chief display,
These most resembling cluster'd stars,
Those the long milky way.

Bright shone the roofs, the domes, the spires,
And rockets flew, self-driven,
To hang their momentary fires
Amid the vault of heaven.

So fire with water to compare,
The ocean serves, on high
Up-spouted by a whale in air,
To express unwieldy joy.

Had all the pageants of the world
In one procession join'd,
And all the banners been unfurl'd
That heralds e'er design'd,

For no such sight had England's Queen
Forsaken her retreat,
Where George, recover'd, made a scene
Sweet always doubly sweet.

Yet glad she came that night to prove,
A witness undescried,
How much the object of her love
Was loved by all beside.

Darkness the skies had mantled o'er
In aid of her design——
Darkness, O Queen! ne'er call'd before
To veil a deed of thine!

On borrow'd wheels away she flies,
Resolved to be unknown,
And gratify no curious eyes
That night except her own.

Arrived, a night like noon she sees,
And hears the million hum:
As all by instinct, like the bees,
Had known their sovereign come.

Pleased she beheld aloft portray'd,
On many a splendid wall,
Emblems of health and heavenly aid,
And George the theme of all.

Unlike the enigmatic line,
So difficult to spell,
Which shook Belshazzar at his wine
The night his city fell.

Soon watery grew her eyes and dim,
But with a joyful tear,
None else, except in prayer for him,
George ever drew from her.

It was a scene in every part
Like those in fable feign'd,
And seem'd by some magician's art
Created and sustain'd.

But other magic there, she knew,
Had been exerted none,
To raise such wonders in her view,
Save love of George alone.

That cordial thought her spirit cheer'd,
And through the cumbrous throng,
Not else unworthy to be fear'd,
Convey'd her calm along.

So, ancient poets say, serene
The sea-maid rides the waves,
And fearless of the billowy scene
Her peaceful bosom laves.

With more than astronomic eyes
She view'd the sparkling show;
One Georgian star adorns the skies,
She myriads found below.

Yet let the glories of a night
Like that, once seen, suffice,
Heaven grant us no such future sight
Such previous woe the price!

THE COCK-FIGHTER'S GARLAND.*

Muse—hide his name of whom I sing,
Lest his surviving house thou bring
For his sake into scorn,
Nor speak the school from which he drew
The much or little that he knew,
Nor place where he was born.

That such a man once was, may seem
Worthy of record (if the theme
Perchance may credit win),
For proof to man, what man may prove
If grace depart, and demons move
The source of guilt within.

This man (for since the howling wild
Disclaims him, man he must be styled)
Wanted no good below;
Gentle he was, if gentle birth
Could make him such, and he had worth,
If wealth can worth bestow.

* Written on reading the following in the obituary of the Gentleman's Magazine, for April, 1789.—' At Tottenham, John Ardesoif, Esq., a young man of large fortune, and in the splendour of his carriages and horses rivalled by few country gentlemen. His table was that of hospitality, where, it may be said, he sacrificed too much to conviviality; but, if he had his foibles he had his merits also, that far outweighed them. Mr. A. was very fond of cock-fighting, and had a favourite cock, upon which he had won many profitable matches. The last bet he laid upon this cock he lost; which so enraged him, that he had the bird tied to a spit and roasted alive before a large fire. The screams of the miserable animal were so affecting, that some gentlemen who were present attempted to interfere, which so enraged Mr. A. that he seized a poker, and with the most furious vehemence declared, that he would kill the first man who interposed; but, in the midst of his passionate asseverations, he fell down dead upon the spot. Such, we are assured, were the circumstances which attended the death of this great pillar of humanity.'

In social talk and ready jest
He shone superior at the feast,
    And qualities of mind,
Illustrious in the eyes of those
Whose gay society he chose,
    Possess'd of every kind.

Methinks I see him powder'd red,
With bushy locks his well-dress'd head
    Wing'd broad on either side,
The mossy rosebud not so sweet;
His steeds superb, his carriage neat,
    As luxury could provide.

Can such be cruel? Such can be
Cruel as hell, and so was he;
    A tyrant entertain'd
With barbarous sports, whose fell delight
Was to encourage mortal fight
    'Twixt birds to battle train'd.

One feather'd champion he possess'd,
His darling far beyond the rest,
    Which never knew disgrace,
Nor e'er had fought but he made flow
The life-blood of his fiercest foe
    The Cæsar of his race.

It chanced at last, when on a day,
He push'd him to the desperate fray,
    His courage droop'd, he fled.
The master storm'd, the prize was lost,
And, instant, frantic at the cost,
    He doom'd his favourite dead.

He seized him fast, and from the pit
Flew to the kitchen, snatch'd the spit,
    And, Bring me cord, he cried;
The cord was brought, and, at his word,
To that dire implement the bird,
    Alive and struggling, tied.

The horrid sequel asks a veil;
And all the terrors of the tale
That can be shall be sunk—
Led by the sufferer's screams aright
His shock'd companions view the sight,
And him with fury drunk.

All, suppliant, beg a milder fate
For the old warrior at the grate:
He, deaf to pity's call,
Whirl'd round him rapid as a wheel
His culinary club of steel,
Death menacing on all.

But vengeance hung not far remote,
For while he stretch'd his clamorous throat,
And heaven and earth defied,
Big with a curse too closely pent,
That struggled vainly for a vent,
He totter'd, reel'd, and died.

'Tis not for us, with rash surmise,
To point the judgment of the skies;
But judgments plain as this,
That, sent for man's instruction, bring
A written label on their wing,
'Tis hard to read amiss.

May, 1789.

TO WARREN HASTINGS, ESQ.

BY AN OLD SCHOOLFELLOW OF HIS AT WESTMINSTER.

Hastings! I knew thee young, and of a mind
While young humane, conversable, and kind,
Nor can I well believe thee, gentle then,
Now grown a villain, and the worst of men.
But rather some suspect, who have oppress'd
And worried thee, as not themselves the best.

VERSES TO THE MEMORY OF DR. LLOYD,*

SPOKEN AT THE WESTMINSTER ELECTION NEXT AFTER HIS DECEASE.

Abiit senex! periit senex amabilis!
  Quo non fuit jucundior.
Lugete vos, ætas quibus maturior
  Senem colendum præstitit,
Seu quando, viribus valentioribus
  Firmoque fretus pectore,
Florentiori vos juventute excolens
  Curâ fovebat patriâ,
Seu quando fractus, jamque donatus rude,
  Vultu sed usque blandulo,
Miscere gaudebat suas facetias
  His annuis leporibus.
Vixit probus, purâque simplex indole,
  Blandisque comis moribus,
Et dives æquâ mente—charus omnibus,
  Unius† auctus munere.
Ite tituli! meritis beatioribus
  Aptate laudes debitas!
Nec invidebat ille, si quibus favens
  Fortuna plus arriserat.
Placide senex! levi quiescas cespite,
  Etsi superbum nec vivo tibi
Decus sit inditum, nec mortuo
  Lapis notatus nomine.

* I make no apology for the introduction of the following lines, though I have never learned who wrote them. Their elegance will sufficiently recommend them to persons of classical taste and erudition, and I shall be happy if the English version that they have received from me be found not to dishonour them. Affection for the memory of the worthy man whom they celebrate alone prompted me to this endeavour.

W. COWPER.

† He was usher and under-master of Westminster near fifty years, and retired from his occupation when he was near seventy, with a handsome pension from the king.

THE SAME IN ENGLISH.

Our good old friend is gone, gone to his rest,
Whose social converse was, itself, a feast.
O ye of riper age, who recollect
How once ye loved, and eyed him with respect,
Both in the firmness of his better day,
While yet he ruled you with a father's sway,
And when, impair'd by time and glad to rest,
Yet still with looks in mild complacence drest,
He took his annual seat and mingled here
His sprightly vein with yours—now drop a tear.
In morals blameless as in manners meek,
He knew no wish that he might blush to speak,
But, happy in whatever state below,
And richer than the rich in being so,
Obtain'd the hearts of all, and such a meed
At length from one,* as made him rich indeed.
Hence, then, ye titles, hence, not wanted here,
Go, garnish merit in a brighter sphere,
The brows of those whose more exalted lot
He could congratulate, but envied not.
  Light lie the turf, good senior! on thy breast,
And tranquil as thy mind was be thy rest!
Though, living, thou hadst more desert than fame,
And not a stone now chronicles thy name.

TO MRS. THROCKMORTON,

ON HER BEAUTIFUL TRANSCRIPT OF HORACE'S ODE, 'AD LIBRUM SUUM.'

Maria, could Horace have guess'd
  What honour awaited his ode
To his own little volume address'd,
  The honour which you have bestow'd;

* See the note in the Latin copy.

Who have traced it in characters here,
  So elegant, even, and neat,
He had laugh'd at the critical sneer
  Which he seems to have trembled to meet.

And sneer, if you please, he had said,
  A nymph shall hereafter arise
Who shall give me, when you are all dead,
  The glory your malice denies;
Shall dignity give to my lay,
  Although but a mere bagatelle;
And even a poet shall say,
  Nothing ever was written so well.

Feb. 1790.

TO THE IMMORTAL MEMORY OF THE HALIBUT,

ON WHICH I DINED THIS DAY, MONDAY, APRIL 26, 1784.

Where hast thou floated, in what seas pursued
Thy pastime? when wast thou an egg new spawn'd,
Lost in the immensity of ocean's waste?
Roar as they might, the overbearing winds
That rock'd the deep, thy cradle, thou wast safe—
And in thy minikin and embryo state,
Attach'd to the firm leaf of some salt weed,
Didst outlive tempests, such as wrung and rack'd
The joints of many a stout and gallant bark,
And whelm'd them in the unexplored abyss
Indebted to no magnet and no chart,
Nor under guidance of the polar fire,
Thou wast a voyager on many coasts,
Grazing at large in meadows submarine,
Where flat Batavia just emerging peeps
Above the brine—where Caledonia's rocks
Beat back the surge—and where Hibernia shoots
Her wondrous causeway far into the main.

—Wherever thou hast fed, thou little thought'st,
And I not more, that I should feed on thee.
Peace, therefore, and good health, and much good fish,
To him who sent thee! and success, as oft
As it descends into the billowy gulf,
To the same drag that caught thee!—Fare thee well!
Thy lot thy brethren of the slimy fin
Would envy, could they know that thou wast doom'd
To feed a bard, and to be praised in verse.

INSCRIPTION FOR A STONE

ERECTED AT THE SOWING OF A GROVE OF OAKS AT CHILLINGTON, THE SEAT OF T. GIFFARD, ESQ., 1790.

Other stones the era tell
When some feeble mortal fell;
I stand here to date the birth
Of these hardy sons of earth.
  Which shall longest brave the sky,
Storm and frost—these oaks or I?
Pass an age or two away,
I must moulder and decay,
But the years that crumble me
Shall invigorate the tree,
Spread its branch, dilate its size,
Lift its summit to the skies.
  Cherish honour, virtue, truth,
So shalt thou prolong thy youth:
Wanting these, however fast
Man be fix'd and form'd to last,
He is lifeless even now,
Stone at heart, and cannot grow.

June, 1790.

ANOTHER,

For a stone erected on a similar occasion at the same place in the following year.

READER! behold a monument
That asks no sigh or tear,
Though it perpetuate the event
Of a great burial here.

Anno 1791.

TO MRS. KING,

On her kind present to the author, a patchwork counterpane of her own making.

THE bard, if e'er he feel at all,
Must sure be quicken'd by a call
Both on his heart and head,
To pay with tuneful thanks the care
And kindness of a lady fair
Who deigns to deck his bed.

A bed like this, in ancient time,
On Ida's barren top sublime,
(As Homer's epic shows)
Composed of sweetest vernal flowers,
Without the aid of sun or showers,
For Jove and Juno rose.

Less beautiful, however gay,
Is that which in the scorching day
Receives the weary swain,
Who, laying his long scythe aside,
Sleeps on some bank with daisies pied,
Till roused to toil again.

What labours of the loom I see!
Looms numberless have groan'd for me!
Should every maiden come
To scramble for the patch that bears
The impress of the robe she wears,
The bell would toll for some.

And oh, what havoc would ensue!
This bright display of every hue
  All in a moment fled!
As if a storm should strip the bowers
Of all their tendrils, leaves, and flowers—
  Each pocketing a shred.

Thanks then to every gentle fair
Who will not come to peck me bare
  As bird of borrow'd feather,
And thanks to one above them all,
The gentle fair of Pertenhall,
  Who put the whole together.

August, 1790.

TRANSLATION OF AN EPIGRAM OF HOMER *

PAY me my price, potters! and I will sing.
Attend, O Pallas! and with lifted arm
Protect their oven; let the cups and all
The sacred vessels blacken well, and, baked
With good success, yield them both fair renown
And profit, whether in the market sold
Or streets, and let no strife ensue between us.
But, oh ye potters! if with shameless front
Ye falsify your promise, then I leave
No mischief uninvoked to avenge the wrong.
Come, Syntrips, Smaragus, Sabactes, come,
And Asbetus, nor let your direst dread,
Omodamus, delay! Fire seize your house,
May neither house nor vestibule escape,
May ye lament to see confusion mar
And mingle the whole labour of your hands

* No title is prefixed to this piece, but it appears to be a translation of one of the Επιγραμματα of Homer called 'Ο Καμινος, or the Furnace. Herodotus, or whoever was the Author of the Life of Homer ascribed to him, observes, 'certain potters, while they were busied in baking their ware, seeing Homer at a small distance, and having heard much said of his wisdom, called to him, and promised him a present of their commodity and of such other things as they could afford, if he would sing to them—when he sang as follows.'

And may a sound fill all your oven, such
As of a horse grinding his provender,
While all your pots and flagons bounce within.
Come hither also, daughter of the sun,
Circe the sorceress, and with thy drugs
Poison themselves, and all that they have made!
Come also, Chiron, with thy numerous troop
Of centaurs, as well those who died beneath
The club of Hercules, as who escaped,
And stamp their crockery to dust; down fall
Their chimney; let them see it with their eyes
And howl to see the ruin of their art,
While I rejoice; and if a potter stoop
To peep into his furnace, may the fire
Flash in his face and scorch it, that all men
Observe, thenceforth, equity and good faith.

Oct. 1790.

IN MEMORY OF
THE LATE JOHN THORNTON, ESQ.

Poets attempt the noblest task they can,
Praising the Author of all good in man,
And, next, commemorating worthies lost,
The dead in whom that good abounded most.
Thee, therefore, of commercial fame, but more
Famed for thy probity from shore to shore,
Thee, Thornton! worthy in some page to shine,
As honest and more eloquent than mine,
I mourn; or, since thrice happy thou must be,
The world, no longer thy abode, not thee.
Thee to deplore were grief misspent indeed;
It were to weep that goodness has its meed,
That there is bliss prepared in yonder sky,
And glory for the virtuous when they die.
What pleasure can the miser's fondled hoard,
Or spendthrift's prodigal excess afford
Sweet as the privilege of healing woe
By virtue suffer'd combating below

That privilege was thine; Heaven gave thee means
To illumine with delight the saddest scenes,
Till thy appearance chased the gloom, forlorn
As midnight, and despairing of a morn.
Thou hadst an industry in doing good,
Restless as his who toils and sweats for food;
Avarice in thee was the desire of wealth
By rust unperishable or by stealth,
And if the genuine worth of gold depend
On application to its noblest end,
Thine had a value in the scales of Heaven
Surpassing all that mine or mint had given.
And, though God made thee of a nature prone
To distribution boundless of thy own,
And still by motives of religious force
Impell'd thee more to that heroic course,
Yet was thy liberality discreet,
Nice in its choice, and of a temper'd heat;
And though in act unwearied, secret still,
As in some solitude the summer rill
Refreshes, where it winds, the faded green,
And cheers the drooping flowers, unheard, unseen.
  Such was thy charity; no sudden start,
After long sleep, of passion in the heart,
But steadfast principle, and, in its kind,
Of close relation to the Eternal Mind,
Traced easily to its true source above,
To Him whose works bespeak his nature, love.
  Thy bounties all were Christian, and I make
This record of thee for the Gospel's sake;
That the incredulous themselves may see
Its use and power exemplified in thee.

Nov. 1790.

THE FOUR AGES.

(A BRIEF FRAGMENT OF AN EXTENSIVE PROJECTED POEM.)

'I COULD be well content, allow'd the use
Of past experience, and the wisdom glean'd
From worn-out follies, now acknowledged such,

To recommence life's trial, in the hope
Of fewer errors, on a second proof!'
Thus, while gray evening lull'd the wind, and call'd
Fresh odours from the shrubbery at my side,
Taking my lonely winding walk, I mused,
And held accustom'd conference with my heart;
When from within it thus a voice replied: [length
'Couldst thou in truth? and art thou taught at
This wisdom, and but this, from all the past?
Is not the pardon of thy long arrear,
Time wasted, violated laws, abuse
Of talents, judgment, mercies, better far
Than opportunity, vouchsafed to err
With less excuse, and, haply, worse effect?'
I heard, and acquiesced: then to and fro
Oft pacing, as the mariner his deck,
My gravelly bounds, from self to human kind
I pass'd, and next consider'd—what is man.
Knows he his origin? can he ascend
By reminiscence to his earliest date?
Slept he in Adam? And in those from him
Through numerous generations, till he found
At length his destined moment to be born?
Or was he not, till fashion'd in the womb? [toil'd
Deep mysteries both! which schoolmen must have
To unriddle, and have left them mysteries still.
It is an evil incident to man,
And of the worst, that unexplored he leaves
Truths useful and attainable with ease,
To search forbidden deeps, where mystery lies
Not to be solved, and useless if it might.
Mysteries are food for angels; they digest
With ease, and find them nutriment; but man,
While yet he dwells below, must stoop to glean
His manna from the ground, or starve and die.

May, 1791.

THE RETIRED CAT.*

A POET'S cat sedate and grave,
As poet well could wish to have,
Was much addicted to inquire
For nooks to which she might retire,
And where, secure as mouse in chink,
She might repose, or sit and think.
I know not where she caught the trick—
Naturé perhaps herself had cast her
In such a mould philosophique,
Or else she learn'd it of her master.
Sometimes ascending, debonnair,
An apple tree, or lofty pear,
Lodged with convenience in the fork,
She watch'd the gardener at his work;
Sometimes her ease and solace sought
In an old empty watering pot:
There, wanting nothing save a fan,
To seem some nymph in her sedan
Apparell'd in exactest sort,
And ready to be borne to court.
But love of change, it seems, has place
Not only in our wiser race,
Cats also feel, as well as we,
That passion's force, and so did she.
Her climbing, she began to find,
Exposed her too much to the wind,

* Cowper's partiality to animals is well known. Lady Hesketh, in one of her letters, states, 'that he had, at one time, five rabbits, three hares, two guinea-pigs, a magpie, a jay, and a starling; besides two goldfinches, two canary birds, and two dogs. It is amazing how the three hares can find room to gambol and frolic (as they certainly do) in his small parlour;' and adds, 'I forgot to enumerate a squirrel, which he had at the same time, and which used to play with one of the hares continually. One evening the cat giving one of the hares a sound box on the ear, the hare ran after her, and having caught her, punished her by drumming on her back with her two feet, as hard as drumsticks, till the creature would have actually been killed, had not Mrs. Unwin rescued her.'

And the old utensil of tin
Was cold and comfortless within:
She therefore wish'd instead of those
Some place of more serene repose,
Where neither cold might come, nor air
Too rudely wanton with her hair,
And sought it in the likeliest mode
Within her master's snug abode.
  A drawer, it chanced, at bottom lined
With linen of the softest kind,
With such as merchants introduce
From India, for the ladies' use,
A drawer impending o'er the rest,
Half open in the topmost chest,
Of depth enough, and none to spare,
Invited her to slumber there;
Puss with delight beyond expression
Survey'd the scene, and took possession.
Recumbent at her ease, ere long,
And lull'd by her own humdrum song,
She left the cares of life behind,
  And slept as she would sleep her last,
When in came, housewifely inclined,
  The chambermaid, and shut it fast;
By no malignity impell'd,
But all unconscious whom it held.
  Awaken'd by the shock—cried Puss,
'Was ever cat attended thus?
The open drawer was left, I see,
Merely to prove a nest for me,
For soon as I was well composed,
Then came the maid, and it was closed,
How smooth these 'kerchiefs, and how sweet!
O what a delicate retreat!
I will resign myself to rest
Till Sol, declining in the west,
Shall call to supper, when, no doubt,
Susan will come and let me out.'
  The evening came, the sun descended,
And Puss remain'd still unattended.
The night roll'd tardily away
(With her indeed 'twas never day),

The sprightly morn her course renew'd,
The evening gray again ensued,
And Puss came into mind no more
Than if entomb'd the day before.
With hunger pinch'd, and pinch'd for room,
She now presaged approaching doom,
Nor slept a single wink, or purr'd,
Conscious of jeopardy incurr'd.
That night, by chance, the poet watching,
Heard an inexplicable scratching;
His noble heart went pit-a-pat,
And to himself he said—'What's tnat?'
He drew the curtain at his side,
And forth he peep'd, but nothing spied
Yet, by his ear directed, guess'd
Something imprison'd in the chest,
And, doubtful what, with prudent care
Resolved it should continue there.
At length a voice which well he knew,
A long and melancholy mew,
Saluting his poetic ears,
Consoled him and dispell'd his fears:
He left his bed, he trod the floor,
He 'gan in haste the drawers explore,
The lowest first, and without stop
The rest in order to the top.
For 'tis a truth well known to most,
That whatsoever thing is lost,
We seek it, ere it come to light,
In every cranny but the right.
Forth skipp'd the cat, not now replete
As erst with airy self-conceit,
Nor in her own fond apprehension
A theme for all the world's attention
But modest, sober, cured of all
Her notions hyperbolical,
And wishing for a place of rest,
Any thing rather than a chest.
Then stepp'd the poet into bed
With this reflection in his head.

MORAL.

Beware of too sublime a sense
Of your own worth and consequence:
The man who dreams himself so great,
And his importance of such weight,
That all around, in all that's done,
Must move and act for him alone,
Will learn in school of tribulation
The folly of his expectation.

1791.

THE JUDGMENT OF THE POETS.

Two nymphs, both nearly of an age,
Of numerous charms possess'd,
A warm dispute once chanced to wage,
Whose temper was the best.

The worth of each had been complete
Had both alike been mild:
But one, although her smile was sweet,
Frown'd oftener than she smiled.

And in her humour, when she frown'd,
Would raise her voice, and roar,
And shake with fury to the ground
The garland that she wore.

The other was of gentler cast,
From all such frenzy clear,
Her frowns were seldom known to last,
And never proved severe.

To poets of renown in song
The nymphs referr'd the cause,
Who, strange to tell, all judged it wrong,
And gave misplaced applause.

They gentle call'd, and kind and soft,
The flippant and the scold,
And though she changed her mood so oft,
That failing left untold.

No judges, sure, were e'er so mad,
Or so resolved to err—
In short, the charms her sister had
They lavish'd all on her.

Then thus the God whom fondly they
Their great inspirer call,
Was heard, one genial summer's day,
To reprimand them all.

'Since thus ye have combined,' he said,
'My favourite nymph to slight,
Adorning May, that peevish maid,
With June's undoubted right,

'The minx shall, for your folly's sake,
Still prove herself a shrew,
Shall make your scribbling fingers ache,
And pinch your noses blue.'

May, 1791.

YARDLEY OAK.

Survivor sole, and hardly such, of all
That once lived here, thy brethren, at my birth
(Since which I number threescore winters past),
A shatter'd veteran, hollow-trunk'd perhaps,
As now, and with excoriate forks deform
Relics of ages! could a mind, imbued
With truth from heaven, created thing adore,
I might with reverence kneel, and worship thee
It seems idolatry with some excuse,
When our forefather druids in their oaks
Imagined sanctity. The conscience, yet

Unpurified by an authentic act
Of amnesty, the meed of blood divine,
Loved not the light, but, gloomy, into gloom
Of thickest shades, like Adam after taste
Of fruit proscribed, as to a refuge, fled.
  Thou wast a bauble once, a cup and ball
Which babes might play with; and the thievish jay,
Seeking her food, with ease might have purloin'd
The auburn nut that held thee, swallowing down
Thy yet close folded latitude of boughs
And all thine embryo vastness at a gulp.
But fate thy growth decreed; autumnal rains
Beneath thy parent tree mellow'd the soil
Design'd thy cradle; and a skipping deer,
With pointed hoof dibbling the glebe, prepared
The soft receptacle, in which, secure,
Thy rudiments should sleep the winter through.
  So fancy dreams. Disprove it, if ye can,
Ye reasoners broad awake, whose busy search
Of argument, employ'd too oft amiss,
Sifts half the pleasures of short life away!
  Thou fell'st mature; and, in the loamy clod
Swelling with vegetative force instinct,
Didst burn thine egg, as theirs the fabled twins,
Now stars; two lobes, protruding, pair'd exact;
A leaf succeeded, and another leaf,
And, all the elements thy puny growth
Fostering propitious, thou becamest a twig.
  Who lived when thou wast such? Oh, couldst thou [speak,
As in Dodona once thy kindred trees
Oracular, I would not curious ask
The future, best unknown, but at thy mouth
Inquisitive, the less ambiguous past.
  By thee I might correct, erroneous oft,
The clock of history, facts and events
Timing more punctual, unrecorded facts
Recovering, and misstated setting right——
Desperate attempt, till trees shall speak again!
  Time made thee what thou wast, king of the woods;
And time hath made thee what thou art—a cave
For owls to roost in. Once thy spreading boughs
O'erhung the champaign; and the numerous flocks

That grazed it stood beneath that ample cope
Uncrowded, yet safe shelter'd from the storm.
No flock frequents thee now. Thou hast outlived
Thy popularity, and art become
(Unless verse rescue thee awhile) a thing
Forgotten, as the foliage of thy youth.
While thus through all the stages thou hast push'd
Of treeship—first a seedling, hid in grass;
Then twig; then sapling; and, as century roll'd
Slow after century, a giant bulk
Of girth enormous, with moss-cushion'd root
Upheaved above the soil, and sides emboss'd
With prominent wens globose—till at the last
The rottenness, which time is charged to inflict
On other mighty ones, found also thee.
What exhibitions various hath the world
Witness'd of mutability in all
That we account most durable below!
Change is the diet on which all subsist,
Created changeable, and change at last
Destroys them. Skies uncertain now the heat
Transmitting cloudless, and the solar beam
Now quenching in a boundless sea of clouds—
Calm and alternate storm, moisture, and drought,
Invigorate by turns the springs of life
In all that live, plant, animal, and man,
And in conclusion mar them. Nature's threads,
Fine passing thought, e'en in their coarsest works,
Delight in agitation, yet sustain
The force that agitates not unimpair'd;
But worn by frequent impulse, to the cause
Of their best tone their dissolution owe.
Thought cannot spend itself, comparing still
The great and little of thy lot, thy growth
From almost nullity into a state
Of matchless grandeur, and declension thence,
Slow, into such magnificent decay.
Time was when, settling on thy leaf, a fly
Could shake thee to the root—and time has been
When tempests could not. At thy firmest age
Thou hadst within thy bole solid contents
That might have ribb'd the sides and plank'd the deck

Of some flagg'd admiral; and tortuous arms,
The shipwrights darling treasure, didst present
To the four-quarter'd winds, robust and bold,
Warp'd into tough knee-timber, many a load!*
But the axe spared thee. In those thriftier days
Oaks fell not, hewn by thousands, to supply
The bottomless demands of contest waged
For senatorial honours. Thus to time
The task was left to whittle thee away
With his sly scythe, whose ever-nibbling edge,
Noiseless, an atom, and an atom more,
Disjoining from the rest, has, unobserved,
Achieved a labour which had, far and wide,
By man perform'd, made all the forest ring.
  Embowel'd now, and of thy ancient self
Possessing nought but the scoop'd rind that seems
A huge throat calling to the clouds for drink,
Which it would give in rivulets to thy root,
Thou temptest none, but rather much forbidst
The feller's toil, which thou couldst ill requite.
Yet is thy root sincere, sound as the rock,
A quarry of stout spurs and knotted fangs,
Which, crook'd into a thousand whimsies, clasp
The stubborn soil, and hold thee still erect.
  So stands a kingdom, whose foundation yet
Fails not, in virtue and in wisdom laid,
Though all the superstructure, by the tooth
Pulverized of venality, a shell
Stands now, and semblance only of itself! [off
  Thine arms have left thee. Winds have rent them
Long since, and rovers of the forest wild
With bow and shaft have burnt them. Some have left
A splinter'd stump bleach'd to a snowy white;
And some memorial none where once they grew.
Yet life still lingers in thee, and puts forth
Proof not contemptible of what she can,
Even where death predominates. The spring
Finds thee not less alive to her sweet force

* Knee-timber is found in the crooked arms of oak, which, by reason of their distortion, are easily adjusted to the angle formed where the deck and the ship's sides meet.

Than yonder upstarts of the neighbouring wood,
So much thy juniors, who their birth received
Half a millennium since the date of thine.
  But since, although well qualified by age
To teach, no spirit dwells in thee, nor voice
May be expected from thee, seated here
On thy distorted root, with hearers none,
Or prompter, save the scene, I will perform
Myself the oracle, and will discourse
In my own ear such matter as I may.
  One man alone, the father of us all,
Drew not his life from woman; never gazed,
With mute unconsciousness of what he saw,
On all around him; learn'd not by degrees,
Nor owed articulation to his ear;
But, moulded by his Maker into man
At once, upstood intelligent, survey'd
All creatures, with precision understood
Their purport, uses, properties, assign'd
To each his name significant, and, fill'd
With love and wisdom, render'd back to Heaven
In praise harmonious the first air he drew.
He was excused the penalties of dull
Minority. No tutor charged his hand
With the thought-tracing quill, or task'd his mind
With problems. History, not wanted yet,
Lean'd on her elbow, watching time, whose course,
Eventful, should supply her with a theme; . . . .

1791.

TO THE NIGHTINGALE,

WHICH THE AUTHOR HEARD SING ON NEW YEAR'S DAY

Whence is it that, amazed, I hear
  From yonder wither'd spray,
This foremost morn of all the year,
  The melody of May?

And why, since thousands would be proud
  Of such a favour shown,
Am I selected from the crowd
  To witness it alone?

Sing'st thou, sweet Philomel, to me,
  For that I also long
Have practised in the groves like thee
  Though not like thee in song?

Or sing'st thou, rather, under force
  Of some divine command,
Commission'd to presage a course
  Of happier days at hand!

Thrice welcome then! for many a long
  And joyless year have I,
As thou to-day, put forth my song
  Beneath a wintry sky.

But thee no wintry skies can harm,
  Who only need'st to sing
To make e'en January charm,
  And every season spring.

1792.

LINES WRITTEN IN AN ALBUM

OF MISS PATTY MORE'S, SISTER OF HANNAH MORE.

In vain to live from age to age
  While modern bards endeavour,
I write my name in Patty's page,
  And gain my point for ever

W. COWPER.

March 6, 1792.

SONNET TO WILLIAM WILBERFORCE, ESQ.

Thy country, Wilberforce, with just disdain,
Hears thee by cruel men and impious call'd
Fanatic, for thy zeal to loose the inthral'd
From exile, public sale, and slavery's chain.
Friend of the poor, the wrong'd, the fetter-gall'd,
Fear not lest labour such as thine be vain.

Thou hast achieved a part; hast gain'd the ear
Of Britain's senate to thy glorious cause; [pause
Hope smiles, joy springs, and, though cold caution
And weave delay, the better hour is near
That shall remunerate thy toils severe
By peace for Afric, fenced with British laws.

Enjoy what thou hast won, esteem and love
From all the just on earth, and all the blest ab[ove]

April 16, 1792.

EPIGRAM

PRINTED IN THE NORTHAMPTON MERCURY.

To purify their wine some people bleed
A lamb into the barrel, and succeed;
No nostrum, planters say, is half so good
To make fine sugar as a negro's blood.
Now lambs and negroes both are harmless things,
And thence perhaps this wondrous virtue springs,
'Tis in the blood of innocence alone—
Good cause why planters never try their own.

TO DR. AUSTIN, OF CECIL STREET, LONDON.

Austin! accept a grateful verse from me,
The poet's treasure, no inglorious fee.
Loved by the muses, thy ingenuous mind
Pleasing requital in my verse may find

Verse oft has dash'd the scythe of time aside,
Immortalizing names which else had died:
And O! could I command the glittering wealth
With which sick kings are glad to purchase health!
Yet, if extensive fame, and sure to live,
Were in the power of verse like mine to give,
I would not recompense his art with less,
Who, giving Mary health, heals my distress.
  Friend of my friend!* 'I love thee, tho' unknown,
And boldly call thee, being his, my own.

May 26, 1792.

CATHARINA:

THE SECOND PART: ON HER MARRIAGE TO GEORGE COURTENAY, ESQ.

Believe it or not, as you choose,
  The doctrine is certainly true,
That the future is known to the muse,
  And poets are oracles too.
I did but express a desire
  To see Catharina at home,
At the side of my friend George's fire,
  And lo—she is actually come.

Such prophecy some may despise,
  But the wish of a poet and friend
Perhaps is approved in the skies,
  And therefore attains to its end.
'Twas a wish that flew ardently forth
  From a bosom effectually warm'd
With the talents, the graces, and worth
  Of the person for whom it was form'd.

Maria† would leave us, I knew,
  To the grief and regret of us all,
But less to our grief, could we view
  Catharina the Queen of the Hall.

* Hayley. † Lady Throckmorton.

And therefore I wish'd as I did,
  And therefore this union of hands
Not a whisper was heard to forbid,
  But all cry—Amen—to the bans.

Since, therefore, I seem to incur
  No danger of wishing in vain
When making good wishes for her,
  I will e'en to my wishes again—
With one I have made her a wife,
  And now I will try with another,
Which I cannot suppress for my life—
  How soon I can make her a mother.

June, 1792.

EPITAPH ON FOP,

A DOG BELONGING TO LADY THROCKMORTON.

Though once a puppy, and though Fop by name,
Here moulders one whose bones some honour claim
No sycophant, although of spaniel race,
And though no hound, a martyr to the chase—
Ye squirrels, rabbits, leverets, rejoice,
Your haunts no longer echo to his voice;
This record of his fate exulting view,
He died worn out with vain pursuit of you.
  'Yes,'—the indignant shade of Fop replies—
'And worn with vain pursuit man also dies.'

August, 1792.

SONNET

TO GEORGE ROMNEY, ESQ.

On his Picture of me in Crayons, drawn at Eartham in the 61st year of my age, and in the months of August and September, 1792.

ROMNEY, expert infallibly to trace
On chart or canvas, not the form alone
And semblance, but, however faintly shown,
The mind's impression too on every face—
With strokes that time ought never to erase
Thou hast so pencil'd mine, that though I own
The subject worthless, I have never known
The artist shining with superior grace.

But this I mark—that symptoms none of woe
In thy incomparable work appear.
Well—I am satisfied it should be so,
Since, on maturer thought, the cause is clear;

For in my looks what sorrow couldst thou see
When I was Hayley's guest, and sat to thee?

October, 1792.

MARY AND JOHN.

IF John marries Mary, and Mary alone,
'Tis a very good match between Mary and John.
Should John wed a score, Oh, the claws and the scratches!
It can't be a match:—'tis a bundle of matches.

EPITAPH

ON MR. CHESTER, OF CHICHELEY.

Tears flow, and cease not, where the good man lies
Till all who knew him follow to the skies.
Tears therefore fall where Chester's ashes sleep;
Him wife, friends, brothers, children, servants, weep—
And justly—few shall ever him transcend
As husband, parent, brother, master, friend.

April, 1793.

TO MY COUSIN, ANNE BODHAM,

ON RECEIVING FROM HER A NETWORK PURSE, MADE BY HERSELF.

My gentle Anne, whom heretofore,
When I was young, and thou no more
Than plaything for a nurse,
I danced and fondled on my knee
A kitten both in size and glee,
I thank thee for my purse.

Gold pays the worth of all things here;
But not of love;—that gem's too dear
For richest rogues to win it;
I, therefore, as a proof of love,
Esteem thy present far above
The best things kept within it.

May 4, 1793.

INSCRIPTION FOR A HERMITAGE IN THE AUTHOR'S GARDEN.

This cabin, Mary, in my sight appears,
Built as it has been in our waning years,
A rest afforded to our weary feet,
Preliminary to—the last retreat.

May, 1793.

TO MRS. UNWIN.

Mary! I want a lyre with other strings, [drew,
Such aid from heaven as some have feign'd they
An eloquence scarce given to mortals, new
And undebased by praise of meaner things,
That, ere through age or woe I shed my wings,
I may record thy worth with honour due,
In verse as musical as thou art true,
And that immortalizes whom it sings.
But thou hast little need. There is a book
By seraphs writ with beams of heavenly light,
On which the eyes of God not rarely look,
A chronicle of actions just and bright;
There all thy deeds, my faithful Mary, shine,
And, since thou own'st that praise, I spare thee mine.

May, 1793.

TO JOHN JOHNSON,

ON HIS PRESENTING ME WITH AN ANTIQUE BUST OF HOMER.

Kinsman beloved, and as a son, by me!
When I behold this fruit of thy regard,
The sculptured form of my old favourite bard,
I reverence feel for him, and love for thee.
Joy too and grief. Much joy that there should be
Wise men and learn'd, who grudge not to reward
With some applause my bold attempt and hard,
Which others scorn; critics by courtesy.
The grief is this, that, sunk in Homer's mine,
I lose my precious years, now soon to fail
Handling his gold, which, howsoe'er it shine,
Proves dross when balanced in the Christian scale.
Be wiser thou—like our forefather Donne,
Seek heavenly wealth, and work for God alone.

May, 1793.

TO A YOUNG FRIEND,

ON HIS ARRIVING AT CAMBRIDGE WET WHEN NO RAIN HAD FALLEN THERE.

If Gideon's fleece, which drench'd with dew he found,
While moisture none refresh'd the herbs around,
Might fitly represent the church endow'd
With heavenly gifts to heathens not allow'd;
In pledge, perhaps, of favours from on high,
Thy locks were wet when others' locks were dry.
Heaven grant us half the omen—may we see
Not drought on others, but much dew on thee!

May, 1798.

A TALE.*

In Scotland's realms, where trees are few,
Nor even shrubs abound;
But where, however bleak the view,
Some better things are found:

For husband there and wife may boast
Their union undefiled,
And false ones are as rare almost
As hedge rows in the wild.

* This tale is founded on an article which appeared in the Buckinghamshire Herald, for Saturday, June 1, 1793:—' Glasgow, May 23. In a block, or pulley, near the head of the mast of a gabert, now lying at the Broomielaw, there is a chaffinch's nest and four eggs. The nest was built while the vessel lay at Greenock, and was followed hither by both birds. Though the block is occasionally lowered for the inspection of the curious, the birds have not forsaken the nest. The cock, however, visits the nest but seldom, while the hen never leaves it, but when she descend to the hull for food.'

In Scotland's realm, forlorn and bare,
The history chanced of late—
This history of a wedded pair,
A chaffinch and his mate.

The spring drew near, each felt a breast
With genial instinct fill'd;
They pair'd, and would have built a nest,
But found not where to build.

The heaths uncover'd and the moors
Except with snow and sleet,
Sea-beaten rocks and naked shores
Could yield them no retreat.

Long time a breeding place they sought,
Till both grew vex'd and tired;
At length a ship arriving brought
The good so long desired.

A ship?—could such a restless thing
Afford them place of rest?
Or was the merchant charged to bring
The homeless birds a nest?

Hush—silent hearers profit most—
This racer of the sea
Proved kinder to them than the coast—
It served them with a tree.

But such a tree! 'twas shaven deal,
The tree they call'd a mast,
And had a hollow with a wheel
Through which the tackle pass'd.

Within that cavity aloft
Their roofless home they fix'd,
Form'd with materials neat and soft,
Bents, wool, and feathers mix'd.

Four ivory eggs soon pave its floor
With russet specks bedight—
The vessel weighs, forsakes the shore,
And lessens to the sight.

The mother-bird is gone to sea,
    As she had changed her kind;
But goes the male? Far wiser, he
    Is doubtless left behind.

No—soon as from the shore he saw
    The winged mansion move,
He flew to reach it, by a law
    Of never-failing love;

Then perching at his consort's side,
    Was briskly borne along,
The billows and the blast defied,
    And cheer'd her with a song.

The seaman with sincere delight
    His feather'd shipmates eyes,
Scarce less exulting in the sight
    Than when he tows a prize.

For seamen much believe in signs
    And from a chance so new
Each some approaching good divines,
    And may his hopes be true!

Hail, honour'd land! a desert where
    Not even birds can hide,
Yet parent of this loving pair
    Whom nothing could divide.

And ye who, rather than resign
    Your matrimonial plan,
Were not afraid to plough the brine
    In company with man.

For whose lean country much disdain
    We English often show,
Yet from a richer nothing gain
    But wantonness and woe.

Be it your fortune, year by year,
    The same resource to prove,
And may ye, sometimes landing here,
    Instruct us how to love!

June, 1793.

ON A SPANIEL, CALLED BEAU, KILLING A YOUNG BIRD.

A SPANIEL, Beau, that fares like you,
  Well fed, and at his ease,
Should wiser be than to pursue
  Each trifle that he sees.

But you have kill'd a tiny bird,
  Which flew not till to-day,
Against my orders, whom you heard
  Forbidding you the prey.

Nor did you kill that you might eat
  And ease a doggish pain,
For him, though chased with furious heat,
  You left where he was slain.

Nor was he of the thievish sort
  Or one whom blood allures,
But innocent was all his sport
  Whom you have torn for yours

My dog! what remedy remains,
  Since, teach you all I can,
I see you, after all my pains,
  So much resemble man?

July 15, 1793.

BEAU'S REPLY.

SIR, when I flew to seize the bird
  In spite of your command,
A louder voice than yours I heard,
  And harder to withstand.

You cried—Forbear—but in my breast
  A mightier cried—Proceed—
'Twas nature, Sir, whose strong behest
  Impell'd me to the deed.

Yet, much as nature I respect,
I ventured once to break
(As you perhaps may recollect)
Her precept for your sake;

And when your linnet on a day,
Passing his prison door,
Had flutter'd all his strength away,
And panting press'd the floor,

Well knowing him a sacred thing,
Not destined to my tooth,
I only kiss'd his ruffled wing,
And lick'd the feathers smooth.

Let my obedience then excuse
My disobedience now,
Nor some reproof yourself refuse
From your aggrieved bow-wow:

If killing birds be such a crime
(Which I can hardly see)
What think you, Sir, of killing time
With verse address'd to me!

TO WILLIAM HAYLEY, ESQ.

Dear architect of fine chateaux in air,
Worthier to stand for ever, if they could,
Than any built of stone, or yet of wood,
For back of royal elephant to bear!

O for permission from the skies to share,
Much to my own, though little to thy good,
With thee (not subject to the jealous mood!)
A partnership of literary ware!

But I am bankrupt now; and doom'd henceforth
To drudge, in descant dry, on others' lays;
Bards, I acknowledge, of unequal'd birth!
But what his commentators' happiest praise?

That he has furnish'd lights for other eyes,
Which they who need them use, and then despise

June 29, 1793.

ANSWER

To Stanzas addressed to Lady Hesketh, by Miss Catharine Fanshawe, in returning a Poem of Mr. Cowper's, lent to her, on condition she should neither show it, nor take a Copy.

To be remember'd thus is fame,
And in the first degree;
And did the few like her the same,
The press might sleep for me.

So Homer, in the memory stored
Of many a Grecian belle,
Was once preserved—a richer hoard,
But never lodged so well.

1793.

ON FLAXMAN'S PENELOPE.

The suitors sinn'd, but with a fair excuse,
Whom all this elegance might well seduce;
Nor can our censure on the husband fall,
Who, for a wife so lovely, slew them all.

September, 1793.

TO THE SPANISH ADMIRAL COUNT GRAVINA,

On his translating the Author's Song on a Rose into Italian Verse.

My rose, Gravina, blooms anew,
And, steep'd not now in rain,
But in Castalian streams by you,
Will never fade again.

1793.

TO MARY

THE twentieth year is well nigh past
Since first our sky was overcast;
Ah would that this might be the last!
My Mary!

Thy spirits have a fainter flow,
I see thee daily weaker grow
'Twas my distress that brought thee low,
My Mary!

Thy needles, once a shining store,
For my sake restless heretofore,
Now rust disused, and shine no more;
My Mary!

For though thou gladly wouldst fulfil
The same kind office for me still,
Thy sight now seconds not thy will,
My Mary!

But well thou play'dst the housewife's part,
And all thy threads with magic art
Have wound themselves about this heart,
My Mary!

Thy indistinct expressions seem
Like language utter'd in a dream;
Yet me they charm, whate'er the theme,
My Mary!

Thy silver locks, once auburn bright,
Are still more lovely in my sight
Than golden beams of orient light,
My Mary!

For, could I view nor them nor thee,
What sight worth seeing could I see?
The sun would rise in vain for me,
My Mary!

Partakers of thy sad decline,
Thy hands their little force resign;
Yet gently press'd, press gently mine,
My Mary!

Such feebleness of limbs thou provest,
That now at every step thou movest
Upheld by two; yet still thou lovest,
My Mary

And still to love, though press'd with ill,
In wintry age to feel no chill,
With me is to be lovely still,
My Mary!

But ah! by constant heed I know,
How oft the sadness that I show
Transforms thy smiles to looks of woe,
My Mary!

And should my future lot be cast
With much resemblance of the past,
Thy worn-out heart will break at last,
My Mary!

Autumn of 1793.

MONTES GLACIALES, IN OCEANO GERMANICO NATANTES.

En, quæ prodigia, ex oris allata, remotis,
Oras adveniunt pavefacta per æquora nostras!
Non equidem priscæ sæclum rediisse videtur
Pyrrhæ, cum Proteus pecus altos visere montes
Et Sylvas, egit. Sed tempora vix leviora
Adsunt, evulsi quando radicitùs alti
In mare descendunt montes, fluctusque pererrant.
Quid verò hoc monstri est magis et mirabile visu?
Splendentes video, ceu pulchro ex ære vel auro
Conflatos, rutilisque accinctos undique gemmis,
Baccâ cæruleâ, et flammas imitante pyropo.
Ex oriente adsunt, ubi gazas optima tellus
Parturit omnigenas, quibus æva per omnia sumptu
Ingenti finxêre sibi diademata reges?

Vix hoc crediderim. Non fallunt talia acutos
Mercatorum oculos: prius et quàm littora Gangis
Liquissent, avidis gratissima præda fuissent.
Ortos unde putemus? An illos Ves'vius atrox
Protulit, ignivomisve ejecit faucibus Ætna?
Luce micant propriâ, Phœbive, per aëra purum
Nunc stimulantis equos, argentea tela retorquent?
Phœbi luce micant. Ventis et fluctibus altis
Appulsi, et rapidis subter currentibus undis,
Tandem non fallunt oculos. Capita alta videre est
Multâ onerata nive et canis conspersa pruinis.
Cætera sunt glacies. Procul hinc, ubi Bruma ferè
Contristat menses, portenta hæc horrida nobis [omnes
Illa strui voluit. Quoties de culmine summo.
Clivorum fluerent in littora prona, solutæ
Sole, nives, propero tendentes in mare cursu,
Illa gelu fixit. Paulatim attollere sese
Mirum cœpit opus; glacieque ab origine rerum
In glaciem aggestâ sublimes vertice tandem
Æquavit montes, non crescere nescia moles.
Sic immensa diu stetit, æternumque stetisset
Congeries, hominum neque vi neque mobilis arte,
Littora ni tandem declivia deseruisset,
Pondere victa suo. Dilabitur. Omnia circum
Antra et saxa gemunt, subito concussa fragore,
Dum ruit in pelagum, tanquam studiosa natandi,
Ingens tota strues. Sic Delos dicitur olim,
Insula, in Ægæo fluitâsse erratica ponto.
Sed non ex glacie Delos; neque torpida Delum
Bruma inter rupes genuit nudum sterilemque.
Sed vestita herbis erat illa, ornataque nunquam
Deciduâ lauro; et Delum dilexit Apollo.
At vos, errones horrendi, et caligine digni
Cimmeriâ, Deus idem odit. Natalia vestra,
Nubibus involvens frontem, non ille tueri
Sustinuit. Patrium vos ergo requirite cœlum!
Ite! Redite! Timete moras; ni lenitèr austro
Spirante, et nitidas Phœbe jaculante sagittas
Hostili vobis, pereatis gurgite misti!

March 11, 1799.

ON THE ICE ISLANDS, SEEN FLOATING IN THE GERMAN OCEAN.

WHAT portents, from what distant region ride,
Unseen till now in ours, the astonish'd tide?
In ages past, old Proteus, with his droves
Of sea-calves, sought the mountains and the groves.
But now, descending whence of late they stood,
Themselves the mountains seem to rove the flood.
Dire times were they, full charged with human woes;
And these, scarce less calamitous than those.
What view we now? More wondrous still! Behold!
Like burnish'd brass they shine, or beaten gold;
And all around the pearl's pure splendour show,
And all around the ruby's fiery glow.
Come they from India, where the burning earth,
All bounteous, gives her richest treasures birth;
And where the costly gems, that beam around
The brows of mightiest potentates, are found?
No. Never such a countless dazzling store
Had left unseen the Ganges' peopled shore.
Rapacious hands, and ever watchful eyes,
Should sooner far have mark'd and seized the prize.
Whence sprang they then? Ejected have they come
From Vesuvius', or from Ætna's burning womb?
Thus shine they self-illumed, or but display
The borrow'd splendours of a cloudless day?
With borrow'd beams they shine. The gales that breathe
Now landward, and the current's force beneath,
Have borne them nearer: and the nearer sight,
Advantaged more, contemplates them aright.
Their lofty summits crested high they show,
With mingled sleet, and long-incumbent snow.
The rest is ice. Far hence, where, most severe,
Bleak winter well nigh saddens all the year,
Their infant growth began. He bade arise
Their uncouth forms, portentous in our eyes.

Oft as dissolved by transient suns, the snow
Left the tall cliff, to join the flood below;
He caught, and curdled with a freezing blast
The current, ere it reach'd the boundless waste.
By slow degrees uprose the wondrous pile,
And long successive ages roll'd the while;
Till, ceaseless in its growth, it claim'd to stand
Tall as its rival mountains on the land.
Thus stood, and, unremovable by skill
Or force of man, had stood the structure still,
But that, though firmly fix'd, supplanted yet
By pressure of its own enormous weight,
It left the shelving beach—and, with a sound
That shook the bellowing waves and rocks around,
Self-launch'd, and swiftly, to the briny wave,
As if instinct with strong desire to lave,
Down went the ponderous mass. So bards of old
How Delos swam the Ægean deep have told.
But not of ice was Delos. Delos bore
Herb, fruit, and flower. She, crown'd with laurel, wore
E'en under wintry skies, a summer smile;
And Delos was Apollo's favourite isle.
But, horrid wanderers of the deep, to you
He deems Cimmerian darkness only due.
Your hated birth he deign'd not to survey,
But, scornful, turn'd his glorious eyes away.
Hence, seek your home, nor longer rashly dare
The darts of Phœbus, and a softer air;
Lest ye regret, too late, your native coast,
In no congenial gulf for ever lost!

March 19, 1799.

THE CASTAWAY.

Obscurest night involved the sky,
The Atlantic billows roar'd,
When such a destined wretch as I
Wash'd headlong from on board,
Of friends, of hope, of all bereft,
His floating home for ever left.

No braver chief could Albion boast
  Than he with whom he went,
Nor ever ship left Albion's coast
  With warmer wishes sent.
He loved them both, but both in vain,
Nor him beheld, nor her again.

Not long beneath the whelming brine,
  Expert to swim he lay;
Nor soon he felt his strength decline,
  Or courage die away:
But waged with death a lasting strife,
Supported by despair of life.

He shouted; nor his friends had fail'd
  To check the vessel's course,
But so the furious blast prevail'd
  That, pitiless perforce,
They left their outcast mate behind,
And scudded still before the wind.

Some succour yet they could afford;
  And, such as storms allow,
The cask, the coop, the floated cord,
  Delay'd not to bestow:
But he, they knew, nor ship nor shore,
Whate'er they gave, should visit more.

Nor, cruel as it seem'd, could he
  Their haste himself condemn,
Aware that flight, in such a sea,
  Alone could rescue them;
Yet bitter felt it still to die
Deserted, and his friends so nigh.

He long survives, who lives an hour
  In ocean, self-upheld:
And so long he, with unspent power,
  His destiny repell'd:
And ever, as the minutes flew,
Entreated help, or cried—'Adieu!'

At length, his transient respite past
  His comrades, who before
Had heard his voice in every blast,
  Could catch the sound no more:
For then, by toil subdued, he drank
The stifling wave, and then he sank.

No poet wept him; but the page
  Of narrative sincere,
That tells his name, his worth, his age,
  Is wet with Anson's tear:
And tears by bards or heroes shed,
Alike immortalize the dead.

I therefore purpose not, or dream,
  Descanting on his fate,
To give the melancholy theme
  A more enduring date:
But misery still delights to trace
Its semblance in another's case.

No voice divine the storm allay'd,
  No light propitious shone;
When, snatch'd from all effectual aid,
  We perish'd, each alone:
But I beneath a rougher sea,
And whelm'd in deeper gulfs than he.

March 20, 1799.

THE SALAD, BY VIRGIL.

The winter night now well nigh worn away,
The wakeful cock proclaim'd approaching day,
When Simulus, poor tenant of a farm
Of narrowest limits, heard the shrill alarm,
Yawn'd, stretch'd his limbs, and anxious to provid
Against the pangs of hunger unsupplied,

By slow degrees his tatter'd bed forsook,
And poking in the dark explored the nook
Where embers slept with ashes heap'd around,
And with burnt fingers'-ends the treasure found.
It chanced that from a brand beneath his nose,
Sure proof of latent fire, some smoke arose;
When trimming with a pin the incrusted tow,
And stooping it towards the coals below,
He toils, with cheeks distended, to excite
The lingering flame, and gains at length a light.
With prudent heed he spreads his hand before
The quivering lamp, and opes his granary door.
Small was his stock, but taking for the day
A measured stint of twice eight pounds away,
With these his mill he seeks. A shelf at hand
Fix'd in the wall, affords his lamp a stand:
Then baring both his arms—a sleeveless coat
He girds, the rough exuviæ of a goat:
And with a rubber, for that use design'd,
Cleansing his mill within—begins to grind;
Each hand has its employ; labouring amain,
This turns the winch, while that supplies the grain.
The stone revolving rapidly, now glows,
And the bruised corn a mealy current flows;
While he, to make his heavy labour light,
Tasks oft his left hand to relieve his right;
And chants with rudest accent, to beguile
His ceaseless toil, as rude a strain the while.
And now, 'Dame Cybale, come forth!' he cries;
But Cybale, still slumbering, nought replies.
From Afric she, the swain's sole serving-maid,
Whose face and form alike her birth betray'd.
With woolly locks, lips tumid, sable skin,
Wide bosom, udders flaccid, belly thin,
Legs slender, broad and most misshapen feet,
Chapp'd into chinks, and parch'd with solar heat.
Such, summon'd oft, she came; at his command
Fresh fuel heap'd, the sleeping embers fann'd,
And made in haste her simmering skillet steam,
Replenish'd newly from the neighbouring stream.
The labours of the mill perform'd, a sieve
The mingled flour and bran must next receive,

Which shaken oft shoots Ceres through refined,
And better dress'd, her husks all left behind.
This done at once, his future plain repast
Unleaven'd on a shaven board he cast,
With tepid lymph first largely soak'd it all,
Then gather'd it with both hands to a ball,
And spreading it again with both hands wide,
With sprinkled salt the stiffen'd mass supplied;
At length the stubborn substance, duly wrought,
Takes from his palms impress'd the shape it ought,
Becomes an orb—and quarter'd into shares.
The faithful mark of just division bears.
Last, on his hearth it finds convenient space,
For Cybale before had swept the place,
And there, with tiles and embers overspread,
She leaves it—reeking in its sultry bed.
Nor Simulus, while Vulcan thus alone
His part perform'd, prove heedless of his own,
But sedulous, not merely to subdue
His hunger, but to please his palate too,
Prepares more savoury food. His chimney side
Could boast no gammon, salted well and dried,
And hook'd behind him; but sufficient store
Of bundled anise, and a cheese it bore;
A broad round cheese, which, through its centre strung
With a tough broom twig, in the corner hung;
The prudent hero, therefore, with address
And quick dispatch, now seeks another mess.
Close to his cottage lay a garden ground,
With reeds and osiers sparely girt around:
Small was the spot, but liberal to produce;
Nor wanted aught that serves a peasant's use,
And sometimes e'en the rich would borrow thence
Although its tillage was his sole expense.
For oft as from his toils abroad he ceased,
Home-bound by weather, or some stated feast,
His debt of culture here he duly paid,
And only left the plough to wield the spade.
He knew to give each plant the soil it needs,
To drill the ground and cover close the seeds;
And could with ease compel the wanton rill
To turn and wind obedient to his will

There flourish'd star-wort, and the branching beet,
The sorrel acid, and the mallow sweet,
The skirret, and the leek's aspiring kind,
The noxious poppy—quencher of the mind!
Salubrious sequel of a sumptuous board,
The lettuce, and the long huge-bellied gourd;
But these (for none his appetite control'd
With stricter sway) the thrifty rustic sold;
With broom twigs neatly bound, each kind apart,
He bore them ever to the public mart:
Whence laden still, but with a lighter load,
Of cash well earn'd, he took his homeward road,
Expending seldom, ere he quitted Rome,
His gains in flesh-meat for a feast at home.
There, at no cost, on onions, rank and red,
Or the curl'd endive's bitter leaf he fed:
On scallions sliced, or with a sensual gust,
On rockets—foul provocatives of lust!
Nor even shunn'd with smarting gums to press
Nasturtium—pungent face-distorting mess!
 Some such regale now also in his thought,
With hasty steps his garden ground he sought;
There delving with his hands, he first displaced
Four plants of garlick, large, and rooted fast;
The tender tops of parsley next he culls,
Then the old rue bush shudders as he pulls;
And coriander last to these succeeds,
That hangs on slightest threads her trembling seeds
 Placed near his sprightly fire he now demands
The mortar at his sable servant's hands;
When stripping all his garlick first, he tore
The exterior coats, and cast them on the floor,
Then cast away with like contempt the skin,
Flimsier concealment of the cloves within.
These search'd, and perfect found, he one by one
Rinsed, and disposed within the hollow stone.
Salt added, and a lump of salted cheese,
With his injected herbs he cover'd these,
And tucking with his left his tunic tight,
And seizing fast the pestle with his right,
The garlick bruising first he soon express'd,
And mix'd the various juices of the rest.

He grinds, and by degrees his herbs below,
Lost in each other, their own powers forego,
And with the cheese in compound, to the sight
Nor wholly green appear, nor wholly white.
His nostrils oft the forceful fume resent,
He cursed full oft his dinner for its scent;
Or with wry faces, wiping as he spoke
The trickling tears, cried, 'vengeance on the smoke!'
The work proceeds: not roughly turns he now
The pestle, but in circles smooth and slow;
With cautious hand, that grudges what it spills,
Some drops of olive oil he next instills.
Then vinegar with caution scarcely less,
And gathering to a ball the medley mess,
Last, with two fingers frugally applied,
Sweeps the small remnant from the mortar's side
And thus complete in figure and in kind,
Obtains at length the salad he design'd.
And now black Cybale before him stands,
The cake drawn newly glowing in her hands,
He glad receives it, chasing far away
All fears of famine for the passing day;
His legs enclosed in buskins, and his head
In its tough casque of leather, forth he led
And yoked his steers, a dull obedient pair,
Then drove afield, and plunged the pointed share.

June, 1799.

TO SIR JOSHUA REYNOLDS.

DEAR President, whose art sublime
Gives perpetuity to time,
And bids transactions of a day,
That fleeting hours would waft away
To dark futurity, survive,
And in unfading beauty live,—

You cannot with a grace decline
A special mandate of the Nine—
Yourself, whatever task you choose,
So much indebted to the Muse.
  Thus say the sisterhood :—We come—
Fix well your pallet on your thumb,
Prepare the pencil and the tints—
We come to furnish you with hints.
French disappointment, British glory,
Must be the subject of the story.
  First strike a curve, a graceful bow,
Then slope it to a point below;
Your outline easy, airy, light,
Fill'd up becomes a paper kite.
Let independence, sanguine, horrid,
Blaze, like a meteor in the forehead:
Beneath (but lay aside your graces)
Draw six-and-twenty rueful faces,
Each with a staring, steadfast eye,
Fix'd on his great and good ally.
France flies the kite—'tis on the wing—
Britannia's lightning cuts the string.
The wind that raised it, ere it ceases,
Just rends it into thirteen pieces,
Takes charge of every fluttering sheet,
And lays them all at George's feet.
  Iberia, trembling from afar,
Renounces the confederate war.
Her efforts and her arts o'ercome,
France calls her shatter'd navies home:
Repenting Holland learns to mourn
The sacred treaties she has torn;
Astonishment and awe profound
Are stamp'd upon the nations round;
Without one friend, above all foes,
Britannia gives the world repose

ON THE AUTHOR OF LETTERS ON LITERATURE.*

The genius of the Augustan age
His head among Rome's ruins rear'd,
And bursting with heroic rage,
When literary Heron appear'd.

Thou hast, he cried, like him of old
Who set the Ephesian dome on fire,
By being scandalously bold,
Attain'd the mark of thy desire.

And for traducing Virgil's name
Shalt share his merited reward;
A perpetuity of fame,
That rots and stinks, and is abhorr'd.

STANZAS

ON THE LATE INDECENT LIBERTIES TAKEN WITH THE REMAINS OF MILTON.† ANNO 1790.

Me too, perchance, in future days,
The sculptured stone shall show,
With Paphian myrtle or with bays
Parnassian on my brow.

* Nominally by Robert Heron, Esq. but supposed to have been written by John Pinkerton. 8vo. 1785.

† The bones of Milton, who lies buried in Cripplegate church, were disinterred; a pamphlet by Le Neve was published at the time, giving an account of what appeared on opening his coffin.

'But I, or ere that season come,
  Escaped from every care,
Shall reach my refuge in the tomb
  And sleep securely there.'*

So sang, in Roman tone and style,
  The youthful bard, ere long
Ordain'd to grace his native isle
  With her sublimest song.

Who then but must conceive disdain,
  Hearing the deed unblest
Of wretches who have dared profane
  His dread sepulchral rest?

Ill fare the hands that heaved the stones†
  Where Milton's ashes lay,
That trembled not to grasp his bones
  And steal his dust away!

O ill-requited bard! neglect
  Thy living worth repaid,
And blind idolatrous respect
  As much affronts thee dead.

August, 1790.

TO THE REV. WILLIAM BULL.

MY DEAR FRIEND, June 22, 1782.

If reading verse be your delight,
'Tis mine as much, or more, to write;
But what we would, so weak is man,
Lies oft remote from what we can.

* Forsitan et nostros ducat de marmore vultus
Nectens aut Paphia myrti aut Pernasside lauri
Fronde comas—At ego secura pace quiescam.
Milton in Manso.

† Cowper, no doubt, had in his memory the lines said to have been written by Shakspeare on his tomb:
'Good friend, for Jesus' sake forbear
To dig the dust inclosed here.
Blest be the man that spares these stones,
And curst be he that moves my bones.'

For instance, at this very time
I feel a wish by cheerful rhyme
To soothe my friend, and, had I power,
To cheat him of an anxious hour;
Not meaning (for I must confess,
It were but folly to suppress)
His pleasure, or his good alone,
But squinting partly at my own.
But though the sun is flaming high
In the centre of yon arch, the sky,
And he had once (and who but he?)
The name for setting genius free,
Yet whether poets of past days
Yielded him undeserved praise,
And he by no uncommon lot
Was famed for virtues he had not;
Or whether, which is like enough,
His Highness may have taken huff,
So seldom sought with invocation,
Since it has been the reigning fashion
To disregard his inspiration,
I seem no brighter in my wits,
For all the radiance he emits,
Than if I saw, through midnight vapour,
The glimmering of a farthing taper.
Oh for a succedaneum, then,
To accelerate a creeping pen!
Oh for a ready succedaneum,
Quod caput, cerebrum, et cranium
Pondere liberet exoso,
Et morbo jam caliginoso!
'Tis here; this oval box well fill'd
With best tobacco, finely mill'd,
Beats all Anticyra's pretences
To disengage th' encumber'd senses.
  Oh Nymphs of transatlantic fame,
Where'er thine haunt, whate'er thy name,
Whether reposing on the side
Of Oroonoquo's spacious tide,
Or listening with delight not small
To Niagara's distant fall,

'Tis thine to cherish and to feed
The pungent nose-refreshing weed,
Which, whether pulverized it gain
A speedy passage to the brain,
Or whether, touch'd with fire, it rise
In circling eddies to the skies,
Does thought more quicken and refine
Than all the breath of all the Nine—
Forgive the bard, if bard he be,
Who once too wantonly made free
To touch with a satiric wipe
That symbol of thy power, the pipe;
So may no blight infest thy plains,
And no unseasonable rains;
And so may smiling peace once more
Visit America's sad shore;
And thou, secure from all alarms,
Of thundering drums, and glittering arms,
Rove unconfined beneath the shade
Thy wide expanded leaves have made;
So may thy votaries increase,
And fumigation never cease.
May Newton with renew'd delights
Perform thine odoriferous rites,
While clouds of incense half divine
Involve thy disappearing shrine;
And so may smoke-inhaling Bull
Be always filling, never full.

MONUMENTAL INSCRIPTION TO WILLIAM NORTHCOT.

Hic sepultus est
Inter suorum lacrymas
GULIELMUS NORTHCOT
GULIELMI et MARIÆ filius
Unicus, unicè dilectus,
Qui floris ritu succisus est semihiantis,
Aprilis die septimo,
1780, Æt. 10.

Care, vale! Sed non æternùm, care, valeto!
  Namque iterùm tecum, sim modò dignus, ero.
Tum nihil amplexus poterit divellere nostros,
  Nec tu marcesces, nec lacrymabor ego.

TRANSLATION.

FAREWELL! "But not for ever," Hope replies,
Trace but his steps and meet him in the skies!
There nothing shall renew our parting pain,
Thou shalt not wither, nor I weep, again.

EPITAPH

ON MRS. M. HIGGINS, OF WESTON.

LAURELS may flourish round the conqueror's tomb,
But happiest they who win the world to come:
Believers have a silent field to fight,
And their exploits are veil'd from human sight.
They in some nook, where little known they dwell,
Kneel, pray in faith, and rout the hosts of hell;
Eternal triumphs crown their toils divine,
And all those triumphs, Mary, now are thine.

1791.

A RIDDLE.

I AM just two and two, I am warm, I am cold,
And the parent of numbers that cannot be told.
I am lawful, unlawful—a duty, a fault,
I am often sold dear, good for nothing when bought
An extraordinary boon, and a matter of course,
And yielded with pleasure when taken by force.

ANSWER FROM THE GENTLEMAN'S MAGAZINE

Vol. lxxvi. p. 1224.

A RIDDLE by Cowper
Made me swear like a trooper;
But my anger, alas! was in vain;
For, remembering the bliss
Of beauty's soft Kiss,
I now long for such riddles again.

J. T.

COWPER had sinn'd with some excuse,
If, bound in rhyming tethers,
He had committed this abuse
Of changing ewes for wethers;*

But, male for female is a trope,
Or rather bold misnomer,
That would have startled even Pope,
When he translated Homer.

IN SEDITIONEM HORRENDAM,

CORRUPTELIS GALLICIS, UT FERTUR, LONDINI NUPER EXORTAM.

PERFIDA, crudelis, victa et lymphata furore,
Non armis, laurum Gallia fraude petit.
Venalem pretio plebem conducit, et urit
Undique privatas patriciasque domos.

* I have heard about my wether mutton from various quarters It was a blunder hardly pardonable in a man who has lived amid fields and meadows, grazed by sheep, almost these thirty years. I have accordingly satirized myself in two stanzas which I composed last night, while I lay awake, tormented with pain, and well dosed with laudanum. If you find them not very brilliant, therefore, you will know how to account for it.—*Letter to Joseph Hill, Esq. dated April 15, 1792.*

Nequicquàm conata suâ, fœdissima sperat
  Posse tamen nostrâ nos superare manu.
Gallia, vana struis! Precibus nunc utere! Vinces
  Nam mites timidis, supplicibusque sumus.

TRANSLATION.

False, cruel, disappointed, stung to the heart,
France quits the warrior's for the assassin's part,
To dirty hands a dirty bribe conveys,
Bids the low street and lofty palace blaze.
Her sons, too weak to vanquish us alone,
She hires the worst and basest of our own.
Kneel, France! a suppliant conquers us with ease,
We always spare a coward on his knees.

TRANSLATIONS OF GREEK VERSES.

FROM THE GREEK OF JULIANUS.

A Spartan, his companion slain,
  Alone from battle fled;
His mother, kindling with disdain
  That she had borne him, struck him dead;
For courage, and not birth alone,
In Sparta, testifies a son!

ON THE SAME-BY PALAADAS.

A Spartan 'scaping from the fight
His mother met him in his flight,
Upheld a falchion to his breast,
And thus the fugitive address'd:

'Thou canst but live to blot with shame
Indelibly thy mother's name,
While every breath that thou shalt draw
Offends against thy country's law;
But, if thou perish by this hand,
Myself indeed throughout the land,
To my dishonour, shall be known
The mother still of such a son;
But Sparta will be safe and free,
And that shall serve to comfort me.'

AN EPITAPH.

My name—my country—what are they to thee?
What, whether base or proud my pedigree
Perhaps I far surpass'd all other men—
Perhaps I fell below them all—what then?
Suffice it, stranger! that thou seest a tomb—
Thou know'st its use—it hides—no matter whom.

ANOTHER.

Take to thy bosom, gentle earth, a swain
With much hard labour in thy service worn
He set the vines that clothe yon ample plain
And he these olives that the vale adorn.
He fill'd with grain the glebe; the rills he led
Through this green herbage, and those fruitful bowers;
Thou, therefore, earth! lie lightly on his head,
His hoary head, and deck his grave with flowers.

ANOTHER.

Painter, this likeness is too strong,
And we shall mourn the dead too long.

ANOTHER.

At threescore winters' end I died
A cheerless being, sole and sad;
The nuptial knot I never tied,
And wish my father never had.

BY CALLIMACHUS.

At morn we placed on his funereal bier
Young Melanippus; and at eventide,
Unable to sustain a loss so dear,
By her own hand his blooming sister died.
Thus Aristippus mourn'd his noble race,
Annihilated by a double blow,
Nor son could hope, nor daughter more to embrace,
And all Cyrene sadden'd at his woe.

ON MILTIADES.

Miltiades! thy valour best
(Although in every region known)
The men of Persia can attest,
Taught by thyself at Marathon.

ON AN INFANT.

Bewail not much, my parents! me, the prey
Of ruthless Ades, and sepulchred here.
An infant, in my fifth scarce-finish'd year,
He found all sportive, innocent, and gay,
Your young Callimachus; and if I knew
Not many joys, my griefs were also few.

BY HERACLIDES

In Cnidus born, the consort I became
Of Euphron. Aretimias was my name.
His bed I shared, nor proved a barren bride,
But bore two children at a birth, and died.
One child I leave to solace and uphold
Euphron hereafter, when infirm and old.
And one for his remembrance sake I bear
To Pluto's realm, till he shall join me there.

ON THE REED.

I was of late a barren plant,
Useless, insignificant,
Nor fig, nor grape, nor apple bore,
A native of the marshy shore;
But gather'd for poetic use,
And plunged into a sable juice,
Of which my modicum I sip
With narrow mouth and slender lip,
At once, although by nature dumb,
All eloquent I have become,
And speak with fluency untired,
As if by Phœbus' self inspired.

TO HEALTH.

Eldest born of powers divine!
Bless'd Hygeia! be it mine
To enjoy what thou canst give,
And henceforth with thee to live:
For in power if pleasure be,
Wealth, or numerous progeny,

Or in amorous embrace,
Where no spy infests the place;
Or in aught that heaven bestows
To alleviate human woes,
When the wearied heart despairs
Of a respite from its cares;
These and every true delight
Flourish only in thy sight;
And the sister Graces three,
Owe, themselves, their youth to thee,
Without whom we may possess
Much, but never happiness.

ON INVALIDS.

Far happier are the dead, methinks, than they
Who look for death, and fear it, every day

ON THE ASTROLOGERS.

The astrologers did all alike presage
My uncle's dying in extreme old age;
One only disagreed. But he was wise,
And spoke not till he heard the funeral cries.

ON AN OLD WOMAN.

Mycilla dyes her locks, 'tis said;
But 'tis a foul aspersion;
She buys them black; they therefore need
No subsequent immersion

ON FLATTERERS.

No mischief worthier of our fear
  In nature can be found
Than friendship, in ostent sincere,
  But hollow and unsound.
For lull'd into a dangerous dream
  We close infold a foe,
Who strikes, when most secure we seem,
  The inevitable blow

ON A TRUE FRIEND.

Hast thou a friend? Thou hast indeed
  A rich and large supply,
Treasure to serve your every need,
  Well managed, till you die.

TO THE SWALLOW.

Attic maid! with honey fed,
  Bear'st thou to thy callow brood
Yonder locust from the mead,
  Destined their delicious food?

Ye have kindred voices clear,
  Ye alike unfold the wing,
Migrate hither, sojourn here,
  Both attendant on the spring

Ah, for pity drop the prize;
  Let it not with truth be said,
That a songster gasps and dies,
  That a songster may be fed.

ON LATE-ACQUIRED WEALTH.

Poor in my youth, and in life's later scenes
  Rich to no end, I curse my natal hour,
Who nought enjoy'd while young, denied the means;
  And nought when old enjoy'd, denied the power.

ON A BATH, BY PLATO

Did Cytherea to the skies
From this pellucid lymph arise?
Or was it Cytherea's touch
When bathing here, that made it such?

ON A FOWLER, BY ISIODORUS.

With seeds and birdlime, from the desert air,
Eumelus gather'd free, though scanty, fare.
No lordly patron's hand he deign'd to kiss,
Nor luxury knew, save liberty, nor bliss.
Thrice thirty years he lived, and to his heirs
His seeds bequeath'd, his birdlime, and his snares.

ON NIOBE.

Charon! receive a family on board
  Itself sufficient for thy crazy yawl,
Apollo and Diana, for a word
  By me too proudly spoken, slew us all.

ON A GOOD MAN.

TRAVELLER, regret not me; for thou shalt find
Just cause of sorrow none in my decease,
Who, dying, children's children left behind,
And with one wife lived many a year in peace:
Three virtuous youths espoused my daughters three
And oft their infants in my bosom lay,
Nor saw I one, of all derived from me,
Touch'd with disease, or torn by death away.
Their duteous hands my funeral rites bestow'd,
And me, by blameless manners fitted well
To seek it, sent to the serene abode
Where shades of pious men for ever dwell.

ON A MISER.

THEY call thee rich—I deem thee poor,
Since, if thou darest not use thy store,
But savest it only for thine heirs,
The treasure is not thine, but theirs.

ANOTHER.

A MISER, traversing his house,
Espied, unusual there, a mouse,
And thus his uninvited guest
Briskly inquisitive address'd:
'Tell me, my dear, to what cause is it
I owe this unexpected visit?'
The mouse her host obliquely eyed,
And, smiling, pleasantly replied:
'Fear not, good fellow, for your hoard!
I come to lodge, and not to board.'

ANOTHER.

Art thou some individual of a kind
Long lived by nature as the rook or hind?
Heap treasure, then, for if thy need be such,
Thou hast excuse, and scarce canst heap too much.
But man thou seem'st, clear therefore from thy breast
This lust of treasure—folly at the best!
For why shouldst thou go wasted to the tomb,
To fatten with thy spoils thou know'st not whom?

ON FEMALE INCONSTANCY.

Rich, thou hadst many lovers—poor, hast none
So surely want extinguishes the flame,
And she who call'd thee once her pretty one,
And her Adonis, now inquires thy name.

Where wast thou born, Sosicrates, and where
In what strange country can thy parents live,
Who seem'st, by thy complaints, not yet aware
That want's a crime no woman can forgive?

ON THE GRASSHOPPER.

Happy songster, perch'd above,
On the summit of the grove,
Whom a dew-drop cheers to sing
With the freedom of a king.
From thy perch survey the fields
Where prolific nature yields
Nought that, willingly as she,
Man surrenders not to thee.

For hostility or hate
None thy pleasures can create.
Thee it satisfies to sing
Sweetly the return of spring,
Herald of the genial hours,
Harming neither herbs nor flowers.
Therefore man thy voice attends
Gladly—thou and he are friends;
Nor thy never-ceasing strains
Phœbus or the muse disdains
As too simple or too long,
For themselves inspire the song.
Earth-born, bloodless, undecaying,
Ever singing, sporting, playing,
What has nature else to show
Godlike in its kind as thou?

ON HERMOCRATIA.

Hermocratia named—save only one—
Twice fifteen births I bore, and buried none;
For neither Phœbus pierced my thriving joys
Nor Dian—she my girls, or he my boys.
But Dian rather, when my daughters lay
In parturition, chased their pangs away.
And all my sons, by Phœbus' bounty, shared
A vigorous youth, by sickness unimpair'd.
O Niobe! far less prolific! see
Thy boast against Latona shamed by me!

FROM MENANDER.

Fond youth! who dream'st that hoarded gold
Is needful, not alone to pay
For all thy various items sold,
To serve the wants of every day;

Bread, vinegar, and oil, and meat,
For savoury viands season'd high;
But somewhat more important yet—
I tell thee what 't cannot buy.

No treasure, hadst thou more amass'd
Than fame to Tantalus assign'd,
Would save thee from a tomb at last,
But thou must leave it all behind.

I give thee, therefore, counsel wise;
Confide not vainly in thy store,
However large—much less despise
Others comparatively poor;

But in thy more exalted state
A just and equal temper show,
That all who see thee rich and great
May deem thee worthy to be so.

ON PALLAS BATHING, FROM A HYMN OF CALLIMACHUS.

Nor oils of balmy scent produce,
Nor mirror for Minerva's use,
Ye nymphs who lave her; she, array'd
In genuine beauty, scorns their aid.
Not even when they left the skies
To seek on Ida's head the prize
From Paris' hand, did Juno deign,
Or Pallas in the crystal plain
Of Simois' stream her locks to trace,
Or in the mirror's polish'd face,
Though Venus oft with anxious care
Adjusted twice a single hair.

TO DEMOSTHENES.

It flatters and deceives thy view,
This mirror of ill polish'd ore;
For were it just, and told thee true,
Thou wouldst consult it never more.

ON A SIMILAR CHARACTER.

You give your cheeks a rosy stain,
With washes dye your hair;
But paint and washes both are vain
To give a youthful air.

Those wrinkles mock your daily toil,
No labour will efface 'em
You wear a mask of smoothest oil,
Yet still with ease we trace 'em.

An art so fruitless then forsake,
Which though you much excel in,
You never can contrive to make
Old Hecuba young Helen.

ON AN UGLY FELLOW.

Beware, my friend! of crystal brook
Or fountain, lest that hideous hook,
Thy nose, thou chance to see;
Narcissus' fate would then be thine,
And self-detested thou wouldst pine,
As self-enamour'd he.

ON A BATTERED BEAUTY.

Hair, wax, rouge, honey, teeth you buy
A multifarious store!
A mask at once would all supply,
Nor would it cost you more.

ON A THIEF.

When Aulus, the noctural thief, made prize
Of Hermes, swift-wing'd envoy of the skies,
Hermes, Arcadia's king, the thief divine,
Who when an infant stole Apollo's kine,
And whom, as arbiter and overseer
Of our gymnastic sports, we planted here;
Hermes,' he cried, 'you meet no new disaster;
Ofttimes the pupil goes beyond his master.'

ON PEDIGREE.

FROM EPICHARMUS.

My mother! if thou love me, name no more
My noble birth! Sounding at every breath
My noble birth, thou kill'st me. Thither fly,
As to their only refuge, all from whom
Nature withholds all good besides; they boast
Their noble birth, conduct us to the tombs
Of their forefathers, and, from age to age
Ascending, trumpet their illustrious race:
But whom hast thou beheld, or canst thou name,
Derived from no forefathers? Such a man
Lives not; for how could such be born at all?
And if it chance that, native of a land
Far distant, or in infancy deprived

Of all his kindred, one, who cannot trace
His origin, exist, why deem him sprung
From baser ancestry than theirs who can?
My mother! he whom nature at his birth
Endow'd with virtuous qualities, although
An Æthiop and a slave, is nobly born.

ON ENVY.

Pity, says the Theban bard,
From my wishes I discard;
Envy, let me rather be,
Rather far, a theme for thee!
Pity to distress is shown,
Envy to the great alone—
So the Theban—But to shine
Less conspicuous be mine!
I prefer the golden mean,
Pomp and penury between;
For alarm and peril wait
Ever on the loftiest state,
And the lowest to the end
Obloquy and scorn attend.

BY MOSCHUS.

I slept when Venus enter'd: to my bed
A Cupid in her beauteous hand she led,
A bashful seeming boy, and thus she said:
'Shepherd, receive my little one! I bring
An untaught love, whom thou must teach to sing.'
She said, and left him. I, suspecting nought,
Many a sweet strain my subtle pupil taught,
How reed to reed Pan first with osier bound,
How Pallas form'd the pipe of softest sound,
How Hermes gave the lute, and how the quire
Of Phœbus owe to Phœbus' self the lyre.

Such were my themes; my themes nought heeded he,
But ditties sang of amorous sort to me,
The pangs that mortals and immortals prove
From Venus' influence, and the darts of love.
Thus was the teacher by the pupil taught;
His lessons I retain'd, and mine forgot.

BY PHILEMON.

Oft we enhance our ills by discontent,
And give them bulk beyond what nature meant.
A parent, brother, friend deceased, to cry—
'He's dead indeed, but he was born to die'—
Such temperate grief is suited to the size
And burthen of the loss; is just and wise
But to exclaim, 'Ah! wherefore was I born,
Thus to be left for ever thus forlorn?'
Who thus laments his loss invites distress,
And magnifies a woe that might be less,
Through dull despondence to his lot resign'd,
And leaving reason's remedy behind.

EPIGRAMS TRANSLATED FROM THE LATIN OF OWEN.

ON ONE IGNORANT AND ARROGANT.

Thou mayst of double ignorance boast,
Who know'st not that thou nothing know'st.

PRUDENT SIMPLICITY.

That thou mayst injure no man, dove-like be,
And serpent-like, that none may injure thee!

TO A FRIEND IN DISTRESS.

I WISH thy lot, now bad, still worse, my friend;
For when at worst, they say, things always mend.

RETALIATION.

THE works of ancient bards divine,
  Aulus, thou scorn'st to read;
And should posterity read thine,
  It would be strange indeed!

WHEN little more than boy in age,
I deem'd myself almost a sage:
But now seem worthier to be styled,
For ignorance, almost a child.

SUNSET AND SUNRISE.

CONTEMPLATE, when the sun declines,
  Thy death with deep reflection!
And when again he rising shines,
  Thy day of resurrection!

TRANSLATIONS FROM THE FABLES OF GAY.

LEPUS MULTIS AMICUS.

LUSUS amicitia est, uni nisi dedita, ceu fit,
  Simplice ni nexus fœdere, lusus amor.
Incerto genitore puer, non sæpe paternæ
  Tutamen novit, deliciasque domûs:

Quique sibi fidos fore multos sperat, amicus,
Mirum est huic misero si ferat ullus opem.
Comis erat, mitisque, et nolle et velle paratus
Cum quovis, Gaii more modoque, Lepus.
Ille, quot in sylvis et quot spatiantur in agris
Quadrupedes, nôrat conciliare sibi;
Et quisque innocuo, invitoque lacessere quenquam
Labra tenus saltem fidus amicus erat.
Ortum sub lucis dum pressa cubilia linquit,
Rorantes herbas, pabula sueta, petens,
Venatorum audit clangores ponè sequentem,
Fulmineumque sonum territus erro fugit.
Corda pavor pulsat, sursum sedet, erigit aures,
Respicit, et sentit jam prope adesse necem.
Utque canes fallat latè circumvagus, illuc,
Unde abiit, mirâ calliditate redit;
Viribus at fractis tandem se projicit ultro
In mediâ miserum semianimemque viâ.
Vix ibi stratus, equi sonitum pedis audit, et, oh spe
Quam lætâ adventu cor agitatur equi!
Dorsum (inquit) mihi, chare, tuum concede, tuoque
Auxilio nares fallere, vimque canum.
Me meus, ut nosti, pes prodit—fidus amicus
Fert quodcunque lubens, nec grave sentit, onus
Belle miselle lepuscule, (equus respondet) amara
Omnia quæ tibi sunt, sunt et amara mihi.
Verum age—sume animos—multi, me pone, bonique
Adveniunt, quorum sis citò salvus ope.
Proximus armenti dominus bos solicitatus
Auxilium his verbis se dare posse negat.
Quando quadrupedum, quot vivunt, nullus amicum
Me nescire potest usque fuisse tibi,
Libertate æquus, quam cedita micus amico,
Utar, et absque metu ne tibi displiceam;
Hinc me mandat amor. Juxta istum messis acervum
Me mea, præ cunctis chara, juvenca manet;
Et quis non ultro quæcunque negotia linquit,
Pareat ut dominæ, cum vocat ipse suæ?
Neu me crudelem dicas—discedo—sed hircus,
Cujus ope effugias integer, hircus adest [languent!
Febrem ait hircus) habes. Heu, sicca ut lumina
Utque caput, collo deficiente, jacet!

Hirsutum mih tergum; et forsan læserit ægrum,
  Vellere eris melius fultus, ovisque venit.
Me mihi fecit onus natura, ovis inquit, anhelans
  Sustineo lanæ pondera tanta meæ;
Me nec velocem nec fortem jacto, solentq
  Nos etiam sævi dilacerare canes.
Ultimus accedit vitulus, suscepero tantam
  Ut periturum alias ocyus eripiat.
Remne ego, respondet vitulus, vitulumque precatur
  Non depulsus adhuc ubere, natus heri?
Te, quem maturi canibus validique relinquunt,
  Incolumem potero reddere parvus ego?
Præterea tollens quem illi aversantur, amicis
  Forte parum videar consuluisse meis.
Ignoscas oro. Fidissima dissociantur
  Corda, et tale tibi sat liquet esse meum.
Ecce autem ad calces canis est! te quanta perempto
  Tristitia est nobis ingruitura!—Vale!

AVARUS ET PLUTUS

Icta fenestra Euri flatu stridebat, avarus
  Ex somno trepidus surgit, opumque memor.
Lata silenter humi ponit vestigia, quemque
  Respicit ad sonitum respiciensque tremit;
Angustissima quæque foramina lampade visit,
  Ad vectes, obices, fertque refertque manum.
Dein reserat crebris junctam compagibus arcam
  Exultansque omnes conspicit intus opes.
Sed tandem furiis ultricibus actus ob artes
  Queis sua res tenuis creverat in cumulum.
Contortis manibus nunc stat, nunc pectora pulsans
  Aurum execratur, perniciemque vocat;
O mihi, ait, misero mens quam tranquilla fuisset,
  Hoc celasset adhuc si modo terra malum!
Nunc autem virtus ipsa est venalis; et aurum
  Quid contra vitii tormina sæva valet?
O inimicum aurum! O homini infestissima pesti;
  Cui datur illecebras vincere posse tuas?

Aurum homines suasit contemnere quicquid honestum est
  Et præter nomen nil retinere boni.
Aurum cuncta mali per terras semina sparsit;
  Aurum nocturnis furibus arma dedit.
Bella docet fortes, timidosque ad pessima ducit.
  Fœdifragas artes, multiplicesque dolos,
Nec vitii quicquam est, quod non inveneris ortum
  Ex malesuadâ auri sacrilegâque fame.
Dixit, et ingemuit; Plutusque suum sibi numen
  Ante oculos, irâ fervidus, ipse stetit.
Arcam clausit avarus, et ora horrentia rugis
  Ostendens; tremulum sic Deus increpuit
Questibus his raucis mihi cur, stulte, obstrepis aures?
  Ista tui similis tristia quisque canit.
Commaculavi egone humanum genus, improbe? Culpa,
  Dum rapis, et captas omnia, culpa tua est.
Mene execrandum censes, quia tam pretiosa
  Criminibus fiunt perniciosa tuis?
Virtutis specie, pulchro ceu pallio amictus
  Quisque catus nebulo sordida facta tegit.
Atque suis manibus commissa potentia, durum
  Et dirum subito vergit ad imperium.
Hinc, nimium dum latro aurum detrudit in arcam,
  Idem aurum latet in pectore pestis edax.
Nutrit avaritiam et fastum, suspendere adunco
  Suadet naso inopes, et vitium omne docet.
Auri et larga probo si copia contigit, instar
  Roris dilapsi ex æthere cuncta beat:
Tum, quasi numen inesset, alit, fovet, reducat orbos,
  Et viduas lacrymis ora rigare vetat.
Quo sua crimina jure auro derivet avarus,
  Aurum animæ pretium qui cupit atque capit?
Lege pari gladium incuset sicarius atrox
  Cæso homine, et ferrum judicet esse reum.

PAPILIO ET LIMAX.

Qui subito ex imis rerum in fastigia surgit
  Nativas sordes, quicquid agatur, olet.

TRANSLATION FROM VIRGIL.

ÆNEID, BOOK VIII, LINE 18.

THUS Italy was moved—nor did the chief
Æneas in his mind less tumult feel.
On every side his anxious thought he turns,
Restless, unfix'd, not knowing what to choose.
And as a cistern that in brim of brass
Confines the crystal flood, if chance the sun
Smile on it, or the moon's resplendent orb,
The quivering light now flashes on the walls,
Now leaps uncertain to the vaulted roof:
Such were the wavering motions of his mind.
'Twas night—and weary nature sunk to rest.
The birds, the bleating flocks, were heard no more.
At length, on the cold ground, beneath the damp
And dewy vault, fast by the river's brink,
The father of his country sought repose.
When lo! among the spreading poplar boughs,
Forth from his pleasant stream, propitious rose
The god of Tiber: clear transparent gauze
Infolds his loins, his brows with reeds are crown'd:
And these his gracious words to soothe his care:
'Heaven-born, who bring'st our kindred home [again,
Rescued, and givest eternity to Troy,
Long have Laurentum and the Latian plains
Expected thee; behold thy fix'd abode.
Fear not the threats of war, the storm is pass'd,
The gods appeased. For proof that what thou hear'st
Is no vain forgery or delusive dream,
Beneath the grove that borders my green bank,
A milk-white swine, with thirty milk-white young,
Shall greet thy wondering eyes. Mark well the place;
For 'tis thy place of rest, there end thy toils:
There, twice ten years elapsed, fair Alba's walls
Shall rise, fair Alba, by Ascanius' hand.
Thus shall it be—now listen, while I teach
The means to accomplish these events at hand.
The Arcadians here, a race from Pallas sprung,
Following Evander's standard and his fate,

High on these mountains, a well-chosen spot,
Have built a city, for their grandsire's sake
Named Pallanteum. These perpetual war
Wage with the Latians: join'd in faithful league
And arms confederate, add them to your camp.
Myself between my winding banks will speed
Your well-oar'd barks to stem the opposing tide.
Rise, goddess-born, arise; and with the first
Declining stars seek Juno in thy prayer,
And vanquish all her wrath with suppliant vows.
When conquest crowns thee, then remember me.
I am the Tiber, whose cærulean stream
Heaven favours; I with copious flood divide
These grassy banks, and cleave the fruitful meads.
My mansion, this—and lofty cities crown
My fountain head.'—He spoke and sought the deep,
And plunged his form beneath the closing flood.
Æneas at the morning dawn awoke,
And, rising, with uplifted eye beheld
The orient sun then dipp'd his palms, and scoop'd
The brimming stream, and thus address'd the skies;
'Ye nymphs, Laurentian nymphs, who feed the source
Of many a stream, and thou, with thy blest flood,
O Tiber, hear, accept me, and afford,
At length afford, a shelter from my woes
Where'er in secret cavern under ground
Thy waters sleep, where'er they spring to light,
Since thou hast pity for a wretch like me,
My offerings and my vows shall wait thee still:
Great horned Father of Hesperian floods,
Be gracious now and ratify thy word.'
He said, and chose two galleys from his fleet,
Fits them with oars, and clothes the crew in arms.
When lo! astonishing and pleasing sight,
The milk-white dam, with her unspotted brood,
Lay stretch'd upon the bank, beneath the grove.
To thee, the pious Prince, Juno, to thee
Devotes them all, all on thine altar bleed.
That livelong night old Tiber smooth'd his flood,
And so restrain'd it that it seem'd to stand
Motionless as a pool, or silent lake,

That not a billow might resist their oars.
With cheerful sound of exhortation soon
Their voyage they begin; the pitchy keel
Slides through the gentle deep, the quiet stream
Admires the unwonted burthen that it bears,
Well-polish'd arms, and vessels painted gay.
Beneath the shade of various trees, between
The umbrageous branches of the spreading groves,
They cut their liquid way, nor day nor night
They slack their course, unwinding as they go
The long meanders of the peaceful tide.
  The glowing sun was in meridian height,
When from afar they saw the humble walls,
And the few scatter'd cottages, which now
The Roman power has equall'd with the clouds;
But such was then Evander's scant domain.
They steer to shore, and hasten to the town.
  It chanced the Arcadian monarch on that day,
Before the walls, beneath a shady grove,
Was celebrating high, in solemn feast,
Alcides and his tutelary gods.
Pallas, his son, was there, and there the chief
Of all his youth; with these, a worthy tribe,
His poor but venerable senate, burnt
Sweet incense, and their altars smoked with blood.
Soon as they saw the towering masts approach,
Sliding between the trees, while the crew rest
Upon their silent oars, amazed they rose,
Not without fear, and all forsook the feast.
But Pallas undismay'd, his javelin seized,
Rush'd to the bank, and from a rising ground
Forbade them to disturb the sacred rites.
'Ye stranger youth! What prompts you to explore
This untried way? and whither do ye steer?
Whence, and who are ye? Bring ye peace or war?'
Æneas from his lofty deck holds forth
The peaceful olive-branch, and thus replies:
'Trojans and enemies to the Latian state,
Whom they with unprovoked hostilities
Have driven away, thou see'st. We seek Evander-
Say this—and say beside, the Trojan chiefs
Are come, and seek his friendship and his aid.

Pallas with wonder heard that awful name,
And 'Whosoe'er thou art,' he cried, 'come forth
Bear thine own tidings to my father's ear,
And be a welcome guest beneath our roof.'
He said, and press'd the stranger to his breast:
Then led him from the river to the grove,
Where, courteous, thus Æneas greets the king:
'Best of the Grecian race, to whom I bow
(So wills my fortune) suppliant, and stretch fort
In sign of amity this peaceful branch,
I fear'd thee not, although I knew thee well
A Grecian leader, born in Arcady,
And kinsman of the Atridæ. Me my virtue,
That means no wrong to thee—the Oracles,
Our kindred families allied of old,
And thy renown diffused through every land,
Have all conspired to bind in friendship to thee,
And send me not unwilling to thy shores.
Dardanus, author of the Trojan state,
(So say the Greeks) was fair Electra's son;
Electra boasted Atlas for her sire,
Whose shoulders high sustain the æthereal orbs.
Your sire is Mercury, whom Maia bore,
Sweet Maia, on Cyllene's hoary top.
Her, if we credit aught tradition old,
Atlas of yore, the selfsame Atlas, claim'd
His daughter. Thus united close in blood,
Thy race and ours one common sire confess.
With these credentials fraught, I would not send
Ambassadors with artful phrase to sound
And win thee by degrees—but came myself—
Me, therefore, me thou seest; my life the stake:
'Tis I, Æneas, who implore thine aid.
Should Daunia, that now aims the blow at thee,
Prevail to conquer us, nought then, they think,
Will hinder, but Hesperia must be theirs,
All theirs, from the upper to the nether sea.
Take then our friendship, and return us thine.
We too have courage, we have noble minds,
And youth well tried, and exercised in arms.'
  Thus spoke Æneas—He with fix'd regard
Survey'd him speaking, features, form, and mien.

Then briedy thus—'Thou noblest of thy name,
How gladly do I take thee to my heart,
How gladly thus confess thee for a friend!
In thee I trace Anchises; his thy speech,
Thy voice, thy countenance. For I well remember
Many a day since, when Priam journey'd forth
To Salamis, to see the land where dwelt
Hesione, his sister, he push'd on
E'en to Arcadia's frozen bounds. was then
The bloom of youth was glowing on my cheek;
Much I admired the Trojan chiefs, and much
Their king, the son of great Laomedon,
But most Anchises, towering o'er them all.
A youthful longing seized me to accost
The hero, and embrace him; I drew near,
And gladly led him to the walls of Pheneus.
Departing, he distinguish'd me with gifts,
A costly quiver stored with Lycian darts,
A robe inwove with gold, with gold imboss'd,
Two bridles, those which Pallas uses now.
The friendly league thou hast solicited
I give thee, therefore, and to-morrow all
My chosen youth shall wait on your return.
Meanwhile, since thus in friendship ye are come,
Rejoice with us, and join to celebrate
These annual rites, which may not be delay'd,
And be at once familiar at our board.'
He said, and bade replace the feast removed;
Himself upon a grassy bank disposed
The crew; but for Æneas order'd forth
A couch spread with a lion's tawny shag,
And bade him share the honours of his throne.
The appointed youth with glad alacrity
Assist the labouring priest to load the board
With roasted entrails of the slaughter'd beeves,
Well-kneaded bread and mantling bowls. Well
Æneas and the Trojan youth regale [pleased,
On the huge length of a well-pastured chine.
Hunger appeased, and tables all despatch'd,
Thus spake Evander: 'Superstition here,
In this old solemn feasting, has no part.
No, Trojan friend, from utmost danger saved,

In gratitude this worship we renew.
Behold that rock which nods above the vale,
Those bulks of broken stone dispersed around,
How desolate the shatter'd cave appears,
And what a ruin spreads the incumber'd plain.
Within this pile, but far within, was once
The den of Cacus; dire his hateful form
That shunn'd the day, half monster and half man.
Blood newly shed stream'd ever on the ground
Smoking, and many a visage pale and wan
Nail'd at his gate, hung hideous to the sight.
Vulcan begot the brute: vast was his size,
And from his throat he belch'd his father's fires.
But the day came that brought us what we wish'd
The assistance and the presence of a God.
Flush'd with his victory, and the spoils he won
From triple-form'd Geryon lately slain,
The great avenger, Hercules, appear'd.
Hither he drove his stately bulls, and pour'd
His herds along the vale. But the sly thief
Cacus, that nothing might escape his hand
Of villany or fraud, drove from the stalls
Four of the lordliest of his bulls, and four
The fairest of his heifers; by the tail
He dragg'd them to his den, that there conceal'd,
No footsteps might betray the dark abode.
And now his herd with provender sufficed,
Alcides would be gone: they as they went
Still bellowing loud, made the deep echoing woods
And distant hills resound: when hark! one ox,
Imprison'd close within the vast recess,
Lows in return, and frustrates all his hope.
Then fury seized Alcides, and his breast
With indignation heaved: grasping his club
Of knotted oak, swift to the mountain top
He ran, he flew. Then first was Cacus seen
To tremble, and his eyes bespoke his fears.
Swift as an eastern blast he sought his den,
And dread, increasing, wing'd him as he went.
Drawn up in iron slings above the gate
A rock was hung enormous. Such his haste,
He burst the chains, and dropp'd it at the door,

Then grappled it with iron work within
Of bolts and bars by Vulcan's art contrived.
Scarce was he fast, when panting for revenge
Came Hercules; he gnash'd his teeth with rage,
And quick as lightning glanced his eyes around
In quest of entrance. Fiery red and stung
With indignation, thrice he wheel'd his course
About the mountain; thrice, but thrice in vain,
He strove to force the quarry at the gate,
And thrice sat down o'erwearied in the vale.
There stood a pointed rock, abrupt and rude,
That high o'erlook'd the rest, close at the back
Of the fell monster's den, where birds obscene
Of ominous note resorted, choughs and daws.
This, as it lean'd obliquely to the left,
Threatening the stream below, he from the right
Push'd with his utmost strength, and to and fro
He shook the mass, loosening its lowest base;
Then shoved it from its seat; down fell the pile;
Sky thunder'd at the fall; the banks give way,
The affrighted stream flows upward to his source.
Behold the kennel of the brute exposed,
The gloomy vault laid open. So, if chance
Earth yawning to the centre should disclose
The mansions, the pale mansions of the dead,
Loath'd by the gods, such would the gulf appear
And the ghosts tremble at the sight of day.
The monster braying with unusual din
Within his hollow lair, and sore amazed
To see such sudden inroads of the light,
Alcides press'd him close with what at hand
Lay readiest, stumps of trees, and fragments huge
Of millstone size. He, (for escape was none)
Wondrous to tell! forth from his gorge discharged
A smoky cloud that darken'd all the den;
Wreath after wreath he vomited amain,
The smothering vapour mix'd with fiery sparks.
No sight could penetrate the veil obscure.
The hero, more provoked, endured not this,
But with a headlong leap he rush'd to where
The thickest cloud enveloped his abode.
There grasp'd he Cacus, spite of all his fires,

Till crush'd within his arms, the monster shows
His bloodless throat, now dry with panting hard,
And his press'd eyeballs start. Soon he tears down
The barricade of rock, the dark abyss
Lies open; and the imprison'd bulls, the theft
He had with oaths denied, are brought to light;
By the heels the miscreant carcass is dragg'd forth,
His face, his eyes, all terrible, his breast
Beset with bristles, and his sooty jaws,
Are view'd with wonder never to be cloy'd.
Hence the celebrity thou seest, and hence
This festal day, Potitius first enjoin'd
Posterity these solemn rites, he first
With those who bear the great Pinarian name
To Hercules devoted, in the grove
This altar built, deem'd sacred in the highest
By us, and sacred ever to be deem'd.
Come, then, my friends, and bind your youthful brows
In praise of such deliverance, and hold forth
The brimming cup; your deities and ours
Are now the same, then drink, and freely too.
So saying, he twisted round his reverend locks
A variegated poplar wreath, and fill'd
His right hand with a consecrated bowl.
At once all pour libations on the board,
All offer prayer. And now the radiant sphere
Of day descending, eventide drew near.
When first Potitius with the priests advanced,
Begirt with skins, and torches in their hands.
High piled with meats of savoury taste, they ranged
The chargers, and renew'd the grateful feast.
Then came the Salii, crown'd with poplar too,
Circling the blazing altars; here the youth
Advanced, a choir harmonious, there were heard
The reverend seers responsive; praise they sung,
Much praise in honour of Alcides' deeds;
How first with infant gripe two serpents huge
He strangled, sent from Juno; next they sung,
How Troja and Œchalia he destroy'd,
Fair cities both, and many a toilsome task
Beneath Eurystheus (so his stepdame will'd)
Achieved victorious. Thou, the cloud-born pair,

Hylæus fierce and Pholus, monstrous twins
Thou slew'st the minotaur, the plague of Crete
And the vast lion of the Nemean rock;
Thee hell, and Cerberus, hell's porter, fear'd,
Stretch'd in his den upon his half-gnaw'd bones.
Thee no abhorred form, not e'en the vast
Typhœus could appal, though clad in arms.
Hail, true-born son of Jove, among the gods
At length enroll'd, nor least illustrious thou,
Haste thee propitious, and approve our songs:—
Thus hymn'd the chorus; above all they sing
The cave of Cacus, and the flames he breath'd.
The whole grove echoes, and the hills rebound.
  The rites perform'd, all hasten to the town.
The king, bending with age, held as he went
Æneas and his Pallas by the hand,
With much variety of pleasing talk
Shortening the way. Æneas, with a smile,
Looks round him, charm'd with the delightful scene,
And many a question asks, and much he learns
Of heroes far renown'd in ancient times.
Then spake Evander. These extensive groves
Were once inhabited by fauns and nymphs
Produced beneath their shades, and a rude race
Of men, the progeny uncouth of elms
And knotted oaks. They no refinement knew
Of laws or manners civilized, to yoke
The steer, with forecast provident to store
The hoarded grain, or manage what they had,
But browsed like beasts upon the leafy boughs,
Or fed voracious on their hunted prey.
An exile from Olympus, and expell'd
His native realm by thunder-bearing Jove,
First Saturn came. He from the mountains drew
This herd of men untractable and fierce,
And gave them laws: and call'd his hiding place
This growth of forests, Latium. Such the peace
His land possess'd, the golden age was then,
So famed in story; till by slow degrees
Far other times, and of far different hue,
Succeeded, thirst of gold and thirst of blood.
Then came Ausonian bands, and armed hosts

From Sicily, and Latium often changed
Her master and her name. At length arose
Kings, of whom Tybris of gigantic form
Was chief; and we Italians since have call'd
The river by his name; thus Albula
(So was the country call'd in ancient days)
Was quite forgot. Me from my native land
An exile, through the dangerous ocean driven,
Resistless fortune and relentless fate,
Placed where thou seest me. Phœbus, and
The nymph Carmentis, with maternal care
Attendant on my wanderings, fix'd me here.

[Ten lines omitted.]

He said, and show'd him the Tarpeian rock,
And the rude spot where now the capitol
Stands all magnificent and bright with gold,
Then overgrown with thorns. And yet e'en then
The swains beheld that sacred scene with awe;
The grove, the rock, inspired religious fear
This grove, he said, that crowns the lofty top
Of this fair hill, some deity, we know,
Inhabits, but what deity we doubt.
The Arcadians speak of Jupiter himself,
That they have often seen him, shaking here
His gloomy Ægis, while the thunder storms
Came rolling all around him. Turn thine eyes,
Behold that ruin; those dismantled walls,
Where once two towns, Ianiculum ——,
By Janus this, and that by Saturn built,
Saturnia. Such discourse brought them beneath
The roof of poor Evander; thence they saw,
Where now the proud and stately forum stands,
The grazing herds wide scatter'd o'er the field.
Soon as he enter'd—Hercules, he said,
Victorious Hercules, on this threshold trod,
These walls contain'd him, humble as they are.
Dare to despise magnificence, my friend,
Prove thy divine descent by worth divine,
Nor view with haughty scorn this mean abode.
So saying, he led Æneas by the hand,

And placed him on a cushion stuff'd with leaves,
Spread with the skin of a Lybistian bear.

[The Episode of Venus and Vulcan omitted.]

While thus in Lemnos Vulcan was employ'd,
Awaken'd by the gentle dawn of day,
And the shrill song of birds beneath the eaves
Of his low mansion, old Evander rose.
His tunic, and the sandals on his feet,
And his good sword well girded to his side,
A panther's skin dependent from his left,
And over his right shoulder thrown aslant.
Thus was he clad. Two mastiffs follow'd him,
His whole retinue and his nightly guard.

OVID. TRIST. LIB. V. ELEG. XII.

Scribis, ut oblectem.

You bid me write to amuse the tedious hours,
And save from withering my poetic powers;
Hard is the task, my friend, for verse should flow
From the free mind, not fetter'd down by woe;
Restless amidst unceasing tempests toss'd,
Whoe'er has cause for sorrow, I have most.
Would you bid Priam laugh, his sons all slain,
Or childless Niobe from tears refrain,
Join the gay dance, and lead the festive train?
Does grief or study most befit the mind
To this remote, this barbarous nook confined?
Could you impart to my unshaken breast
The fortitude by Socrates possess'd,
Soon would it sink beneath such woes as mine,
For what is human strength to wrath divine?
Wise as he was, and heaven pronounced him so,
My sufferings would have laid that wisdom low.
Could I forget my country, thee and all,
And e'en the offence to which I owe my fall,

Yet fear alone would freeze the poet's vein,
While hostile troops swarm o'er the dreary plain.
Add that the fatal rust of long disuse
Unfits me for the service of the muse.
Thistles and weeds are all we can expect
From the best soil impoverish'd by neglect;
Unexercised, and to his stall confined,
The fleetest racer would be left behind;
The best built bark that cleaves the watery way,
Laid useless by, would moulder and decay—
No hope remains that time shall me restore,
Mean as I was, to what I was before.
Think how a series of desponding cares
Benumbs the genius, and its force impairs.
How oft, as now, on this devoted sheet,
My verse constrain'd to move with measured feet,
Reluctant and laborious limps along,
And proves itself a wretched exile's song.
What is it tunes the most melodious lays?
'Tis emulation and the thirst of praise,
A noble thirst, and not unknown to me,
While smoothly wafted on a calmer sea.
But can a wretch like Ovid pant for fame?
No, rather let the world forget my name.
Is it because that world approved my strain,
You prompt me to the same pursuit again?
No, let the Nine the ungrateful truth excuse,
I charge my hopeless ruin on the muse,
And, like Perillus, meet my just desert,
The victim of my own pernicious art;
Fool that I was to be so warn'd in vain,
And shipwreck'd once, to tempt the deep again.
Ill fares the bard in this unletter'd land,
None to consult, and none to understand.
The purest verse has no admirers here,
Their own rude language only suits their ear.
Rude as it is, at length familiar grown,
I learn it, and almost unlearn my own—
Yet to say truth, e'en here the muse disdains
Confinement, and attempts her former strains,
But finds the strong desire is not the power,
And what her taste condemns, the flames devour.

A part, perhaps, like this, escapes the doom,
And though unworthy, finds a friend at Rome·
But oh the cruel art, that could undo
Its votary thus! would that could perish too!

HOR. LIB. I. ODE IX.

Vides, ut alta stet nive candidum
Soracte; . . . .

SEE'ST thou yon mountain laden with deep snow
The groves beneath their fleecy burthen bow,
The streams, congeal'd, forget to flow,
Come, thaw the cold, and lay a cheerful pile
Of fuel on the hearth;
Broach the best cask, and make old winter smile
With seasonable mirth.

This be our part—let Heaven dispose the rest
If Jove command, the winds shall sleep
That now wage war upon the foamy deep,
And gentle gales spring from the balmy west.

E'en let us shift to-morrow as we may,
When to-morrow's pass'd away,
We at least shall have to say,
We have lived another day;
Your auburn locks will soon be silver'd o'er,
Old age is at our heels, and youth returns no more.

HOR. LIB. I. ODE XXXVIII.

Persicos odi, puer, apparatus.

BOY, I hate their empty shows,
Persian garlands I detest,
Bring not me the late-blown rose,
Lingering after all the rest.

Plainer myrtle pleases me,
Thus outstretch'd beneath my vine;
Myrtle more becoming thee,
Waiting with thy master's wine.

HOR. LIB. I. ODE XXXVIII.

Boy! I detest all Persian fopperies,
Fillet-bound garlands are to me disgusting;
Task not thyself with any search, I charge thee,
Where latest roses linger,
Bring me alone (for thou wilt find that readily)
Plain myrtle. Myrtle neither will disparage
Thee occupied to serve me, or me drinking
Beneath my vine's cool shelter.

HOR. LIB. II. ODE XVI.

Otium Divos rogat in patenti.

Ease is the weary merchant's prayer,
Who ploughs by night the Ægean flood,
When neither moon nor stars appear,
Or faintly glimmer through the cloud.

For ease the Mede with quiver graced,
For ease the Thracian hero sighs,
Delightful ease all pant to taste,
A blessing which no treasure buys.

For neither gold can lull to rest,
Nor all a Consul's guard beat off
The tumults of a troubled breast,
The cares that haunt a gilded roof.

Happy the man whose table shows
A few clean ounces of old plate,
No fear intrudes on his repose,
No sordid wishes to be great.

Poor short-lived things, what plans we lay!
  Ah, why forsake our native home!
To distant climates speed away;
  For self sticks close where'er we roam.

Care follows hard, and soon o'ertakes
  The well-rigg'd ship, the warlike steed
Her destined quarry ne'er forsakes,
  Not the wind flies with half her speed.

From anxious fears of future ill
  Guard well the cheerful, happy now;
Gild e'en your sorrows with a smile,
  No blessing is unmix'd below.

Thy neighing steeds and lowing herds,
  Thy numerous flocks around thee graze,
And the best purple Tyre affords
  Thy robe magnificent displays.

On me indulgent Heaven bestow'd
  A rural mansion, neat and small;
This lyre;—and as for yonder crowd,
  The happiness to hate them all.

ON THE BENEFIT RECEIVED BY HIS MAJESTY FROM SEA-BATHING IN THE YEAR 1789.

O Sovereign of an isle renown'd
  For undisputed sway
Wherever o'er yon gulf profound
  Her navies wing their way,

With juster claim she builds at length
  Her empire on the sea,
And well may boast the waves her strength
  Which strength restored to thee.

ADDRESSED TO MISS —— ON READING THE PRAYER FOR INDIFFERENCE.*

And dwells there in a female heart,
By bounteous heaven design'd,
The choicest raptures to impart,
To feel the most refined—

Dwells there a wish in such a breast
Its nature to forego,
To smother in ignoble rest,
At once both bliss and woe!

Far be the thought, and far the strain
Which breathes the low desire,
How sweet soe'er the verse complain,
Though Phœbus string the lyre.

Come, then, fair maid (in nature wise)
Who, knowing them, can tell
From generous sympathy what joys
The glowing bosom swell:

In justice to the various powers
Of pleasing, which you share,
Join me, amid your silent hours,
To form the better prayer.

With lenient balm may Oberon hence
To fairy land be driven,
With every herb that blunts the sense
Mankind received from heaven.

'Oh! if my sovereign Author please,
Far be it from my fate
To live, unbless'd, in torpid ease,
And slumber on in state.

* For Mrs. Greville's Ode, see Annual Register, vol. v. p. 202.

'Each tender tie of life defied
 Whence social pleasures spring,
Unmoved with all the world beside,
 A solitary thing—'

Some Alpine mountain, wrapt in snow,
 Thus braves the whirling blast,
Eternal winter doom'd to know,
 No genial spring to taste.

In vain warm suns their influence shed,
 The zephyrs sport in vain,
He rears unchanged his barren head,
 Whilst beauty decks the plain.

What though in scaly armour dress'd,
 Indifference may repel
The shafts of woe—in such a breast
 No joy can ever dwell.

'Tis woven in the world's great plan,
 And fix'd by heaven's decree,
That all the true delights of man
 Should spring from sympathy.

'Tis nature bids, and whilst the laws
 Of nature we retain,
Our self-approving bosom draws
 A pleasure from its pain.

Thus grief itself has comforts dear
 The sordid never know;
And ecstasy attends the tear
 When virtue bids it flow.

For when it streams from that pure source
 No bribes the heart can win,
To check, or alter from its course,
 The luxury within.

Peace to the phlegm of sullen elves,
 Who, if from labour eased,
Extend no care beyond themselves,
 Unpleasing and unpleased.

Let no low thought suggest the prayer,
  Oh! grant, kind Heaven, to me
Long as I draw ethereal air,
  Sweet sensibility.

Where'er the heavenly nymph is seen,
  With lustre-beaming eye,
A train, attendant on their queen,
  (Her rosy chorus) fly.

The jocund loves in Hymen's band,
  With torches ever bright,
And generous friendship hand in hand,
  With pity's watery sight:

The gentler virtues too are join'd
  In youth immortal warm;
The soft relations, which, combined,
  Give life her every charm.

The arts come smiling in the close,
  And lend celestial fire;
The marble breathes, the canvas glows,
  The muses sweep the lyre.

'Still may my melting bosom cleave
  To sufferings not my own,
And still the sigh responsive heave
  Where'er is heard a groan.

'So pity shall take virtue's part,
  Her natural ally,
And fashioning my soften'd heart,
  Prepare it for the sky.'

This artless vow may heaven receive,
  And you, fond maid, approve:
So may your guiding angel give
  Whate'er you wish or love.

So may the rosy-finger'd hours
  Lead on the various year,
And every joy, which now is yours,
  Extend a larger sphere.

And suns to come, as round they wheel,
Your golden moments bless
With all a tender heart can feel,
Or lively fancy guess.

1762.

FROM A LETTER TO THE REV. MR. NEWTON,

LATE RECTOR OF ST. MARY WOOLNOTH.

Says the pipe to the snuff-box, I can't understand
What the ladies and gentlemen see in your face,
That you are in fashion all over the land,
And I am so much fallen into disgrace.

Do but see what a pretty contemplative air
I give to the company—pray do but note 'em—
You would think that the wise men of Greece were all there,
Or, at least, would suppose them the wise men of Gotham.

My breath is as sweet as the breath of blown roses,
While you are a nuisance where'er you appear;
There is nothing but sniveling and blowing of noses,
Such a noise as turns any man's stomach to hear.

Then lifting his lid in a delicate way,
And opening his mouth with a smile quite engaging,
The box in reply was heard plainly to say,
What a silly dispute is this we are waging!

If you have a little of merit to claim,
You may thank the sweet-smelling Virginian weed,
And I, if I seem to deserve any blame,
The before mentioned drug in apology plead.

Thus neither the praise nor the blame is our own,
No room for a sneer, much less a cachinnus,
We are vehicles, not of tobacco alone,
But of anything else they may choose to put in us.

THE FLATTING MILL.

AN ILLUSTRATION.

When a bar of pure silver or ingot of gold
Is sent to be flatted or wrought into length,
It is pass'd between cylinders often, and roll'd
In an engine of utmost mechanical strength.

Thus tortured and squeezed, at last it appears
Like a loose heap of ribbon, a glittering show
Like music it tinkles and rings in your ears,
And, warm'd by the pressure, is all in a glow.

This process achieved, it is doom'd to sustain
The thump after thump of a gold-beater's mallet
And at last is of service in sickness or pain
To cover a pill for a delicate palate.

Alas for the poet! who dares undertake
To urge reformation of national ill—
His head and his heart are both likely to ache
With the double employment of mallet and mill

If he wish to instruct, he must learn to delight,
Smooth, ductile, and even his fancy must flow,
Must tinkle and glitter like gold to the sight,
And catch in its progress a sensible glow.

After all he must beat it as thin and as fine
As the leaf that enfolds what an invalid swallows,
For truth is unwelcome, however divine,
And unless you adorn it, a nausea follows.

EPITAPH

ON A FREE BUT TAME REDBREAST,

A FAVOURITE OF MISS SALLY HURDIS.

THESE are not dew-drops, these are tears,
 And tears by Sally shed
For absent Robin, who she fears,
 With too much cause, is dead.

One morn he came not to her hand
 As he was wont to come,
And, on her finger perch'd, to stand
 Picking his breakfast-crumb.

Alarm'd, she call'd him, and perplex'd
 She sought him, but in vain—
That day he came not, nor the next,
 Nor ever came again.

She therefore raised him here a tomb,
 Though where he fell, or how,
None knows, so secret was his doom,
 Nor where he moulders now.

Had half a score of coxcombs died
 In social Robin's stead,
Poor Sally's tears had soon been dried,
 Or haply never shed.

But Bob was neither rudely bold
 Nor spiritlessly tame;
Nor was, like theirs, his bosom cold,
 But always in a flame.

March, 1792.

SONNET.

ADDRESSED TO WILLIAM HAYLEY, ESQ.

Hayley—thy tenderness fraternal shown
  In our first interview, delightful guest!
  To Mary, and me for her dear sake distress'd,
Such as it is has made my heart thy own,
Though heedless now of new engagements grown;
  For threescore winters make a wintry breast,
  And I had purposed ne'er to go in quest
Of friendship more, except with God alone.
  But thou hast won me; nor is God my foe,
Who, ere this last afflictive scene began,
  Sent thee to mitigate the dreadful blow,
  My brother, by whose sympathy I know
Thy true deserts infallibly to scan,
Not more to admire the bard than love the man.

June 2, 1792.

AN EPITAPH.

Here lies one who never drew
Blood himself, yet many slew;
Gave the gun its aim, and figure
Made in field, yet ne'er pull'd trigger.
Armed men have gladly made
Him their guide, and him obey'd;
At his signified desire
Would advance, present, and fire—
Stout he was, and large of limb,
Scores have fled at sight of him!
And to all this fame he rose
Only following his nose.
Neptune was he call'd, not he
Who controls the boisterous sea.

But of happier command,
Neptune of the furrow'd land;
And, your wonder vain to shorten,
Pointer to Sir John Throckmorton.

1792.

ON RECEIVING HAYLEY'S PICTURE.

In language warm as could be breath'd or penn'd
Thy picture speaks the original my friend,
Not by those looks that indicate thy mind—
They only speak thee friend of all mankind;
Expression here more soothing still I see,
That friend of all a partial friend to me.

January, 1793.

ON A PLANT OF VIRGIN'S BOWER,

DESIGNED TO COVER A GARDEN-SEAT.

Thrive, gentle plant! and weave a bower
For Mary and for me,
And deck with many a splendid flower
Thy foliage large and free.

Thou camest from Eartham, and wilt shade
(If truly I divine
Some future day the illustrious head
Of him who made thee mine.

Should Daphne show a jealous frown,
And envy seize the bay,
Affirming none so fit to crown
Such honour'd brows as they,

Thy cause with zeal we shall defend
And with convincing power;
For why should not the virgin's friend
Be crown'd with virgin's bower?

Spring of 1793.

ON RECEIVING HEYNE'S VIRGIL

FROM MR. HAYLEY.

I SHOULD have deem'd it once an effort vain
To sweeten more sweet Maro's matchless strain,
But from that error now behold me free
Since I received him as a gift from thee.

Oct. 1793.

ON THE DEATH OF SIR WILLIAM RUSSELL

DOOM'D as I am in solitude to waste
The present moments, and regret the past;
Deprived of every joy I valued most,
My friend torn from me and my mistress lost;
Call not this gloom I wear, this anxious mien,
The dull effect of business or of spleen.
Still, still, I mourn, with each returning day,
Him snatch'd by fate in early youth away;
And her through tedious years of doubt and pain
Fix'd in her choice, and faithful, but in vain.
O prone to pity, generous and sincere,
Whose eye ne'er yet refused the wretch a tear;
Whose heart the real claim of friendship knows,
Nor thinks a lover's are but fancied woes;
See me, ere yet my destined course half done,
Cast forth a wanderer on a world unknown:
See me neglected on the world's rude coast,
Each dear companion of my voyage lost;
Nor ask why clouds of sorrow shade my brow,
And ready tears wait only leave to flow;
Why all that soothes a heart from anguish free,
All that delights the happy, palls with me.

EPIGRAM
ON HIS MISTAKE IN TRANSLATING HOMER

COWPER had sinn'd with some excuse,
  If, bound in rhyming tethers
He had committed this abuse
  Of changing ewes for wethers;

But, male for female is a trope,
  Or rather bold misnomer,
That would have startled even Pope,
  When he translated Homer.

714

ANTI-THELYPHTHORA.

A TALE, IN VERSE.

Ah miser,
Quanta laboras in Charybdi!—*Hor. lib.* 1. *Ode* 27.

Airy del Castro was as bold a knight
As ever earn'd a lady's love in fight.
Many he sought, but one above the rest
His tender heart victoriously impress'd;
In fairy-land was born the matchless dame,
The land of dreams, Hypothesis her name.
There Fancy nursed her in ideal bowers,
And laid her soft in amaranthine flowers;
Delighted with her babe, the enchantress smiled,
And graced with all her gifts the favourite child.
Her woo'd Sir Airy, by meandering streams,
In daily musings and in nightly dreams;
With all the flowers he found, he wove in haste
Wreathes for her brow, and girdles for her waist;
His time, his talents, and his ceaseless care
All consecrated to adorn the fair;
No pastime but with her he deign'd to take,
And,—if he studied, studied for her sake.
And, for Hypothesis was somewhat long,
Nor soft enough to suit a lover's tongue,
He call'd her Posy, with an amorous art,
And graved it on a gem, and wore it next his heart.
  But she, inconstant as the beams that play
On rippling waters in an April day,
With many a freakish trick deceived his pains,
To pathless wilds and unfrequented plains
Enticed him from his oaths of knighthood far,
Forgetful of the glorious toils of war.
'Tis thus the tenderness that love inspires
Too oft betrays the votaries of his fires;
Borne far away on elevated wings,
They sport like wanton doves in airy-rings,
And laws and duties are neglected things.
  Nor he alone address'd the wayward fair;
Full many a knight had been entangled there.
But still, whoever woo'd her or embraced,
On every mind some mighty spell she cast.
Some she would teach (for she was wondrous wise,
And made her dupes see all things with her eyes)
That forms material, whatsoe'er we dream,
Are not at all, or are not what they seem;
That substances and modes of every kind
Are mere impressions on the passive mind;

And he that splits his cranium, breaks at most
A fancied head against a fancied post:
Others, that earth, ere sin had drown'd it all,
Was smooth and even as an ivory ball;
That all the various beauties we survey,
Hills, valleys, rivers, and tne boundless sea,
Are but departures from the first design,
Effects of punishment and wrath divine.
She tutor'd some in Dædalus's art,
And promised they should act his wildgoose part,
On waxen pinions soar without a fall,
Swift as the proudest gander of them all.
But fate reserved Sir Airy to maintain
The wildest project of her teeming brain;
That wedlock is not rigorous as supposed,
But man, within a wider pale enclosed,
May rove at will, where appetite shall lead,
Free as the lordly bull that ranges o'er the mead;
That forms and rites are tricks of human law,
As idle as the chattering of a daw;
That lewd incontinence and lawless rape,
Are marriage in its true and proper shape;
That man by faith and truth is made a slave,
The ring a bauble and the priest a knave.
Fair fall the deed! the knight exulting cried,
Now is the time to make the maid a bride!
'Twas on the noon of an autumnal day,
October hight, but mild and fair as May;
When scarlet fruits the russet hedge adorn,
And floating films envelop every thorn;
When gently as in June, the rivers glide,
And only miss the flowers that graced their side;
The linnet twitter'd out his parting song,
With many a chorister the woods among;
On southern banks the ruminating sheep
Lay snug and warm;—'twas summer's farewell peep.
Propitious to his fond intent there grew
An arbour near at hand of thickest yew,
With many a boxen bush, close clipt between,
And phillyrea of a gilded green.
But what old Chaucer's merry page befits,
The chaster muse of modern days omits.
Suffice it then in decent terms to say,
She saw, and turn'd her rosy cheek away.
Small need of prayer-book or of priest, I ween,
Where parties are agreed, retired the scene,
Occasion prompt, and appetite so keen.
Hypothesis (for with such magic power
Fancy endued her in her natal hour)
From many a steaming lake and reeking bog,
Bade rise in haste a dank and drizzling fog,

That curtain'd round the scene where they reposed,
And wood and lawn in dusky folds enclosed.
  Fear seized the trembling sex; in every grove
They wept the wrongs of honourable love.
In vain, they cried, are hymeneal rites,
Vain our delusive hope of constant knights;
The marriage bond has lost its power to bind,
And flutters loose, the sport of every wind.
The bride, while yet her bride's attire is on,
Shall mourn her absent lord, for he is gone,
Satiate of her, and weary of the same,
To distant wilds, in quest of other game.
Ye fair Circassians! all your lutes employ,
Seraglios sing, and harems dance for joy!
For British nymphs whose lords were lately true,
Nymphs quite as fair, and happier once than you,
Honour, esteem, and confidence forgot,
Feel all the meanness of your slavish lot.
O curst Hypothesis! your hellish arts
Seduce our husbands, and estrange their hearts.
Will none arise? no knight who still retains
The blood of ancient worthies in his veins,
To assert the charter of the chaste and fair,
Find out her treacherous heart, and plant a dagger there!
A knight—(can he that serves the fair do less?)
Starts at the call of beauty in distress;
And he that does not, whatsoe'er occurs,
Is recreant, and unworthy of his spurs.
  Full many a champion, bent on hardy deed,
Call'd for his arms and for his princely steed.
So swarm'd the Sabine youth, and grasp'd the shield,
When Roman rapine, by no laws withheld,
Lest Rome should end with her first founders' lives,
Made half their maids, *sans* ceremony, wives.
But not the mitred few, the soul their charge,
They left these bodily concerns at large;
Forms or no forms, pluralities or pairs,
Right reverend sirs! was no concern of theirs.
The rest, alert and active as became
A courteous knighthood, caught the generous flame;
One was accoutred when the cry began,
Knight of the Silver Moon, Sir Marmadan.
  Oft as his patroness, who rules the night,
Hangs out her lamp in yon cærulean height,
His vow was (and he well perform'd his vow),
Arm'd at all points, with terror on his brow,
To judge the land, to purge atrocious crimes,
And quell the shapeless monsters of the times.
For cedars famed, fair Lebanon supplied
The well-poised lance that quiver'd at his side;

Truth arm'd it with a point so keen, so just,
No spell or charm was proof against the thrust
He couch'd it firm upon his puissant thigh,
And darting through his helm an eagle's eye,
On all the wings of chivalry advanced
To where the fond Sir Airy lay entranced.
He dreamt not of a foe, or if his fear
Foretold one, dreamt not of a foe so near.
Far other dreams his feverish mind employ'd,
Of rights restored, variety enjoy'd;
Of virtue too well fenced to fear a flaw;
Vice passing current by the stamp of law;
Large population on a liberal plan,
And woman trembling at the foot of man;
How simple wedlock fornication works,
And Christians marrying may convert the Turks.
The trumpet now spoke Marmadan at hand,
A trumpet that was heard through all the land.
His high-bred steed expands his nostrils wide,
And snorts aloud to cast the mist aside;
But he, the virtues of his lance to show,
Struck thrice the point upon his saddle-bow;
Three sparks ensued that chased it all away,
And set the unseemly pair in open day.
'To horse!' he cried, 'or, by this good right hand
And better spear, I smite you where you stand.'
Sir Airy, not a whit dismay'd or scared,
Buckled his helm, and to his steed repair'd;
Whose bridle, while he cropp'd the grass below,
Hung not far off upon a myrtle bough.
He mounts at once,—such confidence infused
The insidious witch that had his wits abused;
And she, regardless of her softer kind,
Seized fast the saddle and sprang up behind.
'Oh shame to knighthood!' his assailant cried;
'Oh shame!' ten thousand echoing nymphs replied
Placed with advantage at his listening ear,
She whisper'd still that he had nought to fear;
That he was cased in such enchanted steel,
So polish'd and compact from head to heel,
'Come ten, come twenty, should an army call
Thee to the field, thou shouldst withstand them all.'
'By Dian's beams,' Sir Marmadan exclaim'd,
'The guiltiest still are ever least ashamed!
But guard thee well, expect no feign'd attack;
And guard beside the sorceress at thy back!'
He spoke indignant, and his spurs applied,
Though little need, to his good palfrey's side;
The barb sprang forward, and his lord, whose force
Was equal to the swiftness of his horse,

Rush'd with a whirlwind's fury on the foe,
And, Phineas-like, transfix'd them at a blow.
  Then sang the married and the maiden throng,
Love graced the theme, and harmony the song;
The Fauns and Satyrs, a lascivious race,
Shriek'd at the sight, and, conscious, fled the place:
And Hymen, trimming his dim torch anew,
His snowy mantle o'er his shoulders threw;
He turn'd, and view'd it oft on every side,
And reddening with a just and generous pride,
Bless'd the glad beams of that propitious day,
The spot he loath'd so much for ever cleansed away.

THE DISTRESSED TRAVELLERS;

OR,

LABOUR IN VAIN.

AN EXCELLENT NEW SONG, TO A TUNE NEVER SUNG BEFORE

1.

I SING of a journey to Clifton,
  We would have perform'd if we could,
Without car or barrow to lift on
  Poor Mary and me through the mud:
    Slee sla slud,
    Stuck in the mud,
Oh it is pretty to wade through a flood!

2.

So away we went slipping and sliding,
  Hop, hop, *à la mode de deux* frogs,
'Tis near as good walking as riding,
  When ladies are dressed in their clogs.
    Wheels, no doubt,
    Go briskly about,
But they clatter and rattle, and make such a rout!

3.

SHE.

Well! now I protest it is charming;
  How finely the weather improves!
That cloud, though, is rather alarming;
  How slowly and stately it moves.

HE.

Pshaw! never mind;
'Tis not in the wind;
We are travelling south, and shall leave it behind.

4.

SHE.

I am glad we are come for an airing,
For folks may be pounded and penn'd,
Until they grow rusty, not caring
To stir half a mile to an end.

HE.

The longer we stay,
The longer we may;
It's a folly to think about weather or way.

5.

SHE.

But now I begin to be frighted:
If I fall, what a way I should roll!
I am glad that the bridge was indicted,—
Stop! stop! I am sunk in a hole!

HE.

Nay, never care!
'Tis a common affair;
You'll not be the last that will set a foot there.

6.

SHE.

Let me breathe now a little, and ponder
On what it were better to do.
That terrible lane, I see yonder,
I think we shall never get through!

HE.

So think I;
But, by the bye,
We never shall know, if we never should try.

7.

SHE.

But should we get there, how shall we get home?
What a terrible deal of bad road we have past,
Slipping and sliding; and if we should come
To a difficult stile, I am ruin'd at last.
Oh this lane!
Now it is plain
That struggling and striving is labour in vain.

8.

HE.

Stick fast there, while I go and look.

SHE.

Don't go away, for fear I should fall!

HE.

I have examined it every nook,
And what you have here is a sample of all.
Come, wheel round;
The dirt we have found
Would be an estate at a farthing a pound.

9.

Now, Sister Anne, the guitar you must take;
Set it, and sing it, and make it a song.
I have varied the verse for variety sake,
And cut it off short, because it was long.
'Tis hobbling and lame,
Which critics won't blame,
For the sense and the sound, they say, should be the same.

OF HIMSELF.

TO MISS THEODORA JANE COWPER.

WILLIAM was once a bashful youth;
His modesty was such,
That one might say (to say the truth)
He rather had too much.

Some said that it was want of sense,
And others want of spirit,
(So blest a thing is impudence)
While others could not bear it.

But some a different notion had,
And at each other winking,
Observed, that though he little said,
He paid it off with thinking.

Howe'er it happen'd, by degrees,
He mended, and grew perter;
In company, was more at ease,
And dress'd a little smarter;

Nay, now and then would look quite gay,
  As other people do;
And sometimes said, or tried to say,
  A witty thing or so.

He eyed the women, and made free
  To comment on their shapes;
So that there was, or seem'd to be,
  No fear of a relapse.

The women said, who thought him rough,
  But now no longer foolish,
'The creature may do well enough,
  But wants a deal of polish.'

At length, improved from head to heel,
  'Twere scarce too much to say,
No dancing bear was so genteel,
  Or half so *dégagé*.

Now, that a miracle so strange
  May not in vain be shown,
Let the dear maid who wrought the change
  Even claim him for her own.

WRITTEN AFTER LEAVING HER AT NEW BURNS.

How quick the change from joy to woe!
How chequer'd is our lot below!
Seldom we view the prospect fair;
Dark clouds of sorrow, pain, and care,
(Some pleasing intervals between)
Scowl over more than half the scene.
Last week with Delia, gentle maid,
Far hence in happier fields I stray'd.
Five suns successive rose and set,
And saw no monarch in his state,
Wrapp'd in the blaze of majesty,
So free from every care as I.—
Next day the scene was overcast;
Such day till then I never pass'd,—
For on that day, relentless fate!
Delia and I must separate.
Yet ere we look'd our last farewell,
From her dear lips this comfort fell:
'Fear not that time, where'er we rove
Or absence, shall abate my love.'

Complimentary Poems to Milton,

TRANSLATED FROM THE LATIN AND ITALIAN.

THE NEAPOLITAN, JOHN BAPTIST MANSO, MARQUIS OF VILLA, TO THE ENGLISHMAN, JOHN MILTON.

WHAT features, form, mien, manners, with a mind
O how intelligent! and how refined!
Were but thy piety from fault as free,
Thou would'st no Angle but an Angel be.

AN EPIGRAM

ADDRESSED TO THE ENGLISHMAN, JOHN MILTON, A POET WORTHY OF THREE LAURELS, THE GRECIAN, LATIN, AND ETRUSCAN, BY JOHN SALSILLI, OF ROME.

MELES and Mincio, both your urns depress'
Sebetus, boast henceforth thy Tasso less!
But let the Thames o'erpeer all floods, since he
For Milton famed shall, single, match the three.

TO JOHN MILTON.

GREECE, sound thy Homer's, Rome, thy Virgil's name,
But England's Milton equals both in fame.

SELVAGGI.

AN ODE

ADDRESSED TO THE ILLUSTRIOUS ENGLISHMAN, MR. JOHN MILTON, BY SIGNOR ANTONIO FRANCINI, GENTLEMAN, OF FLORENCE.

EXALT me, Clio, to the skies,
  That I may form a starry crown
Beyond what Helicon supplies
  In laureate garlands of renown;
To nobler worth be brighter glory given
And to a heavenly mind a recompense from heaven.

Time's wasteful hunger cannot prey
 On everlasting high desert,
Nor can oblivion steal away
 Its record graven on the heart;
Lodge but an arrow, virtue, on the bow
That binds my lyre, and death shall be a vanquish'd foe.

In ocean's blazing flood enshrined
 Whose vassal tide around her swells,
Albion, from other climes disjoin'd,
 The prowess of the world excels;
She teems with heroes, that to glory rise,
With more than human force in our astonish'd eyes

To virtue, driven from other lands,
 Their bosom yields a safe retreat;
Her law alone the deed commands:
 Her smiles they feel divinely sweet.
Confirm my record, Milton, generous youth!
And by true virtue prove thy virtue's praise a truth.

Zeuxis, all energy and flame,
 Set ardent forth in his career;
Urged to his task by Helen's fame
 Resounding ever in his ear;
To make his image to her beauty true,
From the collected fair each sovereign charm he drew.

The bee, with subtlest skill endued,
 Thus toils to earn her precious juice
From all the flowery myriads strew'd
 O'er meadow and parterre, profuse;
Confederate voices one sweet air compound,
And various chords consent in one harmonious sound.

An artist of celestial aim,
 Thy genius caught by moral grace,
With ardent emulation's flame
 The steps of virtue toil'd to trace,
Observed in every land who brightest shone,
And, blending all their best, made perfect good thy own.

From all, in Florence born, or taught
 Our country's sweetest accent there,
Whose works, with learned labour wrought,
 Immortal honours justly share,
Thou hast such treasure drawn of purest ore,
That not even Tuscan bards can boast a richer store.

Babel confused, and with her towers
  Unfinish'd spreading wide the plain,
Has served but to evince thy powers
  With all her tongues confused in vain,
Since not alone thy England's purest phrase
But every polished realm thy various speech displays.

The secret things of heaven and earth
  By nature, too reserved, conceal'd
From other minds of highest worth,
  To thee are copiously reveal'd;
Thou know'st them clearly, and thy views attain
The utmost bounds prescribed to moral truths' domain.

Let time no more his wing display,
  And boast his ruinous career,
For virtue rescued from his sway
  His injuries may cease to fear;
Since all events, that claim remembrance, find
A chronicle exact in thy capacious mind.

Give me, that I may praise thy song,
  Thy lyre, by which alone I can,
Which, placing thee the stars among,
  Already proves thee more than man;
And Thames shall seem Permessus, while his stream
Graced with a swan like thee, shall be my favourite theme.

I, who, beside the Arno, strain
  To match thy merit with my lays,
Learn, after many an effort vain,
  To admire thee rather than to praise
And that by mute astonishment alone,
Not by the faltering tongue, thy worth may best be shown.

ADAM:

A SACRED DRAMA.

TRANSLATED

FROM THE ITALIAN OF GIO. BATTISTA ANDREINI,

BY COWPER AND HAYLEY

TO THE COURTEOUS READER.

HAVING satiated and fatigued my eyes, gentle reader, by too intent an observation of what is passing on earth; and raising therefore my thoughts to higher contemplations, to the wonders diffused by the supreme Being, for the benefit of man, through the universe; I felt my heart penetrated by a certain Christian compunction, in reflecting how his inexpressible goodness, though perpetually and grievously offended by us, still shows itself in the highest degree indulgent towards us in preserving those wonders with a continual influence to our advantage; and how, on the first provocation to vengeance, Almighty Power does not enlarge the ocean to pass its immense boundary, does not obscure the light of the sun, does not impress sterility on the earth, to ingulf us, to blind us, and finally to destroy us. Softened and absorbed in these divine emotions, I felt myself transported and hurried by a delightful violence into a terrestrial paradise, where I seemed to behold the first man Adam, a creature dear to God, the friend of angels, the heir of heaven, familiar with the stars, a compendium of all created things, the ornament of all, the miracle of nature, the lord of the animals, the only inhabitant of the universe, and enjoyer of a scene so wonderfully grand. Whence charmed more than ever, I resolved, with the favour of the blessed God, to usher into the light of the world, what I bore in the darkness of my imagination; both to render it known in some measure, that, I know myself, and the infinite obligations that I have to God; and that others, who do not know, may learn, the true nature of man, and from the low contemplation of earthly things, may raise their minds to things celestial and divine.

I remained however a considerable time in doubt if I ought, or if I were able to undertake a composition most difficult to me on many accounts, since in beginning the sacred subject from man's creation to the point where he is driven from the terrestrial paradise, a period of six years (as St. Augustin relates in his book on the City of God), I did not clearly perceive, how an action so brief, could be formed into five acts, especially allowing to every act the number of at least six or seven scenes,—difficult from the dispute that the devil maintained with Eve, first that he might induce her to eat the apple, since we have only the text that mentions it, in saying '*nequaquam moriemini, et eritis sicut Dii scientes bonum et malum*,'—difficult from the words of Eve in persuading Adam (who had indeed the gift of knowledge infused) to taste the apple;—but difficult above all, from my own infirmity, since the composition must remain deprived of those poetic ornaments, so dear to the muses: deprived of the power to draw comparisons from implements of art introduced in the course of years, since in the time of the first man there was no such thing: deprived also of naming (at least while Adam speaks, or discourse is held with him), for example, bows, arrows, hatchets, urns, knives, swords, spears, trumpets, drums, trophies, banners, lists, hammers, torches, bellows, funeral piles, theatres, exchequers, infinite things of a like nature, introduced by the necessities of sin; and yet, as circumstances of affliction and punishment, they ought not to pass through the mind or through the lips of Adam, although he had knowledge infused into him, as one who lived most happy in a state of innocence: deprived moreover of introducing points of history sacred or profane, of relating fictions of fabulous deities, of rehearsing loves, furies, sports of hunting or fishing, triumphs, shipwrecks, conflagrations, enchantments, and things of a like nature, that are in truth the ornament and the soul of poetry: difficult from not knowing in what style Adam ought to speak, since in respect to his knowledge it might be proper to assign to him verses of a high majestic and flowing style; but considering him as a shepherd and inhabitant of the woods, it appears that he should be simple and sweet in his discourse, and I endeavoured on that account to render it such, as much as I could, by variety of versification. And here taking courage in my greatest doubt, I formed, I know not how, a beginning; I advanced, if I may say so, without any determined plan; and arrived at the end before I was aware. Whence I am inclined to believe that the favour of God, regarding rather my good intention than my defects (for as he often withdraws the heart of man from evil, so he conducts it insensibly to good), gave direction to my hand, and completed my work. Wherefore to that alone I am indebted for the little grace that may perhaps be found in the present labour; knowing, that as Omnipotence is accustomed to produce wonders from the rude and unformed chaos, so, from the still ruder chaos of my mind, it may have called forth this production, if not for any other purpose, yet to be sacred, and to make as it were a mute speak in my person, in despite of poverty of genius, as on the other hand it is accustomed to strike mute the most eloquent tongues when they employ themselves on subjects low and profane. Let it be surveyed, therefore, with an eye of indulgence, and blame not the poverty of style, the want of dignity in the conduct of the circumstances, sterility of conceits, weakness of spirit, insipid jokes, and extravagant episodes, to mention (without speaking of an infinitude of other things) that the world, the flesh, and the devil, present themselves in human shapes to tempt Adam, since there was then in the universe no other man or woman, and the serpent discovered himself to Eve with a human similitude; moreover this is done, that the subject may be comprehended by the understanding through the medium of the senses: since the great temptations that Adam and Eve at once sustained, were indeed in the interior of their own mind, but could not be so comprehended by the spectator; nor is it to be believed that the serpent held a long dispute with Eve, since he tempted her rather by a suggestion to her mind than by the conference, saying these words, '*nequaquam moriemini, et eritis sicut Dii scientes bonum et malum*,' and yet it will be necessary, in order to express those internal contentions, to find some expedient to give them an outward representation. But, if it is permitted to the painter, who is a dumb poet, to express by colours God the Father under the person of a man silvered by age, and to describe under the image of a white dove the purity of the Spirit, and to figure the divine messengers, or angels, in the shape of winged youths; why is it not permitted to the poet, who is a speaking painter, to represent in his theatrical production another man and another woman besides Adam and Eve, and to represent their internal conflicts through the medium of images and voices entirely human? not to mention that it appears more allowable to introduce in this work the devil under a human shape, than it is to introduce into it the Eternal Father, and even an angel; and if this is permitted, and seen every day exhibited in sacred representations, why should it not be allowed in the present, where, if the greater evil is allowable, surely the lesser should be allowed? Attend therefore, gentle reader, more to the substance than to the accident, considering in the work the great end of introducing into the theatre of the soul the misery and lamentation of Adam, to make your heart a spectator of them, in order to raise it from these dregs of earth, to the magnificence of heaven, through the medium of virtue and the assistance of God; by whom may you be blessed!

THE CHARACTERS.

Chorus of Seraphim, Cherubim, and Angels.
The Archangel Michael.
Adam.
Eve.
A Cherub, the Guardian of Adam.
Lucifer.
Satan.
Beelzebub.
Seven Mortal Sins.
The World.
The Flesh.
Famine.
Labour.
Despair.
Death.
Vain Glory.
The Serpent.
Volano, *an Infernal Messenger.*
A Chorus of Phantoms.
A Chorus of Fiery, Airy, Aquatic, and Infernal Spirits.

ADAM.

CHORUS OF ANGELS

SINGING THE GLORY OF GOD.

To heaven's bright lyre let Iris be the bow.
  Adapt the spheres for chords, for notes the stars;
  Let new-born gales discriminate the bars,
  Nor let old time to measure times be slow.

Hence to new music of the eternal lyre
  Add richer harmony and praise to praise;
  For him who now his wondrous might displays,
  And shows the universe its awful Sire.

O Thou who, ere the world or heaven was made,
  Didst in thyself, that world, that heaven enjoy,
  How does thy bounty all its powers employ;
  What inexpressive good hast thou display'd!

O Thou of sovereign love almighty source,
  Who know'st to make thy works thy love express
  Let pure devotion's fire the soul possess,
  And give the heart and hand a kindred force.

Then shalt thou hear how, when the world began,
  Thy life-producing voice gave myriads birth,
  Call'd forth from nothing all in heaven and earth,
  Bless'd in thy light as eagles in the sun.

ACT I.

SCENE THE FIRST.

GOD THE FATHER—CHORUS OF ANGELS.

RAISE from this dark abyss thy horrid visage,
O Lucifer! aggrieved by light so potent,
Shrink from the blaze of these refulgent planets,
And pant beneath the rays of no fierce sun;
Read in the sacred volumes of the sky,
The mighty wonders of a hand divine.
Behold, thou frantic rebel,
How easy is the task,
To the great Sire of Worlds,
To raise his empyrean seat sublime;

Lifting humility
Thither whence pride hath fallen.
From thence with bitter grief,
Inhabitant of fire, and mole of darkness,
Let the perverse behold,
Despairing his escape and my compassion,
His own perdition in another's good,
And heaven, now closed to him, to others open'd;
And, sighing from the bottom of his heart,
Let him in homage to my power exclaim,
Ah, this creative Sire,
(Wretch as I am!) I see,
Hath need of nothing but himself alone
To re-establish all.

THE SERAPHIM SING.

O scene worth heavenly musing,
With sun and moon their glorious light diffusing;
Where to angelic voices,
Sphere circling sphere rejoices,
How dost thou rise, exciting
Man to fond contemplation
Of his benign creation!

THE CHERUBIM SING.

The volume of the stars
The sovereign Author plann'd,
Inscribing it with his eternal hand,
And his benignant aim
Their beams in lucid characters proclaim;
And man in these delighting,
Feels their bright beams inviting,
And seems, though prison'd in these mortal bars,
Walking on earth, to mingle with the stars.

GOD THE FATHER

Angels, desert your heaven! with you to earth
That Power descends, whom heaven accompanies;
Let each spectator of these works sublime
Behold, with meek devotion,
Earth into flesh transform'd, and clay to man,
Man to a sovereign lord,
And souls to Seraphim.

THE SERAPHIM SING.

Now let us cleave the sky with wings of gold;
The world be paradise,
Since to its fruitful breast
Now the great Sovereign of our quire descends;
Now let us cleave the sky with wings of gold;

Strew yourselves flowers beneath the step divine,
Ye rivals of the stars!
Summon'd from every sphere,
Ye gems of heaven, heaven's radiant wealth appear;
Now let us cleave the sky with wings of gold!

GOD THE FATHER.

Behold, ye springing herbs and new-born flowers,
The step that used to press the stars alone
And the sun's spacious road,
This day begins, along the sylvan scene,
To leave its grand impression:
To low materials now I stretch my hand,
To form a work sublime.

THE ANGELS SING.

Lament, lament in anguish,
Angel to God rebellious!
See, on a sudden rise
The creature doom'd to fill thy radiant seat!
Foolish thy pride took fire
Contemplating thy birth;
But he o'er pride shall triumph,
Acknowledging he sprung from humble dust.
From hence he shall acquire
As much as thou hast lost;
Since the Supreme Inhabitant of heaven
Receives the humble and dethrones the proud.

GOD THE FATHER.

Adam, arise, since I to thee impart
A spirit warm from my benignant breath;
Arise, arise, first man,
And joyous let the world
Embrace its living miniature in thee!
ADAM. O marvels new, O hallow'd, O divine,
Eternal object of the angel host:
Why do I not possess tongues numerous
As now the stars in heaven?
Now then, before
A thing of earth so mean,
See I the great Artificer divine?
Mighty Ruler supernal,
If 'tis denied this tongue
To match my obligation with my thanks,
Behold my heart's affection,
And hear it speaking clearer than my tongue,
And to thee bending lower
Than this my humble knee.
Now, now, O Lord, in ecstacy devout,

Let my mind mount, and passing all the clouds,
Passing each sphere, even up to heaven ascend,
And there behold the stars, a seat for man!
Thou Lord, who all the fire of genuine love
Convertest to thyself,
Transform me into thee, that I a part
Even of thyself, may thus acquire the power
To offer praises not unworthy thee.

THE ANGELS SING.

To smile in paradise,
Great demi-god of earth, direct thy step;
There, like the tuneful spheres,
Circle the murmuring rills
Of limpid water bright;
There the melodious birds
Rival angelic quires;
There lovely flowers profuse
Appear as vivid stars;
The snowy rose is there
A silver moon, the heliotrope a sun:
What more can be desired,
By earth's new lord in fair corporeal vest,
Than in the midst of earth to find a heaven?
ADAM. O ye harmonious birds!
Bright scene of lovely flowers!
But what delightful slumber
Falls on my closing eyes?
I lay me down, adieu
Unclouded light of day, sweet air adieu!

GOD THE FATHER.

Adam, behold I come,
Son dear to me, thou son
Of an indulgent sire;
Behold the hand that never works in vain:
Behold the hand that join'd the elements,
That added heaven to heavens,
That fill'd the stars with light,
Gave lustre to the moon,
Prescribed the sun his course,
And now supports the world,
And forms a solid stage for thy firm step.
Now sleeping, Adam, from thy open'd side
The substance I will take,
That shall have woman's name, and lovely form.

THE ANGELS SING.

Immortal works of an immortal Maker!
Ye high and blessed seats

Of this delightful world,
Ye starry seats of heaven,
Trophies divine, productions pre-ordain'd:
O power! O energy!
Which out of shadowy horror form'd the sun!

EVE. What heavenly melody pervades my heart,
Ere yet the sound my ear! inviting me
To gaze on wonders, what do I behold,
What transformations new;
Is earth become the heaven?
Do I behold His light
Whose splendour dazzles the meridian sun?
Am I the creature of that plastic hand,
Who form'd of nought the angels and the heavens?
Thou sovereign Lord! whom lowly I adore,
A love so tender penetrates my heart,
That while my tongue ventures on utterance,
The words with difficulty
Find passage from my lips;
For in a tide of tears
(That sighs have caused to flow) they seem absorb'd.
Thou pure celestial love
Of the benignant power,
Who pleased to manifest on earth his glory,
Now to this world descends,
To draw from abject clay
The governor of all created things:
Lord of the hallow'd and conceal'd affection,
Thou in whom love glows with such fervent flame,
Inspirit even my tongue
With suitable reply, that these dear vales
And sylvan scenes may hear
Thanks, that to thee I should devote, my Sire;
But if my tongue be mute, speak thou, my heart.

GOD THE FATHER.

Adam, awake! and cease
To meditate in rapturous trance profound
Things holy and abstruse,
And the deep secrets of the Trinal Lord.

ADAM. Where am I? where have I been? what [Sun
Of triple influence that dims the day
Now from my eye withdraws, where is he vanish'd?
O hallow'd miracles
Of this imperial seat,
Of these resplendent suns,
Which, though divided, form
A single ray of light immeasurable,
Embellishing all heaven,
And giving grace and lustre

To every winged Seraph!
Divine mysterious light,
Flowing from sovereign Good,
To him alone thou art known,
Who mounts to thee an eagle in his faith.
What rose of snowy hue and sacred form,
In these celestial bowers,
Wet with empyreal dews, have I beheld
Opening its bosom to the suns! or rather
One of these suns making the rose its heaven;
And in a moment's space,
(O marvels most sublime!)
With deluges of light,
And in a lily's form,
Rise from that lovely virgin bosom blest!
Can suns be lilies then,
And lilies children of the maiden rose?

GOD THE FATHER.

The heavens too lofty, and too low the world;
Suffice it that in vain
Man's humble intellect
Attempts to sound the depth of deeds divine;
Press in the fond embraces of thy heart
The consort of thy bosom,
And let her name be Eve.

ADAM. O my beloved companion,
Support of my existence,
My glory and my power,
Flesh of my flesh, and of my bone the bone,
Behold I clasp thy bosom
In plenitude of pure and hallow'd love.

GOD THE FATHER.

I leave you now, my children; rest in peace,
Receive my blessing, and so fruitful prove
That for your offspring earth may scarce suffice!
Man, be thou lord of all that now the sun
Warms or the ocean laves; impose a name
On every thing that flies, or runs, or swims.
Now through the ear descending to your soul
Receive the immutable decree; hear, Adam,
Let thy companion hear, and in your hearts,
Made the abode of love,
Cherish the mighty world!
Of fruits whatever from a spreading branch
Each copious tree may offer to your hands,
Of dainty viands whatsoe'er abound
In this delightful garden,
This paradise of flowers

The gay delight of man,
The treasure of the earth,
The wonder of the world, the work of God,
These, O my son, these thou art free to taste
But of the tree comprising good and evil,
Under the pain of dying
To him who knows not death,
Be now the fruit forbidden!
I leave ye now, and through my airy road,
Departing from the world, return to heaven.

THE SERAPHIM SING.

Let every airy cloud on earth descend,
And luminous and light
Repose with God upon this glowing sphere!
Then let the stars descend,
Descend the moon and sun,
Forming bright steps to the empyreal world,
And each rejoice that the supreme Creator
Has deign'd to visit what his hand produced.

ADAM. O scene of splendour, viewing which I see
The glories of my God in lovelier light,
How through my eyes do you console my heart!
See, at a single nod of our great Sire
(Dear partner of my life),
Fire bursting forth with elemental power!
The sea, heaven, earth, their properties assume,
And air grows air, although there were before
Nor fire, nor heaven, nor air, nor earth, nor sea.
Behold the azure sky, in which ofttimes
The lovely glittering star
Shall wake the dawn, attired in heavenly light,
The herald of the morn,
To spread the boundless lustre of the day;
Then shall the radiant sun,
To gladden all the world,
Diffuse abroad his energy of light;
And when his eye is weary of the earth,
The pure and silvery moon
And the minuter stars
Shall form the pomp of night.
Behold where fire o'er every element,
Lucid and light, assumes its lofty seat!
Behold the simple field of spotless air
Made the support of variegated birds,
That with their tuneful notes
Guide the delightful hours!
See the great bosom of the fertile earth
With flowers embellish'd and with fruits mature!
See on her verdant brow she seems to bear

Hills as her crown, and as her sceptre trees!
Behold the ocean's fair cerulean plain,
That 'midst its humid sands and vales profound,
And 'midst its silent and its scaly tribes,
Rolls over buried gold and precious pearl,
And crimson coral raising to the sky
Its wavy head, with herbs and amber crown'd!
Stupendous all proclaim
Their Maker's power and glory.
EVE. All manifest thy might,
O Architect divine!
ADAM. Dear partner, let us go
Where to invite our step
God's other wonders shine, a countless tribe.

SCENE THE SECOND.

LUCIFER. Who from my dark abyss
Calls me to gaze on this excess of light?
What miracles unseen
Show'st thou to me, O God?
Art thou then tired of residence in heaven?
Why hast thou form'd on earth
This lovely paradise?
And wherefore place in it
Two earthly demi-gods of human mould?
Say thou vile Architect,
Forming thy work of dust,
What will befall this naked helpless man,
The sole inhabitant of glens and woods?
Does he then dream of treading on the stars?
Heaven is impoverish'd, and I, alone
The cause, enjoy the ruin I produced.
Let him unite above
Star upon star, moon, sun,
And let his Godhead toil
To re-adorn and re-illume his heaven!
Since in the end derision
Shall prove his works, and all his efforts, vain:
For Lucifer alone was that full light
Which scatter'd radiance o'er the plains of heaven.
But these his present fires are shade and smoke,
Base counterfeits of my more potent beams.
I reck not what he means to make his heaven,
Nor care I what his creature man may be.
Too obstinate and firm
Is my undaunted thought,
In proving that I am implacable
'Gainst heaven, 'gainst man, the angels, and their God.

SCENE THE THIRD.

SATAN, BEELZEBUB, *and* LUCIFER.

SATAN. To light, to light raise the embattled brows,
A symbol of the firm and generous heart
That ardent dwells in the unconquer'd breast!
Must we then suffer such excessive wrong?
And shall we not with hands, thus talon-arm'd,
Tear out the stars from their celestial seat;
And, as our sign of conquest,
Down in our dark abyss
Shall we not force the sun and moon to blaze,
Since we are those, who in dread feats of arms
Warring amongst the stars,
Made the bright face of heaven turn pale with fear?
To arms! to arms! redoubted Beelzebub!
Ere yet 'tis heard around,
To our great wrong and memorable shame,
That by the race of man (mean child of clay)
The stars expect a new sublimity.
BEELZEBUB. I burn with such fierce flame,
Such stormy venom deluges my soul,
That with intestine rage
My groans like thunder sound, my looks are lightning,
And my extorted tears are fiery showers!
'Tis needful therefore from my brow to shake
The hissing serpents that o'ershade my visage,
To gaze upon these mighty works of heaven,
And the new demi-gods.
Silent be he, who thinks
(Now that this man is form'd)
To imitate his voice and thus exclaim,
Distressful Satan, ye unhappy spirits,
How wretched is your lot, from being first,
Fallen and degenerate, lost as ye are,
Heaven was your station once, your seat the stars,
And your great Maker God!
Now abject wretches, having lost for ever,
Eternal morn and each celestial light,
Heaven calls you now the denizens of woe.
Instead of moving in the solar road,
You press the plains of everlasting night;
And for your golden tresses
And looks angelical,
Your locks are snaky, and your glance malign,
Your burning lips a murky vapour breathe,
And every tongue now teems with blasphemy;
And all blaspheming raise
A cloud sulphureous of foam and fire;

Arm'd with the eagle's talon, feet of goat,
And dragon's wing, your residence in fire,
Profoundest Tartarus unblest and dark,
The theatre of anguish,
That shuts itself against the beams of day!
Since the dread angel, born to brook no law,
To desolate the sky,
And raise the powers of hell,
Ought to breathe sanguine fire, and on his brow
Display the ensign of sublimest horror.

SATAN. Though arm'd with talons keen, and eagle beak,
Snaky our tresses, and our aspect fierce,
Cloven our feet, our frames with horror plumed,
And though our deep abode
Be fix'd in shadowy scenes of darkest night,
Let us be angels still in dignity;
As far surpassing others as the Lord
Of highest power, his low and humble slaves.
If far from heaven our pennons we expand,
Let us remember still
That we alone are lords, and they are slaves,
And that resigning meaner seats in heaven,
We in their stead have raised a royal throne
Immense and massy, where the mighty chief
Of all our legions higher lifts his brow
Than the proud mountain that upholds your heaven;
And there with heaven still waging endless war,
Threatening the stars, our adversaries ever,
Bears a dread sceptre kindling into flame,
That, while he wheels it round, darts forth a blaze
More dazzling than the sun's meridian ray.

LUCIFER. 'Tis time to show my power, my brave compeers,
Magnanimous and mighty;
Angels endow'd with martial potency,
I know the grief that gives you living death,
Is to see man exalted
To stations so sublime,
That all created things to him submit;
Since ye already doubt,
That to those lofty seats of flaming glory
(Our treasure once and pride, but now renounced)
This pair shall one day rise,
With all the numerous train
Of their posterity.

SATAN. Great Lord of the infernal deep abyss,
To thee I bow, and speak
The anguish of my soul,
That for this man grows hourly more severe,
Fearing the Incarnation of the Word.

LUCIFER. Can it be true, that from so litte dust
A deity shall rise!
That flesh, that deity, that lofty power,
That chains us to the deep?
To this vile clod of earth,
He who himself yet claims to be adored?
Shall angels then do homage thus to men?
And can then flesh impure
Give to angelic nature higher powers?
Can it be true, and to devise the mode
Escape our intellect, ours who so dear
Have bought the boast of wisdom?
I yet am He, I am,
Who would not suffer, that above in heaven,
Your lofty nature should submit to outrage,
When that insensate wish
Possess'd the tyrant of the starry throne,
That you should prostrate fall,
Before the Incarnate Word:
I am that Spirit, I, who for your sake
Collecting dauntless courage, to the north
Led you far distant from the senseless will
Of him who boasts to have created heaven.
And ye are those, your ardour speaks you well,
And your bold hearts, that o'er the host of heaven
Gave me assurance of proud victory.
Arise! let glory's flame
Blaze in your breast; nor be it ever heard,
That him whom ye disdain
To worship in the sky,
Ye stoop to worship in the depth of hell!
Such were your oaths to me,
By your inestimable worth in arms,
Your worth, alas, so great
That heaven itself deserved not to enjoy it.
Oh, 'twere an outrage and a shame too great
Were we not ready to revenge it all!
I see already, flaming in your looks,
The matchless valour of your ardent hearts;
Already see your pinions spread in air,
To overwhelm the world and highest heaven,
That, all creation sunk in the abyss,
This mortal may be found
Instantly crush'd, and buried in his birth.
SATAN. At length pronounce thy orders!
Say what thou wilt, and with a hundred tongues
Speak, speak! that instant in a hundred works
Satan may toil, and hell strain all her powers. [way
LUCIFER. Behold, to smooth the rough and arduous
By which they deem'd they may ascend to glory,

Behold a God assumes
A human form in vain!
A mode too prompt and easy,
To crush the race of mortals,
The ancient God affords to new-born man.
Nature herself too much inclines, or rather
Forces this creature, to support his life,
Frequent to feed on various viands; hence,
Since on delicious dainties
His bitter fall depends,
He may be tempted now to fruit forbidden,
And by the paths of death,
As he was nothing once, return to nothing.

BEELZEBUB. Great Angel! greatly thought!

LUCIFER. Rather the noble spirit
Of higher towering thought prompts me to speak,
That God perchance indignant that his hands
Have stoop'd to stain themselves in abject clay,
Seeing how different angel is from man,
Repenting of his work,
Forbad him to support his frail existence
Upon this sweet allurement; hence to sin
Prompted by natural motives, though tyrannic,
He should himself the earth's destroyer prove,
Converting his vile clay to dust again;
And plucking up again
The rooted world, thus to the highest heaven
Open a faithful passage,
Repenting of his wrong to us of old
Its ornaments sublime!

SATAN. Pardon, O pardon, if my humble thought,
Aspiring by my tongue
Too high, perhaps offend your sovereign ear!
Long as this man shall rest
Alive, and breathe on earth,
Exhausted we must bear
Fierce war, in endless terror of the Word.

LUCIFER. Man yet shall rest alive, he yet shall breathe,
And sinning even to death,
This new-made race of mortals
Shall cover all the earth,
And reign o'er all its creatures;
His soul shall prove eternal,
The image of his God.
Yet shall the Incarnate Word, I trust, be foil'd.

BEELZEBUB. Oh! precious tidings to angelic ears,
That heal the wounds of all our shatter'd host.

LUCIFER. Let man exist to sin, since he by sinning
Shall make the weight of sin his heritage,

Which shall be in his race
Proclaim'd original;
So that mankind existing but to sin,
And sinning still to death,
And still to error born,
In evil hour the Word
Will wear the sinner's form, if rightly deem'd
The enemy of sin.
Now rise, ye Spirits, from the dark abyss,
You who would rest assured
That man the sinner is now doom'd to death.

SCENE THE FOURTH.

MELECANO, LURCONE, LUCIFER, SATAN, BEELZEBUB.

MELECANO. Command us, mighty Lord; what are thy wishes?
Wouldst thou extinguish the new-risen sun?
Behold what stores I bring
Of darkness and of fire!
Alas! with fury Melecano burns.

LURCONE. Behold Lurcone, thou supreme of hell,
Who 'gainst the highest heaven
Pants to direct his rage, whence light of limb,
Though loaded deep with wrath,
He stands with threatening aspect in thy presence.

LUCIFER. Thou, Melecan, assume the name of Pride;
Lurcone, thou of Envy, both united
(Since power combined with power
Acquires new force) to man direct your way:
Nor him alone essay; it is my will
That woman also mourn;
Contrive that she may murmur at her God,
Because in birth not prior to the man;
Since every future man is now ordain'd
To draw his life from woman, with such thoughts
Let her wax envious, that she cannot soar
Above the man, as high as now below him.
Hence, Lurcon, be it thine to make her proud;
Let her give law to her Creator God,
Wishing o'er man priority of birth.

MELECANO. Behold, where Melecan, a dog in fierceness,
The savage dog of hell,
Darts growling to his prey!
He flies, and he returns
All cover'd and all drench'd with human gore.

LURCONE. I rapid too depart,
And, on a swifter wing
Than through the cloudless air
Darts the keen eagle to his earthly prey.
Behold, I too return;
My beak with carnage fill'd, and talons full.
LUCIFER. Haste, Arfarat and Ruspican, rise all,
Rise from the centre to survey the earth!

SCENE THE FIFTH.

RUSPICAN, ARFARAT, LUCIFER, SATAN, BEELZEBUB.

RUSPICAN. Soon as I heard the name of Ruspican,
With rapid pinions spread, I sought the skies,
To bend before the great Tartarean chief,
And aggravate the woes
Of this new mortal, blest with air and light.
ARFARAT. Scarce had thy mighty voice
Re-echoed through the deep,
When the Tartarean fires
Flying I left for this serener sky,
Forth from my lips, and heart,
Breathing fierce rancour 'gainst the life of man.
LUCIFER. Fly, Ruspican, with all your force and fury!
Since now I call thee by the name of Anger;
Find Eve, and tell her that the fair endowment
Of her free will, deserves not she should live
In vassalage to man;
That she alone in value far exceeds
All that the sun in his bright circle warms;
That she from flesh, man from the meaner dust,
Arose to life—in the fair garden she
Created pure, he in the baser field.
RUSPICAN. I joy to change the name of Ruspican
For Anger, dark and deadly:
Hence now, by my tremendous aid, destructive
And deadly be this day!
Behold I go with all my force and fury;
Behold I now transfuse
My anger all into the breast of woman!
LUCIFER. Of Avarice I give,
O Arfarat, to thee the name and works;
Go, see, contend, and conquer!
Contrive that wandering Eve,
With down-cast eyes, may in the fruitful garden
Search with solicitude for hidden treasure:
Then stimulate her heart

To wish no other Lord,
Except herself, of Eden and the world.
ARFARAT. See me already plumed
With wings of gems and gold;
See with an eye of sapphire
I gaze upon the fair;
Behold, to her I speak,
With lips that emulate the ruby's lustre.
Receive now as thy own
(Thus I accost her) all the world's vast wealth!
If she reject my gift,
Then will I tempt her with a shower of pearls,
A fashion yet unknown;
Thus will she melt, and thus I hope at last
In chains of gold to drag her to destruction.
LUCIFER. Rise Guliar, Dulciato, and Maltia!
To make the band of enemies complete,
That, like a deadly hydra,
Shall dart against this man
Your seven crests portentous and terrific.

SCENE THE SIXTH.

MALTIA, DULCIATO, GULIAR, LUCIFER, SATAN, BEELZEBUB.

BEHOLD! we come with emulation fierce
To your severe command:
In prompt obedience let us rise to heaven;
Let us with wrath assail
This human enemy of abject clay.
LUCIFER. Maltia, thou shalt take the name of Sloth:
Sudden invest thyself with drowsy charms
And mischievous repose;
Now wait on Eve, in slothfulness absorb'd,
Let all this pomp of flowers,
And all these tuneful birds,
Be held by her in scorn;
And from her consort flying,
Now let her feel no wishes but for death.
MALTIA. What shall I say? shall I, to others mute,
Announce to thee my sanguinary works;
Savage and silent, I
Would be loquacious in my deeds alone.
LUCIFER. Thee, Dulciato, we name Luxury;
Haste thou to Eve, and fill her with desires
To decorate her fragile form with flowers,
To bind her tresses with a golden fillet,

With various vain devices to allure
A new-found paramour;
And to her heart suggest,
That to exchange her love may prove delightful.
DULCIATO. Can Lord so mighty, from his humble slave
Demand no higher task?
The way to purchase honour
Now will I teach all hell,
By the completion of my glorious triumph.
Already Eve beside a crystal fount
Exults to vanquish the vermilion rose
With cheeks of sweeter bloom,
And to exceed the lily
By her yet whiter bosom;
Now beauteous threads of gold
She thinks her tresses floating in the air;
Now amorous and charming,
Her radiant eyes she reckons suns of love,
Fit to inflame the very coldest heart.
LUCIFER. Guliar, be thou call'd Gluttony; now go,
Reveal to Eve that the forbidden fruit
Is manna all within,
And that such food in heaven
Forms the repast of angels and of God.
GULIAR. Of all the powerful foes
Leagued against man, Guliar is only he
Who can induce him to oppose his Maker;
Hence rapidly I fly
To work the woe of mortals.
SATAN. To arms, to arms! to ruin and to blood!
Yes, now to blood, infernal leeches all!
Again, again proclaiming war to heaven;
And let us put to flight
Every audacious foe
That ventures to disturb our ancient peace.
BEELZEBUB. Now, now, great chief, with feet
That testify thy triumph,
I see thee crush the sun,
The moon, and all the stars;
For where thy radiance shines,
O Lucifer! all other beams are blind.
LUCIFER. Away. Heaven shudders at the mighty ruin
That threatens it from our infernal host;
Already I behold the moon opaque,
And light-supplying sun,
The wandering stars, and fix'd,
With terror pale, and sinking in eclipse.

ACT II.

SCENE THE FIRST.

CHORUS OF ANGELS SINGING.

Now let us garlands weave
Of all the fairest flowers,
Now at this early dawn,
For new-made man, and his companion dear;
Let all with festive joy,
And with melodious song,
Of the great Architect
Applaud this noblest work,
And speak the joyous sound,
Man is the wonder both of earth and heaven.

FIRST ANGEL.

Your warbling now suspend,
You pure angelic progeny of God,
Behold the labour emulous of heaven!
Behold the woody scene
Deck'd with a thousand flowers of grace divine;
Here man resides, here ought he to enjoy
In his fair mate eternity of bliss.

SECOND ANGEL.

How exquisitely sweet
This rich display of flowers,
This airy wild of fragrance,
So lovely to the eye,
And to the sense so sweet.

THIRD ANGEL.

O the sublime Creator,
How marvellous his works, and more his power!
Such is the sacred flame
Of his celestial love,
Not able to confine it in himself,
He breathed, as fruitful sparks
From his creative breast,
The angels, heaven, man, woman, and the world.

FOURTH ANGEL.

Yes, mighty Lord! yes, hallow'd Love divine!
Who, ever in thyself completely blest,
Unconscious of a want,
Who from thyself alone, and at thy will,
Bright with benignant flames,
Without the aid of matter or of form,

By efficacious power
Hast of mere nothing form'd
The whole angelic host;
With potency endow'd,
And that momentous gift,
Either by sin to fall,
Or by volition stand.

FIFTH ANGEL.

Hence, our Almighty Maker,
To render us more worthy of his heaven,
And to confirm us in eternal grace,
Presented to our homage
The pure Incarnate Word;
That as a recompense for hallow'd toil
So worthily achieved,
We might adore him humble;
For there's a written law
In the records of heaven,
That not a work of God that breathes and lives,
And is endow'd with reason,
Shall hold a seat in heaven,
If it incline not first, with holy zeal,
In tender adoration to the Word.

SIXTH ANGEL.

Justly each spirit in the realms above,
And all of mortal race,
And every foe to heaven,
Should bow the knee in reverence of the Word;
Since this is he whom from eternity
God in the awful depth
Of his sublime and fruitful mind produced;
He is not accident, but substance true,
As rare as perfect, and as truly great
As his high Author holy and divine.

SEVENTH ANGEL.

This living Word, image express of God,
Is a resemblance of his mighty substance;
Whence he is call'd the Son, the Son of God,
Even as the Father, God;
The generated Word
By generation yields not unto time,
Since from eternity the eternal Father
Produced this Son, whence he rejoices there,
Great offspring of great Father there for ever
For ever he is born;
There he is fed, and foster'd
With plenitude of grace
Imparted by his Sire:

There was the Father ever, and the Son
Was ever at his side, or in the Father;
Nor younger is the Son
Than his Almighty Sire,
Nor elder is the Father
Than his eternal Son.

EIGHTH ANGEL.

O Son, O Sire, O God, O Man, O Word,
Let all, with bended knee,
With humble adoration reverence you!

NINTH ANGEL.

O Lucifer, now doom'd to endless pain,
Hadst thou been join'd with us
In worship of the Word,
How hadst thou now been blessed in thy God!
But thou in pride alone, yes, thou alone
In thy great wisdom foolish,
Hast scorn'd the Paragon,
And would'st not reverence the Incarnate God;
Whence by thy folly thou hast fallen as far
As thy proud soul expected to ascend.

TENTH ANGEL.

Monster of fierceness, dwell
In thy obscure recess;
And for thy weighty crime
Incessant feel and infinite thy pain,
For infinite has been thy vast offence.

ELEVENTH ANGEL.

Reside for ever in the deep abyss;
For well the world's eternal Master knows
Again to fill those high celestial seats,
That by your ruin you have vacant left;
Behold man fashion'd from the earth, who lives,
Like plants that vegetate;
See in a moment's space
How the pure breath of life,
Breathed on his visage by the power divine,
Endows the wondrous creature with a soul,
A pure immortal soul,
That graced, and lovely with exalted powers,
Shines the great faithful image of its God.
Behold, it has the gift to merit highly,
The option to deserve or heaven or hell,
In free-will perfect, as the first of angels.

TWELFTH ANGEL.

Yes, man alone was form'd in just derision
Of all the infernal host.

As lord of this frail world and all that lives,
The ornament of all,
The miracle of nature,
The perfect heir of heaven,
Related to the angels,
Adopted son of God,
And semblance of the Holy Trinity;
What could'st thou hope for more, what more attain,
Creature miraculous,
In whom the eternal Lord
Has now vouchsafed to signalize his power?

THIRTEENTH ANGEL.

How singular and worthy is his form,
Upright in stature, meek in dignity;
Well fashion'd are his limbs, and his complexion
Well temper'd, with a high majestic brow,
A brow turn'd upward to his native sky;
In language eloquent, in thought sublime,
For contemplation of his Maker form'd.

FOURTEENTH ANGEL.

Placed in a state of innocence is man;
Primeval justice is his blessed gift;
Hence are his senses to his reason subject,
His body to his mind,
Enjoying reason as his prime endowment,

FIFTEENTH ANGEL.

Supernal love held him too highly dear,
To let him dwell alone:
And thence of lovely woman
(Fair faithful aid) bestow'd on man the gift.
Adam, 'tis thine alone
To keep thy duty to thy Lord unstain'd;
In his command of the forbidden fruit,
Thy gift of freedom keep inviolate;
Since he who fashion'd thee, without thy aid,
Think not without thy aid he means to save thee!
But since, descending from the heights of heaven,
We come as kind attendants upon man,
Now let us haste to Eden's flowery banks.

ALL THE ANGELS SING.

Now take we happy flight
To Paradise, adorn'd with fairest flowers;
There let us almost worship
The mighty lord of this transcendent world,
And joyous let us sing
This flowery heaven, and Adam as its god.

SCENE THE SECOND.

ADAM. O mighty Lord of mighty things sublime
O my supreme Creator!
O bounteous in thy love
To me thy humble servant! such rare blessings
With liberal hand thou givest;
Where'er I turn my eyes,
I see myself revered.
Approach ye animals that range the field!
And ye now close your variegated wings,
Ye pleasing birds! in me you look on Adam,
On him ordain'd to name
All things that gracious God has made for man;
And praise, with justic. praise
Him who created me, who made you all,
And in his bounteous love with me rejoice.
But what do I behold? blest that I am,
My dear, my sweet companion!
Who comes to hail me with a gift of flowers,
And with these sylvan honours crown my brow.
Go, stately lion, go! and thou with scales
Impenetrable arm'd
Rhinoceros, whose pride can strike to earth
The unconquer'd elephant!
Thou fiery courser bound along the fields,
And with thy neighing shake the echoing vale;
Thou camel, and all here, or beast or bird,
Retire, in homage to approaching Eve!
EVE. O what delight more dear,
Than that which Adam in my sight enjoys,
Draws him far off from me? Ye tender flowers,
Where may I find on you
The traces of his step?
LURCONE. See man and woman! hide thyself and watch!
ADAM. No more fatigue my eyes,
Nor with thy animated glances dart,
Such radiant lightning round;
Turn the clear heaven of thy serener face,
To him who loves its light;
See thy beloved Adam,
Behold him, my sweet love:
O thou, who art alone
Joy of the world, and dear delight of man!
LURCONE. Dread the approach of evil!
GULIAR. Dread the deceit of hell!
EVE. By sovereign content
I feel my tongue enchain'd;
But though my voice be mute,

My countenance may seem more eloquent,
Expressing, though in silence, all my joy.
ADAM. O my companion dear!
LURCONE. And soon perchance thy foe!
ADAM. O thou my sweetest life!
GULIAR. Perchance thy bitter death!
EVE. Take, gentle Adam, from my hand these flowers;
With these, my gift, let me entwine thy locks.
ADAM. Ye lilies and ye shrubs of snowy hue,
Jasmine as ivory pure,
Ye spotless graces of the shining field;
And thou most lovely rose
Of tint most delicate,
Fair consort of the morn,
Delighted to imbibe
The genial dew of heaven,
Rich vegetation's vermil-tinctured gem,
April's enchanting herald,
Thou flower supremely blest,
And queen of all the flowers,
Thou form'st around my locks
A garland of such fragrance,
That up to heaven itself
Thy balmy sweets ascend.
Let us in pure embraces
So twine ourselves, my love,
That we may seem united,
One well-compact and intricate acanthus.
LURCONE. Soon shall the fetters of infernal toil
So spread around ye both
The indissoluble bond,
No mortal effort shall have power to break!
EVE. Now, that with flowers so lovely
We have adorn'd our tresses,
Here let us both with humble reverence kneel,
And praise our mighty Maker.
From this my thirsting heart
No longer can refrain.
ADAM. At thy engaging words,
And thy pure heart's desire,
On these pure herbs and flowers
I bend my willing knee in hallow'd bliss.
LURCONE. Away! far off must I
From act so meekly just
Furious depart, and leave the light of day.
GULIAR. I must partake thy flight,
And follow thee, alas! surcharged with grief.
ADAM. Now that these herbs and flowers to our
Such easy rest afford, [bent knees

Let us with zealous ardour raise our eyes,
Contemplating with praise our mighty Maker!
First then, devout and favour'd Eve, do thou
With sacred notes invite
To deeds so fair thy Adam.
EVE. My Lord Omnipotent,
In his celestial essence
Is first, supreme, unlimited, alone,
Eternal, uncompounded,
He no beginning had, no end will have.
ADAM. My sovereign Lord, so great,
Is irresistible, terrific, just,
Gracious, benign, indulgent,
Divine, unspotted, holy, loving, good,
In justice most revered,
Ancient of days, in his sublimest court.
EVE. He rests in highest heaven,
Yet more exalted in his boundless self;
Thence his all-searching eye looks down on all;
Nought is from him conceal'd
Since all exists in him:
Without him nothing could retain existence,
Nor is there aught that he
For his perfection needs,
Except himself alone.
ADAM. He every place pervades,
But is confined in none;
In him the limits of all grandeur lie,
But he exists unlimited by space.
EVE. Above the universe himself he raised,
Yet he behind it rests;
The whole he now encircles, now pervades,
Now dwells apart from all,
So great, the universe
To comprehend him fails.
ADAM. If he to all inclines,
In his just balance all he justly weighs;
From him if all things flow,
All things in him acknowledge their support,
But he on nothing rests.
EVE. To time my great director is not subject,
For time in him sees no vicissitude:
In awful and sublime eternity
One being stands for ever;
For ever stands one instant,
And hence this power assumes the name of God.
ADAM. It is indeed a truth,
That my eternal mighty Lord is God;
This deity incomprehensible
That, ere the heaven was made,

Dwelt only in himself, and heaven in him.
Eve, let us joyous rise; in other scenes,
With admiration of celestial splendour
And of this lovely world,
With notes of hallow'd bliss
Let us again make the glad air resound.
EVE. Lead on, my faithful guide;
Quick is my willing foot to follow thee,
Since my fond soul believes
That I in praising heaven to heaven ascend;
So my pure bosom feels
Full of divine content.
ADAM. To speak on every theme
Our mighty Maker made thee eloquent,
So that in praising heaven thou seemest there.
My fair associate! treasure of my life!
Upon the wings of this exalted praise
Devotion soars so high, that if her feet
Rest on the earth, her spirit reaches heaven.

SCENE THE THIRD.

The SERPENT, SATAN, SPIRITS.

SERPENT. To arms, to battle, O ye sons of power!
Ye warring spirits of the infernal field!
A new and wondrous war
Awaits you now, within the lists of earth;
Most strange indeed the mode
Of warring there, if triumph, war's great end,
Proves its beginning now.
Behold the sun himself turn pale with terror,
Behold the day obscured!
Behold each rapid bird directs his flight
Where thickest foliage spreads,
But shelter seeks in vain;
The leaves of every bough,
As with a palsy struck,
Affright him more, and urge his wings to flight.
I would not as a warrior take the field
Against the demi-goddess girt with angels,
Since she has now been used
To gaze on spirits tender and benign,
Not such as I, of semblance rough and fierce,
For battles born to subjugate the sky.
In human form I would not
Defy her to a great important conflict,
The world she knows contains one only man.

Nor would I of the tiger
Or the imperious lion
Or other animal assume the shape;
For well she knows they could not reason with her,
Who are of reason void.
To make her knowledge vain,
That I exist to the eternal Maker
A source of endless fear,
Wrapt in the painted serpent's scaly folds,
Part of myself I hide, giving the rest
A human semblance and a damsel's face.
Great things I tell thee, and behold I see
My adversary prompt to parley with me.
Of novelty to hear
How eager woman is!
Now, now I lose my tongue,
And shall entangle her in many a snare.
SATAN. But what discordant sound
Rises from hell, where all was lately concord?
Why do hoarse trumpets bellow through the deep?

SCENE THE FOURTH.

VOLAN, *the* SERPENT, SPIRITS, SATAN.

VOLAN. Great lord, ordain'd to found infernal realms,
And look with scorn upon the pomp of heaven,
Behold thy Volan fly
To pay his homage at thy scaly feet!
The chieftains of Avernus,
The prime infernal powers
To rise in rivalship
Of heaven in all, as in that lofty seat,
(The Word to us reveal'd,
The source of such great strife)
They wish, that on the earth
A goddess should prepare a throne for man,
And lead him to contemn
His own Almighty Maker:
Yet more the inhabitants of fire now wish
That having conquer'd man,
And with such triumph gay,
To the great realms of deep and endless flames
Ye both with exultation may descend:
Then shall I see around
Hell dart its rays, and hold the sun in scorn.
But if this man resist,

Then losing every hope
Of farther victory,
They wish that on the throne
Of triumph he may as a victor sit,
Who teaches it to move,
And thou perform the office
With an afflicted partner,
With him, who labours to conduct the car;
That cloth'd in horrid pomp
The region of Avernus
May speak itself the seat of endless pain,
And, at the sound of inauspicious trumpets,
The heavens may shake, the universe re-echo.

SCENE THE FIFTH.

VAIN GLORY *drawn by a Giant*, VOLAN, *the* SERPENT, SATAN *and* SPIRITS.

VAIN GLORY. King of Avernus, at this harp's glad sound
I weave a starry garland for thy locks,
For well I see thy lovely scales portend
Honour to me, ruin and shame to man.
I am Vain Glory, and I sit on high,
Exulting Victress of the mighty Giant:
He has his front in heaven, on earth his feet,
A faithful image of man's mighty worth:
But shake not thou with fear! strong as he is,
So brittle is the crown of glass he wears
That at my breath, which drives him fiercely on,
Man loses power, and falls a prey to death.

SERPENT. Angel, or Goddess, from thy lofty triumph
Descend with me at the desire of hell!
Haste to a human conflict,
You all so light and quick,
That by your movement not a leaf is shaken
In all these woods around,
Your mighty triumphs now together hide;
Now that in silence we may pass unseen,
Quick let us enter neighbouring paradise.

VAIN GLORY. Wherefore delay? Point out the path we go;
Since prompt to follow thee,
Full as I am of haughtiness and pride,
With expeditious foot
I will advance
Among these herbs and flowers;
And let infernal laurels
Circle thy towering crest and circle mine!

SERPENT. What tribes of beauteous flowers,
And plants now new and vivid!
How desolate shall I
Soon make these verdant scenes of plant and flower!
Behold! how with my foot
I now as much depress them,
As they shoot forth with pride to rear their heads.
Behold! their humid life
I wither with my step of blasting fire.
How I enjoy, as I advance through these
Fair bowers of rapid growth,
To poison with my breath the leaf and flower,
Embittering all these sweet and blooming fruits.
We are arrived; behold the lovely tree
Prohibited by heaven;
There mount, and be embower'd
In the thick foliage of a wood so fair!
VAIN GLORY. See, I prepare to climb:
I am already high,
And in the leaves conceal'd.
Climb thou, great chief, and rapidly encircle,
And with thy scaly serpent train ascend
The tree; be quick, since now arising higher
I can discern where lonely Eve advances.
SERPENT. Behold, enraged I twine around the trunk
With these my painted and empoison'd folds;
Behold, I breathe towards this woman, love,
Though hate is in my heart:
Behold me now; more beautiful than ever,
Though now of each pestiferous cruel monster,
In poison and in rage, I am the model;
Now I behold her, now
In silence I conceal my gift of speech,
Among these leaves embower'd.

SCENE THE SIXTH.

EVE, SERPENT, *and* VAIN GLORY.

EVE. I ought, the servant of a mighty Lord,
A servant low and humble,
With reverential knee bending to earth,
I ought to praise the boundless love of him,
Since he has made me queen
Of all the sun delights to view on earth.
But if to heaven I raise my eyes and heart,
Clearly can Eve not see
She was created for these great, eternal,
Celestial miracles?

So that in spirit or in mortal frame,
She ever must enjoy or earth or heaven.
Hence this fair flowering tree
Wreathing abroad its widely branching arms,
As if desirous to contend with heaven,
Seems willing in my locks
To spread a shining heaven of verdant leaves:
And if I pass among the herbs and flowers,
Those, I behold, that by my step are press'
Arise more beautiful; the very buds
Expand, to form festoons
To decorate the grassy scene around.
Other new flowers with freshest beauty fair,
That stand from me sequester'd,
Form'd into groups or scatter'd in the vale,
Seem with delight to view me, and to say,
The neighbouring flowers rejoice
To give thy foot support,
But we, aspiring eagles,
From far behold thy visage,
Mild portraiture of the almighty form;
While other plants and flowers,
Wishing that I may form my seat among them.
Above their native growth
So seem to raise themselves, that of sweet flowers
A fragrant hedge they form;
And others in a thousand tender ties,
Form on the ground so intricate a snare,
That the incautious hand which aims to free
The captive foot, must be itself ensnared.
If food I wish, or draught,
Lo! various fruit, lo! honey, milk, and manna;
Behold from many a fount and many a rill,
The crystal beauty of the cooling stream!
If melody, behold the tuneful birds,
Behold angelic bands!
If welcome day,
Or mild and wish'd for night,
Behold the sun, behold the moon and stars!
If I a friend require,
Adam, sweet friend, replies;
And if my God in heaven, the Eternal Maker
Dwells not unmindful, but regards my speech.
If creatures subject to my will I wish,
Lo! at my side all subject to my will.
What more can I desire, what more obtain?
Now nothing more, my Sovereign;
Eve is with honour loaded.
But what's before me? do I wake or dream?
Among these boughs I see

A human visage fair; what! are there then
More than myself and Adam,
Who view the glorious sun?
O marvellous, though I am distant far,
I yet discern the truth; with arms, with hands,
A human breast it has,
The rest is serpent all;
O, how the sun, emblazing with his rays
These gorgeous scales, with glowing colours bright,
O'erwhelms my dazzled eyes!
I would approach it.
SERPENT. Now, then, at length you see
I have precisely ta'en the semblance fit,
To overcome this woman.
EVE. The nearer I approach, more and more lovely
His semblance seems of emerald and sapphire,
Now ruby and now amethyst, and now
Of jasper, pearl, and flaming chrysolite,
Each fold it waving forms around the trunk
Of this fair flowering tree!
SERPENT. I will assail my foe.
Come to survey me better,
Thou dazzler of the eye,
Enchantress of the soul,
Soft idol of the heart,
Fair nymph, approach! Lo, I display myself,
Survey me all; now satisfy thine eyes!
View me attentive, paragon of beauty,
Thou noblest ornament of all the world,
Thou lovely pomp of nature,
Thou little paradise,
To whom all things do homage!
Where lonely from thy friend, thy Adam, far
Where art thou? now advancing where
The numerous bands of Angels
Become such fond admirers of thy beauty?
Happy I deem myself, supremely happy,
Since 'tis my blessed lot,
With two fond eyes alone to gaze on that,
Which, with unnumber'd eyes, heaven scarce surveys.
Trust me, if all the loveliness of heaven
Would wrap itself within a human veil,
Nought but thy beauteous bosom
Could form a mansion worthy such a guest.
How well I see, full well,
That she above with thy light agile feet
Imprints her step in heaven, and there she smiles
With thy enchanting lip,
To scatter joy around those blessed spheres;
Yes, with thy lips above,

She breathes, she speaks, she pauses,
And with thine eyes communicates a lustre
To all that's fair in heaven or fair on earth.
EVE. And who art thou, so eager
To lavish praise on me?
Yet never did mine eyes see form like thine.
SERPENT. Can I be silent now?
Too much, too much, I pant
To please the lovely model of all grace.
Know, when the world was fashion'd out of nought,
And this most fruitful garden,
I was ordain'd to dwell a gardener here,
By him who cultivates
The fair celestial fields;
Here joyful I ascend,
To watch that no voracious bird may seize
On such delicious fruit;
Here it is my delight,
Though all be marvellously fair around,
Lily to blend with lily, rose with rose,
And now the fragrant hedge
To form, and now between the groups of flowers,
And o'er the tender herb
To guide the current of the crystal stream.
Oh what sweet scenes to captivate the eye
Of such a lovely virgin,
Will I disclose around!
Thou, if thou canst, return
To this alluring spot,
And ever with fresh myrtle and new flowers
More beauteous thou shalt find it;
This wondrous faculty I boast infused
By thy supernal Maker,
To guard in plant and flower their life and fragrance
EVE. Since I have found thee courteous
No less than wise, reveal to me thy name;
Speak it to me, unless
I seek to know too much.
SERPENT. Wisdom, I name myself,
Sometimes I Life am call'd,
For this my double nature, since I am
One part a serpent and the other human.
EVE. Strange things this day I hear; but tell me [why
Thou serpent art combined with human form?
SERPENT. I will inform thee; when the sovereign [God
On nothing resting, yet gave force to all,
To balance all things in an even scale
The sage of heaven desired,
And not from opposite extremities
To pass without a medium 'ustly founded;

Hence 'tween the brute and man
It pleased him to create this serpent kind;
And even this participates in reason,
And with a human face has human speech.
But what can fail to honour with submission
The demi-god of earth?
Oh! if proportion'd to thy charms, or equal
To the desert of man,
You had high knowledge, doubt not but in all
Ye would be reckon'd as immortal gods;
Since the prime power of lofty science is
One of the first and greatest
Of attributes divine; Oh, could this be,
Descending from the base
Of this engaging plant,
How as a goddess should I here adore thee!

EVE. What, dost thou think so little then the sum
Of knowledge given to man? does he not know
Of every living herb and flower and plant,
Of minerals and of unnumber'd gems,
Of fish, of fowl, and every animal,
In water or on earth, of fire, of air,
Of this fair starry heaven,
And of the moon and sun,
The virtues most conceal'd?

SERPENT. Ah, this is nothing; since it only serves
To make the common things of nature known;
And I, although I am
Greatly inferior in my rank to man,
Yet, one by one, even I can number these.
More worthy it would be
To know both good and ill;
This, this is the supreme
Intelligence, and mysteries most high,
That on the earth would make you like to God.

EVE. That which hath power sufficient to impart
This knowledge so sublime of good and ill
(But mixt with mortal anguish),
Is this forbidden tree, on which thou sittest.

SERPENT. And tell me why a law
So bitter rises from a fruit so sweet?
Where, then, where is the sense
That you so lately boasted as sublime?
Observe, if it be just,
That man so brave, so lovely, man that rules
The world with skilful hand, man that so much
Pleased his creating God, when power almighty
Fashion'd the wonders both of earth and heaven,
That man at last a little fruit should crush,
And all be form'd for nothing, or at best

But for a moment's space?
No, no, far from thee, far be such a doubt!
Let colour to thy cheek, and to thy lip
The banish'd rose return!
Say,—but I know—thy heart
Within thee speaks the language that I speak!
  EVE. The Lord commanded me I should not taste
This fruit; and to obey him is my joy.
  SERPENT. If 'tis forbidden thee
To taste a fruit so fair,
Heaven does not choose that man should be a god.
But thou, with courtesy, to my kind voice
Lend an attentive ear: say, if your Maker
Required such strict obedience, that you might
Depend but on his word to move and guard you;
Was there not power sufficient in the laws
Sublime of hope, of faith, and charity?
Why then, fair creature, why, without occasion,
Thus should he multiply his laws for man,
For ever outraging with such a yoke
Your precious liberty, and of great lords
Making you slaves, nay, in one point inferior
Even to the savage beasts,
Whom he would not reduce to any law?
Who does not know that loading you so much
With precepts, he has lessen'd the great blessing
Of joyous being, that your God first gave you?
Perchance he dreaded that ye soon might grow
His equals both, in knowledge, and be gods?
No, for though like to God you might become
By such experiment, the difference still
Between you must be great, since this your know-[ledge
And acquisition of divinity,
Could be but imitation, and effect
Of the first cause divine that dwells above.
And can it then be true,
That such a vital hand
Can do a deadly deed?
Oh hadst thou tasted this, how would'st thou gain
Advantage of the Lord, how then with him
Would thy conversing tongue
Accuse the latent mysteries of heaven!
Far other flowers, and other plants, and fields,
And elements, and spheres,
Far different suns, and different moons, and stars,
There are above, from those thou viewest here,
Buried below these; all to thee are near,
Observe how near! but at the very distance
This apple is from thee. Extend thy hand,
Boldly extend it,—ah! why dost thou pause?

EVE. What should I do? Who counsels me, O God?
Hope bids me live, and fear at once destroys me.
But say, how art thou able
To know such glorious things exist above,
And that on earth, one thus may equal God,
By feeding on this apple,
If thou in heaven wert never,
And ne'er permitted of the fruit to taste?
SERPENT. Ah! is there ought I can deny to her
Whose happiness I wish? Now listen to me.
When of this garden I was made the keeper,
By him who fashion'd thee,
All he has said to thee, to me he said;
And opening to me heaven's eternal bosom.
With all his infinite celestial pomp,
He satiated my eyes, and then thus spake:
Thy paradise thou hast enjoy'd, O Serpent,
No more thou shalt behold it; now retain
Memory of heaven on earth,
Which thou may'st do by feeding on such fruit.
A heavenly seat alone is fit for man,
For that's the seat of beauty;
Since thou art partly man and partly brute,
'Tis just thou dwell on earth;
The world was made for various beasts to dwell in,
He added, nor canst thou esteem it hard,
Serpent and man, to dwell on earth for ever,
Since thou already in thy human portion
Most fully hast enjoy'd thy bliss above.
Thus I eternal live,
Forming my banquet of this savoury fruit,
And paradise is open to my eyes,
By the intelligence through me transfused
From this delicious viand.
EVE. Alas! what should I do? to whom apply?
My heart, what is thy counsel?
SERPENT. 'Tis true, thy sovereign has imposed upon [thee,
Under the pain of death,
To taste not of this fruit;
And to secure from thee
A dainty so delightful,
The watchful guard he made me
Of this forbidden tree;
So that if I consent, both man and thou,
His beautiful companion,
May rise to equal God in happiness.
'Tis but too true that to participate
In food and beverage with savage beasts,
Gives us in this similitude to them;
It is not just you both,

Works of a mighty Maker,
Great offspring of great God,
Should in a base condition,
Among these groves and woods,
Lead a life equal to the lowest beast.
Eve. Ah! why art thou so eager
That I should taste of this forbidden food?
Serpent. Wouldst thou that I should tell?
Eve. 'Tis all my wish.
Serpent. Now lend thine ear, now arch,
With silent wonder, both thy beauteous brows!
For two proud joys of mine,
Not for thy good alone, I wish to make thee
This liberal overture, and swear to keep
Silence while thou shalt seize the fruit denied.
First to avenge that high unworthy wrong
Done me by God, in fashioning my shape;
For I was deem'd the refuse of his heaven,
For these my scaly parts,
That ever like a snake I trail behind;
And then, because he should to me alone
Have given this world, and o'er the numerous beasts
Have made me lord, not wholly of their kind;
But this my empire mighty and supreme,
O'er all these living things,
While man is doom'd
To breathe on vital air,
Must seem but low and servile vassalage;
Since man, and only man
Was chosen high and mighty lord of all
This wondrous scene, and he thus raised to grandeur
Was newly form'd of nought.
But when the fairest of all Eden's fruits
Is snatch'd and tasted, when you rise to gods,
'Tis just that both ascending from this world
Should reach the higher spheres;
So that on earth to make me
Of every creature lord,
Of human error I my virtue make:
Know, that command is grateful even to God,
Grateful to man, and grateful to the serpent.
Eve. I yield obedience: ah! what is't I do?
Serpent. Rather, what do you not? Ah, boldly taste,
Make me a god on earth, thyself in heaven.
Eve. Alas, how I perceive
A chilling tremour wander through my bones,
That turns my heart to ice!
Serpent. It is thy mortal part that now begins
To languish, as o'ercome by the divine,

Which o'er its lowly partner
In excellence ascends.
Behold the pleasant plant,
More lovely and more rich
Than if it raised to heaven branches of gold,
And bore the beauteous emerald as leaves,
With roots of coral and a trunk of silver
Behold this jewell'd fruit,
That gives enjoyment of a state divine'
How fair it is, and how
It takes new colours from the solar rays
Bright as the splendid train
Of the gay peacock, when he whirls it round
Full in the sun, and lights his thousand eyes!
Behold how it invites!
'Tis all delicious, it is sweetness all
Its charms are not deceitful,
Thine eye can view them well.
Now take it! Now I watch
If any angel spy thee! Dost thou pause?
Up! for once more I am thy guide; at last
The victory is thine!
Eve. At length behold me the exalted mistress
Of this most lovely fruit!
But why, alas, does my cold brow distil
These drops, that overwhelm me?
Serpent. Lovely Virgin,
Will not our reason tell us
Supreme felicity is bought with pain?
Who from my brow will wipe
These drops of keener pain?
Who dissipate the dread that loads my heart?
Eve. Tell me what would'st thou? tell me who afflicts thee?
Serpent. The terror of thy Lord; and hence I pray thee
That when thou hast enjoy'd
That sweet forbidden fruit,
When both of you become eternal gods,
That you would guard me from the wrath of Heaven;
Since well indeed may he,
Whom we call God, kindle his wrath against me,
Having to you imparted
Taste of this fruit against his high command.
But tell him, my desire
To make me lord of this inferior world,
Like man a god in heaven,
Render'd me mute while Eve attain'd the apple.
Eve. The gift I owe thee, Serpent, well deserves
That I should ne'er forget thee.

SERPENT. Now in these verdant leaves I hide my-
Till thou with sounds of joy [self
Shalt call and re-assure me.
EVE. Now then conceal thyself: I promise thee
To be thy shield against the wrath of God.
O what delicious odour! 'tis so sweet
That I can well believe
That all the lovely flowers
From this derive their fragrance.
These dewy leaves to my conception seem
Moistened with manna, rather than with dew.
Ah, it was surely right
That fruit so exquisite
Should flourish to impart new life to man,
Not waste its sweets upon the wind and sun.
Nothing for any ill
To man could spring from God's creative hand:
Since he for man assuredly has felt
Such warmth of love unbounded, I will taste it.
How sweet it is! how far
Surpassing all the fruits of every kind,
Assembled in this soil!
But where is Adam now? O, Adam! Adam!
He answers not; then thou with speed depart
To find him; but among these flowers and leaves
Conceal this lovely apple, lest the angels,
Descrying it, forbid
Adam to taste its sweets,
And so from man be made a mighty god.
SERPENT. Extinguish in the waves thy rays, O sun
Nor more distribute light!
Thus Lucifer ordains, and thus the apple!
Man, Man is now subdued!
VAIN GLORY. O joyous day! O day
To hell of triumph, and of shame to heaven
Eve has enjoy'd the apple,
And now contrives that man may taste it t:
Now see by direst fate
Life is exchanged for death!
Now I exulting sing,
And hence depart with pride,
Since man's high boast is crush'd,
And his bright day now turn'd to hideous night!

ACT III.

SCENE THE FIRST.

ADAM *and* EVE.

ADAM. OH, my beloved companion!
Oh thou of my existence,
The very heart and soul!
Hast thou, with such excess of tender haste,
With ceaseless pilgrimage,
To find again thy Adam,
Thus solitary wander'd?
Behold him! Speak! what are thy gentle orders?
Why dost thou pause? what ask of God? what dost
thou?
EVE. Adam, my best beloved!
My guardian and my guide!
Thou source of all my comfort, all my joy!
Thee, thee alone I wish,
And in these pleasing shades
Thee only have I sought.
ADAM. Since thou hast call'd thy Adam
(Most beautiful companion!)
The source and happy fountain of thy joy;
Eve, if to walk with me
It now may please thee, I will show thee, love,
A sight thou hast not seen;
A sight so lovely, that in wonder thou
Wilt arch thy graceful brow.
Look thou, my gentle bride, towards that path
Of this so intricate and verdant grove,
Where sit the birds embower'd;
Just there, where now, with soft and snowy plumes,
Two social doves have spread their wings for flight,
Just there, thou shalt behold (oh, pleasing wonder!)
Springing amid the flowers,
A living stream, that with a winding course
Flies rapidly away;
And as it flies, allures
And tempts you to exclaim, Sweet river, stay!
Hence, eager in pursuit
You follow, and the stream, as if it had
Desire to sport with you,
Through many a florid, many a grassy way,
Well known to him, in soft concealment flies:
But when at length he hears
You are afflicted to have lost his sight,
He rears his watery locks, and seems to say,
Gay with a gurgling smile,

'Follow! ah follow still my placid course!
If thou art pleased with me, with thee I sport.'
And thus with sweet deceit he leads you on
To the extremest bound
Of a fair flowery meadow; then at once,
With quick impediment,
Says, 'Stop! Adieu! for now, yes, now I leave you:
Then down a rock descends:
There, as no human foot can follow farther,
The eye alone must follow him, and there,
In little space you see a mass of water,
Collected in a deep and fruitful vale,
With laurel crown'd and olive,
With cypress, oranges, and lofty pines.
The limpid water in the sun's bright ray
A perfect crystal seems;
Hence in its deep recess,
In the translucent wave,
You see a precious glittering sand of gold,
And bright as moving silver,
Innumerable fish;
Here with melodious notes
The snowy swans upon the shining streams
Form their sweet residence;
And seem in warbling to the wind to say,
'Here let those rest who wish for perfect joy!'
So that, my dear companion,
To walk with me will please thee.

EVE. So well thy language to my sight has brought
What thou desir'st to show me,
I see thy flying river as it sports,
And hear it as it murmurs.
And beauteous also is this scene, where now
Pleased we sojourn; and here, perhaps, even here
The lily whitens with the purest lustre,
And the rose reddens with the richest hue.
Here also bathed in dew
Plants of minutest growth
Are painted all with flowers.
Here trees of amplest leaf
Extend their rival shades
And stately rise to heaven.

ADAM. Now by these cooling shades,
The beauty of these plants,
By these delightful meadows,
These variegated flowers,
By the soft music of the rills and birds,
Let us sit down in joy!

EVE. Behold then I am seated!
How I rejoice in viewing not alone

These flowers, these herbs, these high and graceful plants
But Adam, thou, my lover,
Thou, thou art he, by whom the meadows seem
More beautiful to me,
The fruit more blooming, and the streams more clear.
ADAM. The decorated fields
With all their flowery tribute cannot equal
Those lovelier flowers, that with delight I view
In the fair garden of your beauteous face.
Be pacified, you flowers,
My words are not untrue;
You shine besprinkled with ethereal dew,
You give the humble earth to glow with joy
At one bright sparkle of the blazing sun;
But with the falling sun ye also fall:
But these more living flowers
Of my dear beauteous Eve
Seem freshen'd every hour
By soft devotion's dew,
That she with pleasure sheds
Praising her mighty Maker:
And by the rays of two terrestrial suns
In that pure heaven, her face,
They rise, and not to fall,
Decking the paradise
Of an enchanting visage.
EVE. Dear Adam, do not seek
With tuneful eloquence
To soothe my ear by speaking of thy love!
The heart is confident,
That fondly flames with pure and hallow'd ardour.
In sweet exchange accept, my gentle love,
This vermeil-tinctured gift, you know it well;
This is the fruit forbidden,
This is the blessed apple.
ADAM. Alas! what see I? ah! what hast thou done,
Invader of the fruit
Forbidden by thy God?
EVE. It would be long to tell thee
The reason that induced me
To make this fruit my prey; let it suffice
I gain'd thee wings to raise thy flight to heaven.
ADAM. Ne'er be it true, ah never,
That to obtain thy favour,
I prove to heaven rebellious and ungrateful,
And to obey a woman,
So disobey my Maker and my God!
Then did not death denounced
With terror's icy paleness blanch thy cheek?
EVE. And think'st thou, if the apple

Were but the food of death,
The great Producer would have raised it there,
Where being is eternal?
Think'st thou, that if of error
This fruit-tree were the cause,
In man's delighted eye
So fertile and so fair
He would have form'd it flourishing in air?
Ah! were it so, he would indeed have given
A cause of high offence;
Since nature has ordain'd
(A monitress sagacious),
That to support his being, man must eat,
And trust in what looks fair, as just and good.

ADAM. If the celestial tiller,
Who the fair face of heaven
Has thickly sown with stars,
Amidst so many plants fruitful and fair,
Placed the forbidden apple,
The fairest and most sweet,
'Twas to make proof of man,
As a wise keeper of his heavenly law,
And to afford him scope for high desert;
For he alone may gain the name of brave,
Who rules himself and all his own desires.
Man might indeed find some excuse for sin,
If scantily with fruits
This garden were supplied;
But this abounding in so many sweets,
Man ought not to renounce
The clear command of heaven.

EVE. And is it thus you love me?
Ne'er be it true, ah never,
That I address you as my heart, my life!
From you I'll only wander,
Bathed in my tears, and sighing,
And hating even myself,
I'll hide me from the sun.

ADAM. Dear Eve! my sweetest love!
My spirit and my heart!
Oh haste to dry thine eyes;
For mine are all these tears
That bathe thy cheek, and stream upon thy bosom.

EVE. Ah, my unhappy state!
I that so much have said, so much have done
To elevate this man
Above the highest heaven, and now so little
Can he or trust or love me!

ADAM. Ah, do not grieve, my life!
Too much it wounds my soul
To see thee in affliction.

EVE. I know your sole desire
Is to be witness to my sighs and tears;
Hence to the winds and seas
I pay this bitter tribute.
ADAM. Alas! my heart is splitting.
What can I do? When I look up to heaven,
I feel an icy tremour
Even to my bones oppress me,
Anxious alone to guard the heavenly precept:
If I survey my partner,
I share her tears and echo back her sighs.
'Tis torture and distraction
To wound her with refusal: my kind heart
Would teach my opening hand to seize the apple,
But in my doubtful breast
My spirit bids it close.
Adam! thou wretch! how many
Various desires besiege thy trembling heart!
One prompts thee now to sigh,
Another to rejoice; nor canst thou know
Which shall incline thee most,
Or sighs, or joyous favour,
From woman, or from God.
EVE. Yet he reflects, and wishes
That Eve should now forsake
Her hope of being happy
In elevating man
Even while I hold the fruit of exaltation!
ADAM. Though mute, yet eloquent
Are all your looks, my love!
Alas! whate'er you ask
You're certain to obtain;
And my heart grants before your tongue can speak.
Eyes, that to me are suns,
The heaven of that sweet face
No more, no more obscure!
Return! alas! return
To scatter radiance o'er that cloudy cheek!
Lift up, O lift thy brow
From that soft mass of gold that curls around it,
Locks like the solar rays,
Chains to my heart and lightning to my eyes!
O let thy lovely tresses,
Now light and unconfined,
Sport in the air, and all thy face disclose
That paradise, that speaks a heart divine!
I yield thee full obedience;
Thy prayers are all commands;
Dry, dry thy streaming eyes, and on thy lips
Let tender smiles like harmless lightning play
EVE. Ah, misbelieving Adam,

Be now a kind receiver
Of this delightful fruit!
Hasten, now hasten to extend thy hand
To press this banquet of beatitude!
ADAM. Oh, my most sweet companion,
Behold thy ardent lover!
Now banish from his heart
The whirlpool of affliction, turn'd to him
His dearest guide, his radiant polar star!
Show me that lovely apple,
Which, 'midst thy flowers and fruits,
Ingenious plunderer, thy hidest from me!
EVE. Adam, behold the apple!
What say'st thou? I have tasted, and yet live.
Ah, 'twill insure our lives,
And make us equal to our God in heaven.
But first the fruit entire
We must between us eat;
And when we have enjoy'd it,
Then to a radiant throne, a throne of stars,
Exalting angels will direct our flight.
ADAM. Give me the pilfer'd fruit,
Thou courteous pilferer,
Give me the fruit that charms thee,
And let me yield to her,
Who to make me a god has toil'd and wept!
—— Alas! what have I done?
How sharp a thorn is piercing to my heart
With instantaneous anguish!
How am I overwhelm'd
In a vast flood of sorrow!
EVE. Alas! what do I see?
Oh bitter knowledge! unexpected sight!
All is prepared for human misery.
ADAM. O precious liberty! where art thou fled?
EVE. O precious liberty! O dire enthralment!
ADAM. Is this the fruit so sweet,
The source of so much bitter?
Say, why would'st thou betray me?
Ah, why of heaven deprive me!
Why make me forfeit thus
My state of innocence,
Where cheerful I enjoy a blissful life?
Why make me thus a slave
To the fierce arms of death,
Thou, whom I deem'd my life?
EVE. I have been blind to good,
Quick-sighted but to evil,
An enemy to Adam,
A rebel to my God;

For daring to exalt me
To the high gates of heaven,
I fall presumptuous to the depths of hell.
ADAM. Alas, what dart divine appears in heaven,
Blazing with circling flame?
EVE. What punishment,
Wretch that I am, hangs o'er me? Am I naked?
And speaking still to Adam?
ADAM. Am I too naked? hide me! hence!
EVE. I fly.

SCENE THE SECOND.

VOLANO. Thou'rt fallen, at length thou'rt fallen,
O thou presuming
With new support from the resplendent stars,
To mount to seats sublime!
Adam, at length thou'rt fallen to the deep,
As far as thy ambition hoped to soar;
Now see thou hast attain'd,
To learn the distance between heaven and hell.
Now let Avernus echo
To the hoarse sound of the funereal trumpet!
Joyful arise to light,
And pay your homage to the prince of hell.

SCENE THE THIRD.

SATAN, VOLANO, *Chorus of* SPIRITS, *with their flags flying and infernal instruments.*

VOLANO. Man is subdued, subdued!
Palms of eternal glory!
Why pause ye now? to your infernal reeds
And pipes of hoarsest sound, with pitch cemented,
And various instruments of discord,
Now let the hand and lip be quick applied!
Behold how triumph now to us returns,
As rightly he foretold
Our Stygian Emperor! Spread to the wind
Your fluttering banners! Oh thou festive day
To hell of glory, and to heaven of shame!

SCENE THE FOURTH.

SERPENT, VAIN GLORY, SATAN, VOLANO, *and* SPIRITS.

SERPENT. To pleasures and to joys,
Ye formidable dark sulphureous warriors!

Let fame to heaven now on her raven plumes
Direct her rapid flight,
Of man's completed crime
The mournful messenger.

SATAN. Behold, again expanded in the air
The insignia of hell!
Hear now the sounds of triumph,
And voices without number
That raise to heaven the shout of victory!

SERPENT. Lo, I return, ye spirits of Avernus,
And, as I promised, a proud conqueror!
Lo, to these deep infernal realms of darkness
I bring transcendent light, transcendent joy;
Thanks to my fortitude, which from that giant
Now wretched, and in tears,
Forced his aspiring crown of fragile glass;
And thanks to her, this martial heroine,
Vain Glory, whom to my proud heart I press.

SATAN. The torrent hastes not to the sea so rapid,
Nor yet so rapid in the realm of fire
Flashes kindle and die,
As the quick circling hours
Of good are join'd to evil
In life's corrupted state;
The work of my great lord, nor less the work
Of thee, great goddess of the scene condemn'd;
Up, up with homage quick
To show ourselves of both the blest adorers!

SERPENT. Now, from their bended knees let all [arise,
And to increase our joys,
Let thy glad song, Canoro,
Now memorize the prosperous toil of hell.

CANORO. Happy Canoro, raised to matchless bliss,
Since 'tis thy lot to speak
The prosperous exploits of Lucifer!
Behold, I bend the knee,
And sing thy triumph in a joyous strain!
Behold, the glorious triumph
Of that unconquer'd power
Who every power surpasses,
The mighty monarch of the deadly realm!
Now raise the tumid form,
Avernus, banish grief;
Man is involved in snares,
And Death is glutted with his frail existence.
This is the potent, brave,
And ancient enemy
Of man, the dauntless foe,
And dread destroyer of the starry court.
No more contentment dwell

In the terrestrial seat:
Thou moon and sun be darken'd,
And every element to chaos turn!
Man is at length subdued.
From a corrupted source,
A weak and hapless offspring,
Thanks to the fruit, his progeny shall prove.
To that exalted seat
By destiny our due,
Can death's vile prey ascend,
Who now lies prostrate at the feet of hell?
SERPENT. Silence, no more! Now in superior joys
Ye quick and fluttering spirits,
Now, now, your wings expand,
And, active in your pleasure,
Weave a delightful dance!

SCENE THE FIFTH.

A Chorus of SPRIGHTS *in the shape of* ANTICS, SERPENT, SATAN, VOLANO, CANORO, VAIN GLORY, *and* SPIRITS.

To thee behold us flying,
Round thee behold us sporting,
O monarch of Avernus!
To recreate thy heart in joyous dance.
Come, let us dance, happy and light,
Ye little Sprights;
Man was of flesh, now all dust,
Such is the will of hideous death;
A blessed lot
No more is his, wretched in all.
Now let us weave, joyous and dancing,
Ties as many
As now hell's prosperous chieftain
Spreads around man, who weeps and wails,
And now lifeless
Is almost render'd by his anguish.
Enjoy, enjoy in fragile vesture,
Man, O heaven;
Stygian Serpent has o'erwhelm'd him;
Wherefore let each dance in triumph,
Full of glory,
Since our king has proved victorious.
But, what think'st thou? Heaven in sorrow,
On the sudden,
He will spring to scenes celestial;
And he there will wreak his vengeance
On the Godhead,

That is now in heaven so troubled.
SERPENT. Ah, what lofty sounding trumpets
Through the extensive fields of heaven rebellow?
VAIN GLORY. Ah, from my triumph now I fall to hell,
Through subterraneous scenes exhaling fire,
With all my fatal pomp at once I sink!
SERPENT. And I, alas, am plunging
With thee to deepest horror!
SATAN. Avoid, avoid, companions,
This unexpected lustre,
That brings, alas, to us a night of horror!
VOLANO. Alas, why should we tarry?
Fly all, O fly with speed
This inimical splendour,
These dread and deadly accents,
The utterance of God!

SCENE THE SIXTH.

GOD THE FATHER, ANGELS, ADAM *and* EVE.

GOD THE FATHER.

And is it thus you keep the law of heaven,
Adam and Eve? O ye too faithless found,
Ye children of a truly tender father;
Thou most unhappy, how much hast thou lost,
And in a moment, Adam!
Fool, to regard the Serpent more than God.
Ah could repentance e'er belong to Him
Who cannot err, then might I well repent me
Of having made this man.
Now, Adam, thou hast tasted
The apple, thou hast sinn'd,
Thou hast corrupted God's exalted bounty:
The elements, the heavens,
The stars. the moon, the sun, and whatsoever
Has been for man created,
Now seems by man abhorr'd; and as unworthy
Now to retain existence,
To his destruction he solicits death.
But since 'tis just that I, who had proportion'd
Reward to merit, should now make chastisement,
Keep pace with guilt, contemplating myself,
I view Astrea, in whose righteous stroke
Lo, I myself descend, for I am justice.
Why pausest thou, O sinner, in his presence,
Who on a starry throne,
As an offended judge prepares thy sentence?

Appear! to whom do I address me? Adam,
Adam, where art thou? say! dost thou not hear?
Adam. Great Sovereign of Heaven! if to those accents,
Of which one single one form'd earth and heaven,
My God, if to that voice,
That call'd on Adam, a deaf asp I seem'd,
It was terror struck me dumb:
Since to my great confusion,
I was constrain'd, naked, to come before thee.

GOD THE FATHER.

And who with nakedness has made acquainted
Him, who although he was created naked,
With innocence was clothed?
Adam. Of knowledge the dread fruit that I have tasted;
The fault of my companion!
Eve. Too true it is, that the malignant serpent
Made me so lightly think of thy injunction,
That the supreme forbiddance
Little or nought I valued.

GOD THE FATHER.

Adam, thou sinner! O thou bud corrupted
By the vile worm of error!
Though eager to ascend celestial seats,
An angel in thy pride, thy feeble wings
Left thee to fall into the depths of hell.
By thy disdain of life,
Death is thy acquisition;
Unworthy now of favour,
I strip thee of thy honours;
And soon thou shalt behold the herbs and flowers
Turn'd into thorns and thistles,
The earth itself this day by me accurst.
Then shalt thou utter sighs in want of food,
And from thy alter'd brow thou shalt distil
Streams of laborious sweat,
A supplicant for bread;
Nor ever shall the strife of man have end,
Till, as he rose from dust, to dust he turn.
And thou, first author of the first offence,
With pain thou shalt produce the human birth,
As thou hast taught, with anguish infinite,
The world this fatal day to bring forth sin.
Thee, cruel Serpent, I pronounce accursed;
Be it henceforth thy destiny to creep
Prone on the ground, and on the dust to feed.
Eternal strife between thee and the woman,
Strife barbarous and deadly,

This day do I denounce:
If one has fallen, the other, yet victorious,
Shall live to bruise thy formidable head.
Now, 'midst the starry spheres,
Myself I will seclude from human sight.

SCENE THE SEVENTH.

An ANGEL, ADAM, *and* EVE.

ANGEL. Ah Eve, what hast thou lost,
Of thy dread Sovereign slighting the commands!
Thou Adam, thou hast sinn'd;
And Eve too sinning with thee,
Ye have together, of the highest heaven
Shut fast the gates, and open'd those of hell!
In seeking sweeter life,
Ye prove a bitter death;
And for a short delight
A thousand tedious sufferings.
How much it had been better for this man
To say, I have offended, pardon, Lord!
Than to accuse his partner, she the serpent:
Hence let these skins of beasts, thrown over both,
Become your humble clothing;
And hence let each be taught
That God approves the humble,
And God in anger punishes the proud.

ADAM. O man! O dust! O my frail destiny
O my offence! O death!

EVE. O woman! O of evil
Sole gluttonous producer!
O fruit! my sin! O serpent! O deceit!

ANGEL. Now let these skins that you support upon [you,
Tell you the grievous troubles
That you have to sustain;
Rude vestments are these skins,
From whence you may perceive
That much of misery must be endured
Now in the field of life,
Till death shall reap ye both.
Now, now lament and weep,
From him solicit mercy,
For still your mighty Maker may be found
Gracious in heaven, indulgent to the world,
Most merciful to man,
If equal to the pride
That made him err, his penitence will weep.

ADAM. Ah whither art thou fled?
Where lonely dost thou leave me?
O too disgusting apple,

If thou canst render man to angels hateful.
Alas, my dread destruction
Springs from a source so high,
That it will find no end.
Most miserable Adam! if thou fallest,
Ah, who will raise thee up?
If those eternal hands
That should uphold the heaven, the world, and man,
Closed for thy good, are open for thy ill,
How much should'st thou express! but tears and grief
Fetter the tongue and overwhelm the heart!
O sin! O agony!
EVE. Adam, my Adam, I will call thee mine,
Although I may have lost thee!
Unhappy Eve acknowledges her error,
She weeps, and she laments it.
She sees thee in great anguish:
O could her tears wash out the grievous stain
Thou hast upon thy visage!
Adam! alas thou answerest not, and I
Suffer in seeing thee so pale and pensive,
Thy hands united in the folds of pain!
But if through deed of mine thou hast occasion
For endless shame and silence,
Wilt thou reply to me? do I deserve it?
I merit only woe by being woman;
Eve has invented weeping,
Eve has discover'd anguish,
Labour and lassitude,
Distraction and affright;
Eve, Eve has minister'd to death and hell!
ADAM. Enjoy, enjoy, O woman,
My anguish, my perdition, and my death;
Banish me hence for loving thee too well!
Ah, if thou wert desirous of my tears,
Now, now extend thy hands, receive these streams
That I must pour abundant from mine eyes;
If thou didst wish my sighs, lo! sighs I give thee;
If anguish, view it; if my blood, 'tis thine;
Rather my death, it will be easy to thee,
Now to procure my death,
If thou hast render'd me of life unworthy.

SCENE THE EIGHTH.

The ARCHANGEL MICHAEL, ADAM *and* EVE.

MICHAEL. Why this delay? come on, be quick, depart,
Corrupted branches, from this fair and beauteous
Terrestrial paradise! Are ye so bold,

Ye putrid worms? come on, be quick, depart,
Since with a scourge of fire I thus command you.
ADAM. Alas! I am destroy'd
By the fierce blow of this severe avenger!
EVE. Now sunk in vital power
I feel my sad existence,
Even at the menace from this scourge of fire. [foot
MICHAEL. These stony plains now must thy naked
Press, in the stead of sweet and beauteous flowers,
Since thy erroneous folly
Forbids thy dwelling in this pleasant garden.
Behold in me the punisher of those
Who 'gainst their God rebel, and hence I bear
These radiant arms that with tremendous power
Make me invincible. I was the spirit
Who, in the mighty conflict,
Advancing to the north,
Struck down great Lucifer, the haughty leader
Of wicked angels, so that into hell
They plunged precipitate and all subdued;
And thus it has seem'd good to my tremendous
Celestial chief, that I shall also drive
Man, rebel to his God, with this my sword
Of ever-blazing fire,
Drive him for ever from this seat of bliss.
You angels all depart, and now with me
Expand your plumes for heaven;
As it has been your lot,
Like mine, on earth here to rejoice with man,
Man once a demi-god, and now but dust,
Here soon with falchions arm'd,
Falchions that blaze with fire,
As guardians of these once delightful gates,
The brave and active Cherubim shall aid you.

SCENE THE NINTH.

Chorus of ANGELS *that sing*, ARCHANGEL, ADAM, *and* EVE.

ADIEU, remain in peace!
O thou that liv'st in war!
Alas, how much it grieves us,
Great sinner, to behold thee now but dust.
Weep! weep! indulge thy sighs,
And view thy lost possession now behind thee;
Weep! weep! for all thy sorrow
Thou yet may'st see exchanged for songs of joy:
This promise to the sinner heaven affords
Who contrite turns to heaven with holy zeal.

ACT IV.

SCENE THE FIRST.

VOLANO, *Chorus of* FIERY, AIRY, EARTHLY, *and* AQUATIC SPIRITS.

VOLANO. Forth from a thousand clouds of flame
and smoke,
From the deep bosom of the spacious earth,
I to these scenes a messenger return.
Now to the fatal sound
Of these entwisted pipes,
By hissing snakes united,
And all attuned to the fierce notes of death,
Now cease, now cease ye all,
Ye potent spirits, to reside in fire,
Or in the air, in water, or in earth.
Appear! why pause ye? such is the command
Of your brave emperor, the chief of hell.
Hark! hear ye not the sound
That calls you forth from out your various dwellings?
Behold! how from the sphere of blazing fire
Arsiccio, of the blazing legion prince,
Comes to pay homage to his mighty lord.
ARION. Lo, from the field of air I too descend,
I who am called Arion,
The mighty ruler of this winged band,
At the command of hell.
TARPALCE. Of the infernal palace
To bend before the prince,
Forth from a thousand subterraneous paths
The great Tarpalce, chief of earthly sprights,
Raises his brow to heaven.
ONDOSO. From many a vein of water,
From many a rising fount,
From rills, and rivers, torrents, floods and streams,
And from a thousand marshes, pools, and lakes,
Such as I am, Ondoso, of soft spirits
The humid, floating ruler, now on wing,
Here even I attend, to reverence
The subterranean power.
VOLANO. Lo, from the dark abyss to lightsome air
Great Lucifer now rising, and with him
The most sagacious band
Of hellish counsellors.

SCENE THE SECOND.

LUCIFER, FIERY, AIRY, EARTHLY, AQUATIC, INFERNAL SPIRITS, *and* VOLANO.

LUCIFER. Ah light! detested light!
Yet once again I look towards thy rays,
The sightless mole of hell,
And like a frantic angel,
Dazzled and grieved at heart,
Immortally I die.

BELIAR. Of what dost thou complain? why grieves our god?
Clear up thy countenance, and see around
How thy palms shake; thy banners float in air,
Signs of that valour which has conquer'd heaven,
And now in triumph may enjoy the world;
Ah, too imperfect is the victor's glory,
If he exult not in his victory.

LUCIFER. Destructive victory! unworthy boast!
Laughter to weeping turn'd,
Is that which thou esteem'st the praise of hell.
Ah, heaven's high power has found
A new expedient to our endless shame,
To make our vanquish'd foe remain the victor,
And triumph, though defeated.

MIRIM. What barbed arrows in my wounded heart,
Great lord, hast thou enfix'd!

LUCIFER. Ah! for no other purpose have I call'd [you
From realms of air and fire,
From earth, from water, and the central depths,
Save that we might project in council here
How man may fall entirely overwhelm'd,
If to destroy him by the fruit I fail'd.

DIGRIGNAN. Ah, how can Adam live,
If he indeed has eat the fruit forbidden,
Condemning him to death?
Now well may we exclaim,
That heaven this day inures itself to falsehood.

LUCIFER. Hear it, oh hell, and shudder at the sound,
And let thy lively joys now turn to languor.
Tell me, thou Beliar, how seems to thee,
After the tasted fruit, man on the sudden
Discover'd naked, and amid the branches
Of thickest growth hastening to hide his shame?

BELIAR. In viewing his own nakedness, he shows us
The tasted fruit has robb'd him of all grace;
The very foliage where he hides informs him
He is become a beast,

And, like a beast, is doom'd in death to lose
His body and his soul.
LUCIFER. Thou, Coriban, relate why man has
With the fig's ample leaf [form'd
A mantle for his waist.
CORIBAN. I'll tell you,—'tis the nature of the fig
To rise not high, and prove of short duration;
Still less may man expect to glory's height
To raise himself; for short shall be his date.
All the contentious elements at war,
Occasion'd by his sin, now in their conflict
Shall overwhelm him, and the hope with souls
More to embellish heaven shall be in vain. [pent,
LUCIFER. And thou, Ferea, what denotes the ser-
Whom in his anger God is pleased to curse?
FEREA. I will be brief in telling all that's true:
When he pronounced a curse upon the serpent,
Man had already heard his malediction;
And thus to that he added,
Prone on thy belly, Serpent, thou shalt grovel,—
As if to man suggesting,
Dark as a riddling god, man is of clay;
And clay shall now be destitute of soul,
As destitute of soul each other reptile.
LUCIFER. Thou, Solobrico, tell me, what think'st thou
Of this strange speech to man—
Thou by thy sweat must gain
The bread that forms thy food.
SOLOBRICO. This bread to us discovers
The life of man's frail body,
A body form'd of earth, as now indeed
Grain must be drawn from earth to make this bread,
The vital element:
His sweat denotes the element of water,
His countenance is air, his labour fire;
So that this dark expression
Of being doom'd to gain his bread by sweat,
To man says, Thou shalt live,
In many griefs and troubles,
A short space in the world;
Then is thy lot to die,
Turning again to earth, air, water, fire.
LUCIFER. And, Gismon, thou, to woman when he
That with the pangs of birth [said,
She should produce her offspring, say what meaning
Lurk'd in that new expression to bring forth?
GISMON. This said expression birth
Denotes the being born,
When her young progeny shall rise to light:

He also might denote a new partition
By this new word bring forth,
Innumerable pains,
In which the suffering parents
Shall both participate to rear their children.
Of body and of soul
The certain death I see in this expression:
That this may be, turning to man he said,
That he should die, and then to Eve he added,
That she with bitter anguish should bring forth.
Now this mysterious saying nothing means,
If not that man is meant
By death corporeal, and his frail companion
By death that strikes the soul;
Thus from mortality,
With loss reciprocal, the soul is taken:
And thus, when each has languish'd,
The body in its dying,
The soul in its departure,
Leaving at length its transient dear abode;
So verified shall be the mighty sentence
From him, the mighty Judge,
Of bringing forth with dire excess of pain.

LUCIFER. All you, that most sagacious
I reckon'd once in my infernal kingdoms,
I find now least sagacious.
To thee I turn, Arsiccio, tell me now
What means that mystery,
The cursing of the earth?

ARSICCIO. And to the blame of man I too return
Can it be true this cursing of the earth?
What does the mystery mean?
Means it indeed the earth?
Foolish is he who thinks so! what offence
Has she committed? no, 'twas not the earth
Was cursed, but only man, who is of earth;
And human nature all is cursed with him;
And that decree, it should no more bear fruit,
Was utter'd for no purpose
But to proclaim to man,
That, as a sinner, heaven is shut against him.

LUCIFER. Arion, thou exalt thyself in air;
Do thou inform me why with skins of beasts
This man and his companion were array'd.

ARION. This clearly shows to us
That God no longer makes account of man.
Hear me, unconquer'd sovereign:
This clothing Adam with the lifeless skins
Of fleeced animals to us imports,
That, as with dying beast,

The body, soul, and spirit, also die,
So death shall also prove
The dread destroying ravager of men
By the dread fruit's effect.

LUCIFER. Ondoso, thou who art profest a diver
Canst thou pervade the depth
Of these confused decrees? inform me now
What means the mystery
Of cherubim with fiery falchions
Forbidding entrance to the gates of Eden.

ONDOSO. No mystery, great king,
But the destruction of the human rac
Portended by these falchions
They mean indeed the death
Of man's terrestrial form,
And their fierce blades of fire
Damnation to his soul:
So that when struck by death
The body shall be ashes, and the soul
Shall by eternal justice
Within the dark Avernus
Become a prisoner, lost to light and heaven.
Now blest are we, since we behold it clear,
That, rising to the realms above, 'tis ours
To make Olympus joyful, since when we
Resign'd our seat in heaven,
At those exalted gates
No armed cherubim was placed to guard;
Thus all is justly weigh'd,
And in an even balance;
For now the world's inhabitants shall be
The birds, the fish, the beasts;
Of the Tartarean gulf
Man and his numerous race;
We only on gay wing shall soar to heaven,
On this supreme condition,
That heaven's great Lord shall pardon ask of thee,
Repenting of his error, and that both
Shall rule the realm of heaven,
Both Lucifer and God.

LUCIFER. Tarpalce, say what thinkest thou of man?

TARPALCE. 'Tis not my sentiment man can be saved.
In short, this man has sinn'd;
And he who draws from man his flesh and life,
He shall be call'd a sinner;
And he who is a sinner shall be damn'd;
And since it is denied
That these the seats of heaven, that once were ours,
Neglected shall be left, and void of glory,
Well may we re-ascend, with brave condition,

The heaven once more returning to itself.
Sufficiently we know
It otherways would still be void of splendour,
Since God no longer knows
What to achieve that may embellish heaven.
LUCIFER. Alas, 'tis fit that I
From a deep silence now
Loose this chill'd tongue, chill'd though it seems to
With cruel deadly rage! [burn
My heart is bursting only at the thought
Of what I must relate;
Now with great efforts vanquishing myself,
Let that be heard which anguish bids me utter!
The fear he felt to show himself when naked
Was from the mighty shame
To see himself bespotted
With sin's deformity.
His flight with rapid steps towards the woods,
As to the sea the swollen torrent flies,
Denotes his great repentance of his sin.
That leafy screen in which he hid himself
Denotes his coarse and rustic penitence,
Till with long abstinence he shall atone
With punishment for sin.
The harsh and ample leaf
Of fig, still more expressive,
Tells it will be man's lot
With coarse and hairy vest
To cover every fault;
And as upon the fig,
Among its harshest leaves, a dulcet fruit
Arises, thus at last shall man himself,
'Midst all his penitence, enjoy the fruit
So sweet and dear of heaven, that he had lost:
The verdure of the leaf
Affords a certain hope
That man may have of God's returning grace;
That he at length in heaven
Shall know a blooming spring of highest glory
The double summons, thus bestow'd on man,
Tells us he shall have time
To weep, though sinning, his repented sin.
If he was pleased to execrate the serpent,
There hell may understand
That it was not the serpent
Who then offended God; from whence he said,
Prone on thy belly, Serpent, thou shalt creep!
Alas, too clearly saying,
Quit every hope, O ye that now abide
By the infernal streams,

Quit every hope of heaven!
And when between this woman and the serpent
His word denounced, alas! eternal war,
Ah then he comprehended human nature,
Which bears a female name.
What then are now our direst enemies?
Inhabitants of heaven!
So that our most tormenting adversary
Is now no other but this human nature,
Made an eternal denizen of heaven.
What more, alas! (have I the force to speak it?)
The saying that the woman
Shall one day bruise his head,
With mystery severe
Shows us the incarnation of the Word.
Saying to man his bread
He now by sweat must earn, is it not saying
After hard toil thou shalt to heaven ascend?
Alas! perhaps it means
That bread may life denote,
Since man is destined to have life in heaven.
If for the apple God was pleased to say
That man transgressing shall be doom'd to death,
He of the body spake;
The spirit is immortal.
When in his speech to Eve
He doom'd her to bring forth, that indicates
Eternity assign'd to human nature.
The guard of cherubim that wheel around
Their fiery swords, forbidding
All feet to tread on that delicious garden,
I would declare to mean——
But to cold marble turns my faltering tongue.
  BRIAR. Shall it be said that Briar checks his tongue?
Believe not thou, our lord,
That man to heaven shall soar;
Too feeble are his wings;
Had he no other bar,
I am alone prepared to give him death,
Arm'd with a mighty club, or with a stone,
Though sure to be condemn'd
Myself alone to all the pains of hell;
Since I can well discern,
That in continual thinking of my glory,
Infernal pain will turn to heavenly joy.
  LUCIFER. O noble, generous ardour!
Trust me, not less avails
A heart magnanimous for glory panting,
Than a decided triumph.
Let us remain in hell,

Since there is more content
To live in liberty, though all condemn'd,
Than, as his vassals, blest.
Up from these filthy dregs,
A hideous mass, sulphureous, rough, and round,
Let there be raised to light;
So wills the mighty chieftain of damnation.

SCENE THE THIRD.

The infernal Cyclops, armed with hammers, and all those of the preceding Scene.

BEHOLD the smiths of hell,
That, worn with toil and smoke,
To heaven are raising this enormous ball,
Now fashion'd in Avernus.
LUCIFER. Now as a perfect rival
Of God, I will, that Lucifer be seen.
He highly seated, on his throne in heaven,
To us reveal'd the world, and thence arose
Our banishment from heaven, and I this day,
Raising Vain Glory to a throne of splendour,
Have now contrived to exterminate mankind.
If he from nothing made the ample world,
I too a nothing will now make of worlds,
Or of the world a nothing.
Now let this dark and misty mass dissolve,
And in the place of elements, and heavens,
Of all the stars, the moon, and radiant suns,
Let there come forth a strange unfinish'd monster.
ONDOSO. O what a stormy burst, what monsters rise,
All horrible and hissing,
With forms enormous howling,
And breathing blasts of fire!
LUCIFER. Thou that now seem'st a dark and hideous monster,
I will array thee in a human semblance,
Though but of vapour form'd;
Thou shalt be call'd the World.
Instead of shags, and vestments wild,
Sweat thou beneath a load of gems and gold,
For well I know how henceforth in my service
Gold may be used in tempting man to sin.
Such thou shalt have around thee;
On thee I will bestow voice, gesture, snares,
In strictest tie to catch
The human foot of clay that walks incautious;
And all that thou canst wish

To overwhelm this man, all thou shalt have.
Thou beast of monstrous shape,
Thou like a lovely damsel shalt appear,
Thou shalt be call'd the Flesh,
With wiles, deceits, and ardours, in thy train,
Whence man may fall in unbecoming errors:
And, monster, thou that art
So hideous and so meagre, Death be call'd:
Be thou all human bone,
All ice, all madness, all a mass of horror
To the unhappy sinner.
Ye four terrific forms, of wildest semblance,
For horrid deeds I choose you,
Ill omen'd words, and acts of cruel nature,
Your fashion to display.
Up, up, let each return
To his own element, his proper sphere!
Come! why delay to fire?
Haste all with me,
And hence in silence glide,
Abandoning the light.

SCENE THE FOURTH.

ADAM. Wretch that thou art! now cast thine eyes [around,
No longer shalt thou see
Aught to console thy pain.
Ah! in that very thought,
Sorrow so wounds my heart,
My tears so overwhelm me,
That in a sigh I seem to breathe my last.
Where, Adam, is thy beauty? where thy grace,
That made thee dear to angels and to God?
Ah! thou alone hast dared
To stain thy nature, and to wound thy soul!
Is this, is this the way
To please that Being who on thee bestow'd
Whate'er thou seest around thee, with a promise
To give thee in the stars a heavenly mansion?
Rather on fruit forbidden
To feed, than on the living words of God,
Has been thy choice; and lo,
Thou from an angel to a beast art changed!
And, more than other beasts
Driven as a monster from this pleasant garden,
And thus in skins array'd! Alas! I dare not
Lift up my eyes to heaven, yet it becomes me,
Low on my knees, to view the good I lost,

And in lamenting say,—
Dear seat of God, thou should'st have been the seat
Of Adam also; but thou art lost to me,
Thee have I lost, alas! and found instead
Of thee, both death and hell.
O hide, in pity hide, thy splendour, heaven!
Since Adam is a sinner.
Conceal your light, ye stars;
Vanish, thou moon and sun;
Eternal horror be the fate of man,
Since Adam is a sinner.
Now in the faithful choir of angels cease,
Ye soothing melodies,
Since Adam is a sinner.
Behold, with pain behold,
How, from thy dread offence,
All things this day appear to change their form,
All hold thee in abhorrence,
All from thy aspect fly!
Ah, thou may'st well exclaim,
There, from the verdant stem and parent tree,
The rose is fled, and leaves thee but the thorn!
There sinks each flower, within the grassy earth
Hiding its head precipitate, and scarce
Where it display'd its pride now shows its stalk;
Well may'st thou add, in plucking here the apple
Thou gavest a fatal shake to every tree,
Then bringing to the ground
Each leaf, each flower, and every blooming fruit.
Ah, how despoil'd and waste
All now appears to me; all shade and horrors;
Produced by man's rebellion to his God.
Where, where are now the gay and sprightly birds
That on their painted plumes
Round me were used to sport and flutter here?
Ah, your closed wings I see
Amidst the thickest leaves, and fearing all
The deadly snares of Adam.
Where, where is now the tiger, bear, and lion,
The wolf, the pard, and thousand other beasts,
Obedient all to man, and in his train?
Alas! now made voracious
Of human carnage and of smoking blood
I now behold you all,
Sharpening 'gainst man the talon and the tooth.
Where now, ah where, their young
May all the fleecy kind
Let fall in safety? for, alas, I see
No longer will they offer
Their milky dugs to thee, their dugs or offspring
Since to escape from man,

Now, now, I see them eager,
Man turn'd into a wolf
By having seized an apple.
All fly, and all abhor thee,
And from thee, barbarous, learn barbarity.
Hence in the earth and sea,
Beyond their custom, now
All fish, and all the beasts,
To battle seem to invite thee;
See now the wolf and lamb,
She who of late not far from him might wander,
See how she bleating flies from his unfaithful
Tusk, now expecting bloody violence!
Behold the hare, behold
How timid she is made, and the dog fierce
In striving for her life,
While more than native fear to flight inclines her.
Behold that dusky beast,
That with white tusks of an enormous size
Extends its weighty jaw,
That now forgetting to revere the moon,
Intractable, ferocious,
Beyond its native temper,
Rushes in anger with its fibrous trunk
That serves it for a nose,
Against the horn which the rhinoceros
Sharpens of hardest stone!
Behold the sea enraged,
Now, by thy rage, the very sea inflamed
Takes up the fish within its watery arms,
And in a thousand caverns,
Against the mossy stones
Now strikes, and now entombs them.
At length, behold that ox,
That now beneath thy crooked yoke of wood
To turn the sterile earth
Thou must contrive to couple,
See how he darts an eye of fire upon thee,
And foaming now, and panting, fiercely points
His crooked horn, and threatens thee with death.
And more, yet more, the earth
Provokes thee now to conflict,
Thanks to thy dire offence;
And since her bosom must by thee be wounded,
Strives with thee for thy viands, arm'd herself
With thistles and with thorns.
I've sinn'd, O Lord, I've sinn'd!
I've sinn'd, and for my fault
My mournful heart in weeping I distil.
Why wretched do I speak? see what a band

Of beasts made barbarous,
Of hostile beasts, now wet
With crimson's deadly stain,
I see around me, darting from their caves!
Alas! what see I more? wretch that I am!
Behold, from them affrighted Eve is flying!

SCENE THE FIFTH.

ADAM *and* EVE.

EVE. Ah whither shall I fly? and where conceal [me?
ADAM. Haste to my arms, O haste!
Let him who sinn'd like thee,
Like thee become of savage beasts the prey!
EVE. Ah, every path becomes
The pass of death to one of life unworthy;
Here in this cavern's depth,
Here let us plunge, O Adam.
ADAM. Ah, they at length depart; yet not from [man
Will misery depart, or mortal anguish.
Oh wondrous wretchedness, even pleasure weeps,
Joy wears the form of sorrow,
And life itself now dies.
EVE. Ah, how I grieve, O Adam!
Oh heaven! what tears I shed,
How do I sigh, O God, wounded in heart,
Now, nor alive nor dead!
ADAM. But hark, what horrid roarings
Make air rebellow, and the valleys shake!

SCENE THE SIXTH.

FAMINE, THIRST, LASSITUDE, DESPAIR, ADAM, EVE.

FAMINE In vain from our quick grasp
You strive to fly, vile offspring of the earth!
And from the thousand ills that heaven intends thee;
Fly not, for 'tis in vain. Ye now around
Block up the paths, and guard each avenue!
Famine am I, who in this hideous form
Now show myself to man,
To prove how keen I am,
With bitterness to poison all his sweets;
And from the semblance I reveal, thou wretch,
Clearly shalt thou perceive,
Beyond all other creatures,

How sharply Famine's piercing shaft shall wound
And as I now devour these tender shoots [thee;
Of the young fruitful vine,
And suck, with eager thirst, the dulcet juice,
So from thy feeble bones, that now derive
Infirmity from sin,
Soon will I tear the flesh,
And suck thus fiercely from thy veins the blood.
And this fierce monster that you now behold,
Keen at the limpid fountain
To satiate its thirst, and foil'd, attempting
With harpy talon to pollute the water,
This is call'd Thirst; and now, in such a form,
Both horrible and fierce,
To thee appears, that thou may'st comprehend
How wildly raging thou shalt feel its fury.
And this is Lassitude,
That Lassitude which now on thee shall pour
The mighty streams of sorrow.
See how her figure melts in drops of anguish,
In raising on her back
That heavy burden of enormous weight!
'Tis hers to make thee, Adam,
So worn with toil, that from thy pallid visage
The copious streams of painful sweat shall pour;
And Lassitude shall so annoy thy frame,
That thou shalt hate thy life.
Hence, at the last, perforce ye both shall pass
Through unaccustom'd ways of wretchedness
To this dire monster, savage and tremendous,
Who henceforth on the earth
Shall bear of Desperation
The desperate name; look, and behold how fiercely
He in convulsion rolls, and shrieks, and roars;
See how he tears his hair and grinds his teeth,
Wounds all his frame, and makes his breast re-echo
With his repeated blows!
This fierce, relentless monster
Shall so afflict thee, that thou shalt be eager
To turn, and hasten to an end more wretched:
And if, perchance, thou think'st I speak not true,
See him, who from his deep and dark domain
In blackest vapour wrapt,
Circled with globes of fire, appears before thee!

SCENE THE SEVENTH.

DEATH, ADAM, *and* EVE.

DEATH. Thou art the creature, Woman,
Who first hast summon'd me,
And with a sinful voice,
From the Tartarean shades;
Thou, perishable flesh and form of clay,
Hast call'd this fearful monster,
Of human bones compacted,
This day to look upon the light of heaven.
Say now what would'st thou speak?
Dost thou abhor thy life?
Behold the sickle-bearer, and the sickle
That now invites thee to desert the day.
Now with a lynx's eye,
I see, in looking into future time,
To my dread name and these ungodly arms,
What fatal trophies rise.
But what! not here shall end the full perdition
With which heaven threatens thee; such mighty evils
Hell now prepares for thee,
And such excess of horrors,
That I, I who am Death,
Wish for destruction to escape their sight.
Thou art condemn'd to die,
Thy residence is hell,
Become a rebel to thy mighty Maker.

ADAM. Oh source of tears! Oh sorrow!
Oh miserable sinner!

EVE. Ah me! most wretched Eve!
The origin of sin. [withdraws

ADAM. Ah, how the heaven grows dark, how it
Its light from us, who are of light unworthy!
But ah! what flame in heaven quickens and dies,
Dazzling our sight, and sudden darts away,
A serpent all of fire?

EVE. Alas! not here the wrath of heaven shall
First we must suffer death. [end,

ADAM. Ah, what rebellowing sounds I hear above!
Perchance with such a voice
Offended Heaven now drives us from the world,
And sends us banish'd to the gulfs below!
What shafts, how numberless
Strike down the woods and groves! with what wild
The raging winds contend! [force
Now rushes from the sky
Water congeal'd to forceful globes of hail!

EVE. Alas! how from on high
The swelling waters pour,
That rising o'er their banks,
The proud o'erflowing rivers
Now put the beasts to flight,
And in the groves and woods
Precipitately drive the fish to dwell!
ADAM. Fly! let us haste to fly
Up to those lofty mountains,
Where heaven now seems at last
Satiate with ceaseless thundering to repose!

ACT V.

SCENE THE FIRST.

THE FLESH *and* ADAM.

THE FLESH.

IF in a bosom form'd in lonely woods,
An amorous lure, the engine of deceit,
May wake a blazing spark,
And raise an inextinguishable fire;
This day to me shall shine a day of triumph,
When in desire's fierce flames
I shall behold that heart,
Which love's devouring flame yet has not touch'd
And now, if aught of potency resides
In golden-tresses or a breast of snow,
A radiant eye, a cheek of rose and lily,
And teeth of pearl, and lips that vie with coral,
In beauty, grace, allurements, arts and gestures,
To make a wretched mortal heart their captive,
Such tresses, such a breast,
A cheek, and teeth, and lips,
And my intelligent engaging manners,
Will hold thee fetter'd in a thousand snares.
Behold, not distant far, the simple bird
I opportunely see,
Who for my tempting lure
His habitation quits, and his companion,
To fall at once by amorous deceit:
O how to earth dejected,
He bends his watery eyes in deep affliction!
Thou art not yet transfix'd
By my prevailing shaft, but now it seeks thee.

SHE SINGS.

Dearest Adam, grieved and fainting,
Let my song thy spirit comfort!
And with thee,
O let me
Lead a life of true enjoyment!
Gentle Adam, son of glory,
Hearken, hearken! meek and humble
Sounds the artless song unpolish'd
That invites thee
But to kindness;
Give, O give me ease and quiet,
Gentle Adam, son of glory!
But if thou with different feelings
Wish to wound this tender bosom,
See it naked!
Strike! O cruel,
Wherefore pause you? Haste to kill me!
By your hand I fall contented.

ADAM. O thou all-seeing Lord,
If real grief may touch thee,
Survey the contrite sinner,
Who through his eyes distils his heart in tears.
No! of thy mercy do not close the hand,
Since what sustains me now must fall and perish.
Behold, behold, dread Lord! unhappy man,
Who from the fatal fruit
Has to encounter all the snares of hell;
Defend him; he is thine, thine thou hast call'd him,
And having once been thine, thou must have loved him.

THE FLESH.

Go, full of terror and desire! I must
With the impetuous be meek and coy,
And with the timid bold, and urge him on
Till love's keen canker-worm
Prey on the simple heart,
That never yet has felt the sting of passion.

ADAM. Who may this be? alas, both hope and fear
Urge me to seek, and bid me still be silent.

THE FLESH.

This lowliness, and this affected coyness
With an undaunted lover, this presumption
With one more soft and timid, are so prevailing
They seem two strong incentives
To kindle the fierce flame of love's desire:
Whence I a skilful mistress
Brandish my tongue,

And give a mortal wound.
Say, why art thou so pensive,
O my most gentle Adam?
ADAM. Restrain, restrain thy step,
Whoe'er thou art, nor with thy songs inveigle
Him, who has only cause for ceaseless tears.

THE FLESH.

Without thy strict injunction,
Creature of noble semblance,
To stand aloof from thee
Grieves me; I want the courage to approach
The flowery bloom of thy engaging face,
Fearing lest serpents in thy radiant eyes
For ever on the watch,
With stings devoid of pity pierce my heart.
But every bitter root
That leads thee to suspicion,
I from thy breast will pluck; for know, I am
The very soul of love; yes! of that love
Which has induced thy Maker
From nothing to make all:
And since in that debased
Condition into which thy sorrows sunk thee,
This love alone can draw thee,
To the low world I took my flight from heaven.
Perchance thou may'st suppose, enjoying love,
That thou must therefore lead a savage life,
A lover of the brutes;
No, no, adorning all thy form with flowers,
And wearing on thy locks a wreath of palm,
Thou shalt enjoy a vest of gold and silver,
Such as I wear, and such as high in heaven
The radiant tissue shines, when sun and moon
Weave their united rays.
Thine eyes shall sparkle with resplendent fire,
On thy warm cheek a graceful blush shall glow
And when in ecstacy thy lip is press'd,
Its richer hues shall make the coral pale.
Say, at the very sound dost thou not feel
Thy heart dissolve in amorous joy? I see
Thou art delighted, Adam.
ADAM. I love, in truth I love,
But only burn with love
For my almighty Maker.

THE FLESH.

The soul alone can love,
Can love this heavenly Lord:
But in these sublunary woodland scenes,
Love has delights of a corporeal kind.

ADAM. The love thou speak'st of it is mine to prove
With my beloved consort.

THE FLESH.

Yes! that is true; yet only sons of death
Can spring from your affection.
ADAM. Sad fruit of my offence!

THE FLESH.

Ah, but immortal children
From me shall spring, if thou wilt yield to me.
Amidst these herbs and flowers
Be ours sublimest love!
Simple! extend thy hand,
Behold, and touch my breast, that thou wilt find
Far different from the breast of mortal Eve.
If thou wilt love, shall I not make thee worthy
Of the unbounded joy
To steal thee from thyself? Ah come, ah come,
To this pure bosom that I show thee, Adam!
Oh say to me, I love thee!
Perchance thou may'st believe,
Each man to spring from thee
Ought to be happy with a single woman;
Each woman too contented
To love one man alone!
Simple, if such thy thought:
For all the sweets of love
Become more poignant by the change of lovers.
See how each animal, that dwells on earth,
Leads a delicious life,
By changing its affection;
And thou, sole sovereign of each living creature,
Shalt thou content thee with a single lover?
ADAM. Let sorrow's flame convert my heart to ashes,
Rather than it may burn with double love!
Hence then! depart! for a blind mole am I
To all thy proffer'd beauty;
And truly in thy presence
I feel no touch of love.

THE FLESH.

O thou most icy heart!
Now kindle with the flame of my affection.
Behold this ample cavern of the earth;
Lo, it was made for love; whate'er it holds
Within its spacious circuit,
Of love perceives the fire.
Love rules the earth, the sea, the air, and fire;

With endless love a hundred genial stars,
Not moving from their sphere,
Scatter their flames through heaven;
And other wandering planets
Through those exalted regions
Direct their golden steps.
What river, fount, or stream,
Unconscious flows, and destitute of love?
What frozen sea does love not penetrate
With his imperious ardour?
What glowing ocean does not oft discover
A visage pale and wan,
As if infirm with love?
What flower, what plant, or stone,
Wishes for love in vain, of love deprived?
Whate'er inhabits heaven, or earth, or sea,
Burns in the flame of love.
Behold that sportive bird of painted wing,
That goes with fluttering joy from bough to bough,
And in his song declares he sings of love!
Behold the sweet and oft-repeated kisses
Of those two doves, what dost thou think of them?
Of love they are the kisses.
The beauteous peacock see,
That gaily fondles his attractive mate;
He whirls the plume of love.
Hear you that nightingale, does she not mourn?
Now does she not exult? now 'tis her joy
With her melodious warble
To stun the valleys, and make glad the hills.
Simple, what dost thou think?
'Tis love that makes her tuneful.
Behold that river with its banks of flowers,
Its stream of purest silver,
And of fine gold its sand;
Behold, dost thou not see within its bosom
A thousand fishes glide?
They lead the dance of love.
Behold that sportive goat, that butting runs
Exulting o'er the plain,
His conflicts are from love.
Look there, and see amidst a thousand folds
Those close entwisted snakes,
That in a single being seem combined:
Coy Adam, even these
Weave the close web of love.
Behold, at length where yonder clustering vine
Her amorous arms around the elm extends;
She also burns with love.
Even that flower, that ever courts the sun,

Thus in its glances speaks,
I dart the glance of love!
And thou unmelting soul! wilt thou alone,
Wilt thou disdain to feel
That which all creatures prove?
Nought can resist my golden pungent dart,
Nor air, nor fire, nor sea, nor earth, nor heaven.

SCENE THE SECOND.

LUCIFER, THE FLESH, *and* ADAM.

THE FLESH.

Now burn with love, and bless the fond desire
Of her, whom the Creator
Made blazing all with love. [locks
ADAM. And who art thou, whose thick and bushy
And beard of silver shade thy head and face?
LUCIFER. Adam, I am a man; I am thy brother,
But of a higher rank;
Since I have drawn the vital air of heaven—
Thou, in this lower world;
For well thou know'st, that station
Affords an airy grandeur to our birth.
In years too I surpass thee;
My voice, too, and my language
Declare me old, as these my locks of silver;
Now if all elder things
Are deem'd superior to their successors,
In this my merit must be more than thine.
ADAM. How I should answer thee, my tongue knows
Thou lofty Lord of Heaven! [not
Since my sad error with so thick a cloud
Of ever-during fear
O'ershades my eyes and heart.
LUCIFER. Oh, Adam, do not fear!

THE FLESH.

Wait thou a little! soon
That shall be known to thee, which now is hid:
All for thy good alone,
And to save man from many griefs and pains.
LUCIFER. Now, Adam, understand
How having made me in his lofty heaven,
He next created thee;
For a new wish he form'd
To make another man, and give the world

To be his grateful residence, and then
Clay he made flesh, and of that flesh made man;
Then from the side of man he woman drew,
And then ordain'd the law,
Prohibiting the apple,
Which if he tasted, man
Must be deprived of his celestial home.
Hence is it thou hast felt,
Hence is it thou hast seen
Clouds rolling through the air,
And fiery scintillations in the sky,
Rebellowing thunder and its rattling bolts,
And the tempestuous crash.
These mournful pomps of horror,
Say, say, what canst thou think
That they portend below to new-made man?
All these appear'd in heaven, because from heaven
Now the celestial Adam is dislodged.
As to terrestrial man
(As if the world would drive him from the world),
The earth itself grew barren,
And every fruit grew harsh,
The waters full of turbulence and gall,
And every creature sharpen'd
His beak, or tusk, or talon.
Behold at last, O heaven! a pair of brothers,
The citizens of earth.
O, Adam, do not grieve,
That I by fault of thine have now lost heaven,
Since to have haply found
Thee, my beloved brother,
Now makes me not to feel the loss of heaven:
And happy we will live
In this, a sylvan, and a sunny scene;
Or emulous of heaven, in God's own heaven
Raised to a noble seat,
I will, that we ascend,
And underneath our feet
Joy to behold the congregated choirs,
Even like the blessed choirs,
The children of this man.
Now if we wish success to our desires,
And should delight to see
Springing like grass, and frequent as the flowers,
Our children rapidly arise to light,
Turn we our eyes and heart
To this fair goddess of delightful love!
For easy 'tis to her
To form in sweet array the troops we wish.
A plant so sweetly fruitful

Is not; nor is the earth herself so fertile;
Nor does it raise so soon
Its nutritive production,
As she will raise, if we are so disposed,
The fruit of lovely children.
Then to the lily whiteness
Of her enchanting cheek
Advance the living roses of the lip!
And of so sweet a flower
For this love's goddess let us form a garland!
Oh to the living ruby
Of this sweet fount of kisses,
If he for kisses thirst,
The hart of love shall run,
There bathe his thirsty lip,
And there on kisses quench his mighty ardour.

THE FLESH.

Why this delay, O Adam?
Approach, approach, my heart!
Satiate thy thirst of love!
LUCIFER. What! dost thou fear, and tremble?
Now let the empty cloud
Of all thy vain suspicion
Disperse before the sun of heavenly truth!
Extend, extend thy arms
And in one dear embrace encircle both!
Happy who pants for thee! alas, what dost thou?
At once thou givest, and again draw'st back
Thy blandishments, like lightning,
That in appearing flies and vanishes.
ADAM. What fear assaults my heart I cannot tell,
But feel that like a timid deer I pant
At the dire barking of blood-thirsty hounds.

SCENE THE THIRD.

CHERUBIM, GUARDIAN OF ADAM, ADAM, THE FLESH, *and* LUCIFER.

CHERUBIM. 'Tis time to succour man. Alas! what dost thou,
Most miserable Adam?
LUCIFER. Why dost thou silent stand? what are thy thoughts?
ADAM. I seem'd to hear a plaintive, pleasing voice,
That in this manner spoke: Alas! what dost thou?
Most miserable Adam!

THE FLESH.

A vain desire, and dread,
Now lords it o'er thy heart,

CHERUBIM. Since thy heart trembles, evils must be
ADAM. I tremble at deceit. [nigh.

LUCIFER. Thou must have lost thy reason,
If thou canst fear thy mistress, and thy brother.

CHERUBIM. Fear! for they are thy foes.

ADAM. Thou say'st thou art my brother, she my
But if ye were my foes!— [mistress;

THE FLESH.

Cruel to treat us so!
What enemy can man now have on earth?

CHERUBIM. The enemy of Eve.

ADAM. He, who occasion'd misery to Eve,
And he, who was the cause, that from this brow
The painful sweat must now descend in streams.

LUCIFER. So little wilt thou trust us?
So lightly dost thou love us?
Yet it is fit thy fault
Call forth the tears to flow into thy bosom.

THE FLESH.

With treachery 'tis fit to treat with man
In gesture, tears, and voice,
Only to plunge him in Tartarean fires.

ADAM. They weep in such abundance
That every tear they shed strikes on my bosom;
And though like marble hard,
I fear, I fear, that if it does not split,
It may at least be soften'd.

ANGEL. These are the poisonous waters of Avernus,
(Incautious man!) that from their eyes distil.

LUCIFER. Ah heaven! why didst thou form me?
Why didst thou join my lot
With this ungrateful, misbelieving Adam,
That feels not his own good, or my affliction?

ADAM. Restrain thy grief, thy tears! and suffer me
(If it is true, thy soul desires my good)
To speak to thee apart,
And I to thee will open all my thoughts.

LUCIFER. Hast thou no other wish?

ADAM. No! I require no more.

LUCIFER. Behold us now apart! behold us far!
If any other wish
Strike thee, command! behold! we are obedient
Not to thy words alone, but to thy nod.

ADAM. What would'st thou, O my heart?
What is thy wish, my soul?
Now quiet thy desires! quiet thy pains!

CHERUBIM. Tell him, if he's thy brother,
And both descendants from the starry sphere,
They should with thee, in pure and perfect zeal,
Adore the Maker of the heaven and earth.
ADAM. That which my heart suggests, I now will do.

THE FLESH.

O tempter! now I fear
Some singular mischance.
CHERUBIM. Now, now the fraud is known.
ADAM. Now, brother, if you wish,
With this your pure celestial paramour,
Hail'd as the soul of love,
That I should think the one a heavenly Adam,
And her the only love of our great Maker,
Now bend with me your humble knees to earth.
LUCIFER. How in one instant can two opposites,
Humility and pride,
Together reign in me?
ADAM. Can Adam so delay?
LUCIFER. I'll tell thee; ah, it seems a thing unfit
That a celestial knee
Should bend to this vile earth.
ADAM. Thou hast already told me,
That in the high celestial plains above
Thou must no longer dwell,
But here with me enjoy delightful days,
Amid these sunny spots;
Let it not then displease thee
With earthly habitudes
To have thy breast, O Adam, fraught like mine!

THE FLESH.

Well dost thou speak, O Adam! I am ready
To pay thee prompt obedience.
LUCIFER. And I will also show,
This fair one's pleasure shall my pleasure be.
ADAM. Behold I bow myself! behold me bend!
Now let united hands be raised to heaven.
LUCIFER. To make palm meet with palm, in vain we strive.
ADAM. In truth there seems much pain.
LUCIFER. Perhaps you wish
Our hands united thus?
ADAM. No! what,—do you not see
That both united form a knot together,
Finger entwisting finger?

THE FLESH.

Perhaps you choose them thus?

ADAM. Alas! the example,
That with my hands before your eyes I show you,
Serves it so little? heavens! what do I see?
So destitute of sense
Are heavenly creatures?
LUCIFER. Now behold them join'd.

THE FLESH.

In truth I cannot tell,
If hell this day more tries the strength of Adam,
Or Adam more torments the powers of hell.
LUCIFER. Vigour! soul! animation!
For in proportion as our strife is bloody,
So will our palm of conquest rise in glory.
ADAM. Why do you thus apart
In such confusion speak?
Now raise your eyes to heaven,
And with delight contemplate
Of all those starry sapphires
The pure resplendent rays,
And those fair blessed seats!
Alas, thou shutt'st thine eyes,
That stream upon the ground.
LUCIFER. O Adam, cease at length.
Those rays so splendid dazzle us too much.
ADAM. This is my foe: I now discern him well.
The eagle of the sun
Is used with pleasure on the sun to gaze;
And thou, a heavenly eagle,
Accustom'd to the brightest rays of heaven,
Dost thou disdain or shun them,
Dazzled, and in confusion?

THE FLESH.

Who knows what splendours in high heaven are [kindled?
He, who surveys them oft,
Is satiated at last;
There's nought created so divine and dear,
That in long intercourse becomes not tiresome.
ADAM. Celestial good ne'er satiates, but delights,
And magnifies itself in God's perfection;
As the fair landscape's beauty
(Though 'tis a low example)
Becomes more perfect, and more flowery seems,
When the sun gilds the valleys and the hills.
But as I wish what ye too both desire,
Now let your eyes be closed;
And with your opening lips pronounce these words:
'Thee I adore.'
LUCIFER. Go on!

ADAM. Say, then, 'Thee I adore.'
LUCIFER. Go on! for such a memory have I,
That by a single effort
I will repeat thy words.
ADAM. I am contented;
Yet thou observe my words! Thee I adore,
Thus with my knees to earth, and streaming eyes,
Lord of the empyrean!
Great sovereign of the heavens, and only God!
Holy, firm, formidable, just, and pious!—
And still dost thou delay?
LUCIFER. I meditate thy speech,
Which to me seems so long,
I doubt my power to speak it,
ADAM. Shall I again pronounce it?
LUCIFER. This I cannot desire,
But find a great defect
In this imploring speech.
ADAM. Pray tell me what?
LUCIFER. No humble worshipper, not the adorer,
But the adored, 'tis just that I should be.
Alas! I can no longer
Such outrages endure:
No! who I am, I must at length reveal.

THE FLESH.

Alas! the same thing even I must do.
ADAM. Alas! what do I see?
What horrid form, amidst the clustering trees,
Does this false denizen of heaven assume?
And his immodest partner?
Alas! their winged feet
The false ones move to me,
And from their pomp and gold
Breathe forth infuriate flame!
Succour me! help, O God!
Take pity on my failing!
LUCIFER. Fly, as thou canst, from these my rapid [wings
Thy flying must be vain.
Alas! to my great grief, this day I see
Who has the prize of conquest,
Who soonest yields, and from his rival flies.
So that I well can say
To the eternal gulf,
That in this hard and perilous contention,
The toil belongs to hell; to man the glory.
I lose, alas! I lose: now with what face
Can this my foot be turn'd again to hell?

THE FLESH.

Ah! sad and dire event! ah strife! ah death!

LUCIFER. Yes, yes, 'tis just that my infernal rage
Should all now turn on me,
Since I have vainly tried
To work the condemnation of this man.
But can this be? (ah! hard is my belief!)
Exalted providence!

CHERUBIM. Thou canst not mount, fierce monster!
I affirm it,
By this high brandish'd dart of penal fire.

LUCIFER. Ah, for the seats of hell
I spread my rapid wings.

CHERUBIM. And I these happier wings, lucid and [light,
Will exercise around,
For man's protection, and in scorn of hell.

SCENE THE FOURTH.

THE WORLD.

How fine I now appear! no more I seem
A monster now of horror,
But of a lofty spot
The blissful habitant, and call'd *The World*;
That so adorn'd and splendid,
Amidst thy prime delights,
Laughter, and songs, and amorous affections,
My snares of silver, and my nets of gold
I may extend for man,
That he may slide and fall, to rise no more;
And try in vain to heaven
Again to rise upon the wings of zeal.
And should he seem for ever
Bent to survey the lovely azure heaven,
The sun's bright lustre, and the lunar ray,
And trembling stellar fires,
I will delude him so
With other lovely skies, that from the first
Quick he shall turn his view.
I will that my fair heaven
Shall be of living sapphire; there shall shine
A sun of bright pyropus, and a moon
Form'd of the beamy diamond's spotless light.
A thousand and a thousand sparkling stars,
Of jewels rich and rare;
And if amidst this lightning it may thunder,
And burning bolts may seem to dart around,
My lightning be the ruby,
My thunder sounding silver,

With thunderbolts of gold, and storms of pearl!
As a proud sovereign of so rich a heaven,
The World shall still exult,
And this new man shall bend to me in worship;
And thus of these my pomps,
My luxuries, and joys,
The numerous sons of man become enamour'd,
Shall never know repose;
But with destructive force
Each shall endeavour of his wretched brother
To gain the envied finery and wealth.
Man I behold already for this gold,
And for the world's delights,
In horrid mansion full of smoke and fire,
Tempering the deadly steel;
Now at the anvil, see!
How striking frequent with his iron mace,
He forms the coat of mail; makes it his vest,
And for destruction draws the blade of steel.
Another see, converting
Cold iron into fire,
Tapers and twists it round;
And now a hatchet forms; now see him eager
To level trees and woods;
And now, with numerous planks,
Behold him raise a work
Fit to sustain the fury of the sea.
Others I see toiling to pass o'er alps,
To pass o'er mountains and the riven rock:
Leeches that prey on ore,
And from earth's bosom suck great veins of gold.
Lo! others in the deep
Trying the fertile sea, plunge through the waves,
Fearless encountering its tempestuous pride,
If they from crusted shell, or craggy rock
May coral draw, or pearl.
Ah, labour as thou wilt, and sigh, or sweat,
In this pursuit of gold,
Thy cares and woes shall gather in proportion
To all thy gather'd wealth.
Lo! to preserve thy jewels and thy wealth,
Thou hidest them under earth,
And gold forbids thee to enjoy thy gold.
Hence treacherous we see
The servant to his lord,
And through his breast and heart
He thrusts the faithless sword,
Through eagerness of gold.
Hence on the table of a royal house
There stands the statue of a unicorn,

As if in scorn of man;
Since, giving safety to a mighty lord,
The beast exposes human cruelty.
Hence is it that the son,
Greedy of gold, becomes his father's foe,
Wishes him short existence,
Flies him, and steals his wealth,
So that to make him glad, his sire may pine
Hence is it that, for gold,
Brothers, becoming frantic,
Brandish the hostile steel,
And deem this gold more precious than their blood
Here by the blaze of gold
The eyes of woman dazzled
See not her husband, nor regard her children,
While, on the wings of passion,
She with the adulterer flies, nor yet perceives
That for this gold (vile dust!)
She has resolved to quit her very flesh.
What more? what more? not only
By gold's possession thou shalt prove the foe
Of wife, of father, brother, and of friend,
But rebel even to God;
Since with intemperate zeal
Mere idols form'd of gold
Thou shalt proclaim the only powers of heaven.
But what do I behold? blest that I am!
I see fair Eve approach! on her soft back
Bearing a load of many leafy boughs:
What she now means to do
Here will I watch, conceal'd amidst this bower.

SCENE THE FIFTH.

EVE *and* THE WORLD.

EVE. Canst thou presume, afflicted, wretched Eve,
To the bright sun to raise again thine eyes?
No! no! thou art unworthy well thou seest:
Thou could'st behold him once,
And gaze delighted on his golden splendour;
Now if thou darest to view him,
His radiance dazzles thee; rather thou seem'st,
When thou hast dared to meet his potent beams,
To have thy fading eyes
Wrapt in a dusky veil.
Alas! it is too true,
That I in darkness dwell,

And in the formidable clouds of sin
I have o'erwhelm'd the light of innocence.
Ah, wretched, mournful Eve!
If now thou turn'st thy foot,
Eager to taste the pure and limpid stream,
Alas, how troubled dost thou find the water,
Or else the fountain dry!
If with quick appetite thou chance to turn,
Anxious from lovely plants to pluck the fruit,
How dost thou find it crude,
Or made the dark recess of filthy worms!
If weary, 'midst the flowers
Thou seek'st to close thine eyes,
Behold! with fluttering pinions at thy feet,
A serpent 'midst the flowers darts and hisses.
Now to avoid the heat
Of the fierce sun if thou would'st seek the shade
Of the thick wood, or of the leafy grove,
Thou fear'st the rage of monsters, and must tremble
Like the light leaf that shakes at every breeze.
And hence it is, thy wish
To fasten bough to bough, and trunk to trunk,
Raising some safe asylum
From serpents, monsters, tempests, and the sun.
To you then will I turn me, verdant boughs,
That hither on my back with toil I bore,
Do you defend me now! now rise you here,
Afford a safe retreat
To Eve so wretched! Lo! I thus begin.
It will suffice, if I with tender hand
Just shadow, what with far superior strength
And more enlighten'd sense,
The sinner, Adam, here may terminate.

THE WORLD.

Abode more firm and faithful,
Hell now prepares for thee, or rather Death.
Behold, behold, how she
Employs herself in placing these green boughs!
To Eve I will unveil me. Ah! what dost thou?
Why art thou raising thus,
Eve, gentle fair one, these thy leafy boughs?
Tell me, what would'st thou do,
Why dost thou toil and sigh?
EVE. Alas! what do I see?
Do not approach me! no! from me be far!

THE WORLD.

What canst thou fear, O lovely,
Sweet angel of the earth?

Joy of all hearts, and honour of the world?
EVE. Thou Lord, who didst create me,
This stranger, who now rich in gold and gems
Courteous accosts me with a human face,
Do thou to me reveal;
Nor let our God consent,
That Eve again, or man,
Precipitately fall in fatal error!
Alas! with human face
An artful base deceiver,
Led me to taste the interdicted apple;
And thence my heart must dread
Other infernal guile,
Since in the world one man alone exists.

THE WORLD.

Before my light, as at the radiant sun
Darkness itself is used to disappear,
Drive from thy heart this cloud,
That makes thy visage pale;
And from the lovely cave of glowing rubies,
Now closed to guard, as in the depth of Ganges,
The treasure of inestimable pearls,
Send forth thy tender sighs;
And if, thou fair one, 'tis thy wish to sigh,
Let all thy sighs be sweet!
EVE. And who art thou, so eager
To change the tears of woman into smiles?

THE WORLD.

Know, gentle fair one, you in me behold
As much as you can see,
Raising your eyes to heaven,
Or turning them to earth;
An indigested mass,
Chaos I once was call'd, now fair and fine,
Heaven, earth, and sea, salute me as *The World*.
I too have had my residence amidst
The miracles above;
But O! a fault of mine,
Which now to tell thee would be out of season,
Induced the sacred Resident above
From his eternal dome in wrath to drive me;
And from a bright and fine
Trophy of paradise,
Into a shapeless mass
Of hideous matter he converted me.
At last my mighty Maker, having seen
That my condition balanced my offence,
Bestow'd upon me soon another form,

Far from his highest heaven, and thus at once
Annihilated that tremendous prison,
Dreary and dark; he made me in exchange
The luminous gay World.
  EVE. Alas! my first alarm
So deeply wounds and lords it o'er my heart,
I know not what to credit, what to do.

THE WORLD.

Now, since there's nothing that to me affords
Such infinite disgust,
As to behold aught dirty and neglected,
I pray thee, lovely fair, be it thy study
With purple, gold, and robes adorn'd with pearl,
To grace thy gentle form, and cast to earth
Those skins of animals that shock the sight.
Observe how much more pleasing and majestic
Man may be render'd by a graceful dress!
Compared to me dost thou not seem a beast?
Rather among the beasts
Dost thou not seem the vilest animal?
Dost thou not see, that every abject creature,
Or of the foaming sea,
Or of the fields of air,
Or of the woods and mountains
Are deck'd with humid scales,
Gay feathers, shaggy skins, or painted bristles?
And if on earth thou wert created naked,
Yet well array'd with reason
Appear'd thy noble soul, by which thou might'st
(Made empress of the world)
Deck thee with radiant gems, and robes of gold.
Too vile a mansion are the woods for thee,
In nakedness surpassing even the beasts.
For what end dost thou think,
The great exalted hand
Created in a moment
Gold, silver, and rich gems?
Perchance, perchance thou think'st
It may be right that these
Bright wonders of the world
Rest ever buried in a blind oblivion.
No! no! thou simpleton, it is that man,
Sweating in their pursuit,
May decorate himself; and as the sun
Flames in full splendour in a sapphire sky,
Or 'mid the stars of gold
The bright and silvery moon,
He thus may glitter in this earthly heaven.
What more! behold what gems the sea conceals,

Or the rich earth embraces,
Which, tempting man to joy,
Display their rare endowments:
Whence it is just to say,
They were for man created; and if blind
Through ignorance he slights them,
Or shows himself ungrateful,
Why has such treasure been for man created?
Shall it be true, that you, the sovereign fair,
The gentle ruler of this worldly realm,
Can prove to God ungrateful? to the World
Like earth's vile offspring? Rise! assume this gold,
The topaz, ruby, pearls, and splendid purple,
Bright robes of gold, and rich habiliments!
In worldly trophies like our lofty queen
Shine, Eve, and let all creatures worship thee!
O how in viewing thee, thou radiant fair,
Cover'd with gems and gold,
I seem to joy! O how,
While you majestically move along,
The flowers appear before your feet to weave
A sweet impediment!
Rather I seem to see the stars from heaven
Innumerous descend,
Here for your feet to form a bright support.
What dost thou, pensive fair?
Now of thy radiant locks, that stream at length,
A store of jewels, of fine threads you weave
For hearts a net of gold.
Now let a charming smile
Enliven thy sweet cheek!
Then shalt thou hear in accents of delight
The birds around miraculously say,—
'O what a lip of coral!
And what fair teeth of pearl,
Has Eve's sweet mouth, so delicately small!
How sweet is her discourse,
That seems to be below, what, in high heaven,
The voice of God is to the blessed host.'
Arise, arise! be warm,
Thou spring of tenderness, and flame of souls!
Come! leave! O leave the woods
To creatures of the forest;
And with resplendent brass,
And snowy shining marble,
Let a proud palace now be raised to heaven,
To form a worthy mansion for thy merit!
To make this easy to thee
The World will not find difficult. That wood,
Which you have wish'd to join,

Fearing the fury of the savage beasts,
Let that now form a seat
With walls of silver, and a roof of gold,
Of emerald its pillars,
And hung on golden hinges, gates of pearl
EVE. Oh heaven! what do I see? what's this,
O God?

THE WORLD.

What hast thou more to say? Ah, simple, enter
With light and speedy foot, there, where alone
Thou find'st a fit abode!
Then wilt thou truly be of thy great Maker
The image and ingenious imitator,
Since he among so many
Legions in heaven, as much as he excels them
In majesty, so much himself he raised
On his exalted throne, in highest heaven.
Thus here below let man amid these tribes
Of fishes and of birds,
And of unnumber'd beasts,
Possess a mansion worthy
Both of his name and empire!
EVE. In truth, when I behold your mighty pomps,
That might so soon be counted as my own,
I will not say that my high heart feels not
The goading of ambition; but in turning
My eyes upon the precept of my Father,
I will disdain, and from your proffers fly,
As from vile dirt the snowy ermine flies;
And this poor skin alone
Shall be my golden robe adorn'd with pearl;
A cave my proud abode;
The troubled water and rude herbs to me
Dear beverage and food.
No! no! I will not to my first dread fault
Now add a second like it; making thus
A path more recent to the gulf of ruin.

THE WORLD.

O simple fair, come forth!
Come forth, ye fair and gentle virgins all,
From this my golden palace!
Be you devoted handmaids
Around this fair, and 'midst your tuneful songs
Present to her rich robes, adorn'd with gold!

SCENE THE SIXTH.

CHORUS OF NYMPHS, EVE, THE WORLD, *and* ADAM.

BEHOLD in dance, O joyful World,
Little virgins;
See these maidens,
With their treasure bright and cheerful;
Hearken now how they are singing,
Eve alone invoke, and honour!
See their robes with gold inwoven;
See their vestments
Shedding lustre
From the treasure of their jewels!
Bright the crown and rich the sceptre,
That to Eve is now presented.
If in heaven, nor sun nor planet
Shed its ardour
And its radiance,
Heaven would be a mass of horror;
But with light so pure and radiant
Heaven is term'd the seat of splendour.
He, who made so many wonders,
Fair and beauteous,
Is desirous
All that's fair to have before him:
Deck thyself then, O thou coy one,
If thy God delights in beauty.

ADAM. What dost thou, Eve, not see
That if uncautious to these charms thou yield st,
We shall sink deeper in the snares of hell?

EVE. Alas! what do I hear?

ADAM. Hence, ye rebellious crew!
By virtue of my God depart confounded,
To the infernal realms!

CHORUS. Ah, thou must then avoid this light of day
Thou sightless mole of hell!

THE WORLD.

Ah flesh infected!
Await, O yet await
Fit punishment to your presumptuous rage!
And hast thou dared so highly,
Thou creature of corruption,
That this bright palace which for Eve I raised,
Speaking thou hast ingulf'd,
And from the day hast banish'd
A numerous group of fair and graceful nymphs?
Come forth, now all come forth,
Ye horrid monsters, from the caves of hell!

Let us this hour display
Our utmost fortitude, and force supreme.
Now let this man be chain'd;
Fix him a prisoner in the depths of hell,
And let his victor reap the glory due.
EVE. Succour, O God! O succour!
Lord show thy mercy to my great offence!
ADAM. Ah, do not fear, my love,
But hope, still hope in heaven; hope, for at last
Celestial grace was never slow to save.

SCENE THE SEVENTH.

LUCIFER, DEATH, THE WORLD, CHORUS OF DEMONS *armed with various arms.*

LUCIFER. Thou fool, in vain thou toil'st
To invocate high heaven; thy God may arm,
If he is not abased, and with him arm
His flying warriors all,
From our infernal chains
And these sharp talons, now to draw thee forth;
To his first loss, and first discomfiture,
A second like the first shall soon be join'd.
Of his supernal loss has he not heal'd
The painful memory,
The ruin of his angels?
That now, inflamed with anger,
He seeks in heaven another mightier ruin?
To arms! at length to arms,
Satanic warriors all!
And let his wretched residue of angels,
All falling out of heaven,
Be all ingulf'd in hell!
Lo, meteors in the air and storms at sea
I kindle and I raise:
Lo, Tartarus his wings
Spreads for celestial seats:
Behold the stars of God
By Lucifer's proud foot crush'd and extinguish'd;
And girt for war and glory,
Let Tartarus through heaven proclaim a triumph!

SCENE THE EIGHTH.

ARCHANGEL MICHAEL, CHORUS OF ANGELS, CHORUS OF DEMONS.

MICHAEL. Tremble, thou son of wrath,
At this sharp dart's inevitable glance,
At the dread stroke of the celestial leader;
Not against God, against thyself alone,
Thou raisest wrath, and wounding wound'st thyself.
Sink into shade, misguided, wretched spirit!
Utterly void of all angelic light,
Be blind in gazing on that heavenly lustre,
To me imparted by the Lord of light,
The dazzler of the sun.
Fly, ye infected crew,
Ye enemies of God,
Nor let the breathing whirlwind,
With blast from hell, the yet unruin'd life
Of man o'erwhelm with deeper shades of darkness.
No more thy fatal hiss, thou snake of hell,
Shall by its discord stun;
Since pierced and panting now
Thou faintest, poison'd by thy own contagion.
LUCIFER. Heaven's talking minister,
With rays more loaded than inspired with courage·
Soft creature of the sky,
Thou angel of repose,
In solemn indolence,
Humility's calm nest, a seat of peace,
A warrior but in name,
Whose countenance is fear, whose heart confusion?
Spread, spread thy pinions for the arms of God,
Take refuge there, and there be confident!
For too unequal would the combat be
'Twixt cowardice and valour,
The warrior and the slave,
Infirmity and strength, and, let me say,
Betwixt vile Michael and brave Lucifer.
But if such daring can inflame thy heart,
As now to rescue from this warlike arm
That man, mere flesh and clay,
That animated dust, I warn thee well
Of mortal conflict sharp, where thou shalt see,
By this avenging hand
All the large family of God extinguish'd.
MICHAEL. Such mournful victory,
O Belial, in thy frenzy desperate,
As once in heaven thou gain'st, now with mankind

Subduing the deceived,
And hence the conquer'd conquers,
Freed is the captive, and thyself ensnared.
Now be it manifest
What palms of victory 'tis thine to raise.
Behold against thee, thou unfaithful spirit,
Michael become compassionately cruel.
LUCIFER. If at the early sound of war, the first
Encounter of our arms,
'Twas given a mighty warrior to destroy
A third part of the stars,
See in what brief assault
I can demolish the great seat of God!
Be dazzled now before this warlike blaze,
That from the brow of death I now diffuse,
Whirling in bloody circle
From my high front these death-denouncing comets!
Behold! behold at length
Heaven yields no more a refuge to its angels!
Since to a fate more joyous,
A happy pass expands, and seems to say,
Begone, at length begone,
Ye frighten'd angels, now relinquish heaven!
The warrior doom'd to hell
Becomes the blessed lord of these bright seats.
MICHAEL. Why longer pause to crush the proud loquacity
Of this presumptuous and insulting rebel?
Soon with a pen of adamant, with striking
Dread characters of blood,
Within the volume of eternal woe
The glory shall be blazon'd
Of thy lost victory.
To arms! at length to arms,
To spread dismay through hell!
Joy, man! smile, heaven! and Tartarus, lament!
LUCIFER. Seldom upon the vaunting
Of a proud tongue too bold
Boldness of hand attends. To arms! to arms!
Thou fight with me; and you, my followers, all
Unconquerable warriors,
Transpierce and put to flight this abject crew,
The timid partisans
Of an unwarlike leader!
Ah! him who favours brief and endless shame
Possess'd in heaven, and now on earth display'd
Great fortitude but with unequal force,
Him a celestial stroke
Now drives confounded to the blind abyss;
And justice here decrees

That he who lost the fight should lose the sun.
Angels and God, at length ye are triumphant!
Now, now is Lucifer
O'erwhelm'd, and all his legion
Sinks from the light of day to endless night.
MICHAEL. Fall thou at length, fall wounded and
Fierce monster of the shades, [subdued,
To death's deep horrors, there be doom'd to die
By an immortal death!
Nor hope thy wings to heaven
Ever to spread again! that wish, too bold
For thee, so desperate and unrepenting.
Thou'rt fallen, at length thou'rt fallen,
Most arrogant of monsters!
In pain thou sink'st as low,
As high in joy it was thy hope to soar.
Again thou learn'st to fall,
Transfix'd with thunder to the drear abyss.
Fool! thou hast wish'd to take this man thy captive,
And thou alone hast plunged
Within the deepest gulf:
Hence pierced and overwhelm'd,
Sinking to Tartarus,
The flame of wrath eternal
Bore thee to hell, the hell of hottest fires.
A spotless angel, O thou prince of falsehood,
Thy folly hoped to put to flight and wound;
But thou, opposed to him,
Hast yielded, plying thy wing'd feet in haste.
Thou too hast hoped to turn the spacious world,
In hostile flame, to ashes,
And at thy ardent blast and baleful breathing
Clouds, lightning, and tempestuous bursts of thunder,
With rattling deadly bolts of arrowy flame,
Roll'd through the air, whence all the mountains
And all the vales re-echoed in convulsion. [shook,
And yet, behold, in heaven
The spheres move round more musical than ever,
And all the azure sky
The lucid sun with brighter beam adorns:
Behold the ocean, tremulously placid,
And from his Persian gulf
In gay abundance scattering pearl and coral;
Nor weary are the sportive fish in gliding
Along the trembling sapphire.
Behold, what verdant and what flowery brows
These pleasant vales in exultation raise!
Hark, to the grateful accents
Of every flying songster.
Inhabitant of air,

That in his flight now gives
Voice to the woods and music to the vales.
Now, all rejoicing in a day so noble,
To the confusion and the shame of hell,
Let every spotless ensign rise to heaven,
And fluttering sport with the exulting winds;
Let all the instruments of heavenly glory
Sound through the sky the victories of heaven!

SCENE THE NINTH.

ADAM, EVE, CHORUS OF ANGELS.

ADAM. O sounds beloved, that call us now in joy,
To scenes we left in sorrow; ah! I fear
To taint the fragrance of the heavenly host,
Stain'd as I am with sin.
O thou, that haply of celestial ruby
Wearest the blazing mail,
Hallow'd and brave Archangel,
Brave, yet compassionate, thy golden locks,
Radiant as light, thy glittering helmet covers;
Thou in thy right hand shakest the spear of victory
And raisest in thy left a golden balance;
Close, close thy painted plumes so rich in gold,
And cast a gentle look
On him who, prostrate, honours and adores thee

EVE. O happy dawn of the eternal sun,
Thou courteous kind restorer,
To these my blinded eyes
With sorrow darken'd, and bedew'd with tears;
Now, of thy rays a fix'd contemplator,
The mole of error stands;
Now on your voice depends
An asp, once deaf to heaven's most friendly dictates
I, wavering wanderer,
Who undissembling own
The fault in which I fell, to thee I bend,
Nor in my speech deny
That I am Eve, the cause
Of human kind's perdition.
Now let thy guardian hand
(O in the deeds of God thou faithful servant!)
Relieve me from the depth
Of my so great offences.

ADAM. Of heavenly mysteries
And secret will of God,
Thou hallow'd blest revealer,

Angel of eloquence!
The fatal presages
Of mournful Eve and Adam
Now quiet with the breath
Of thy exalted converse;
So that this troubled flood
That strikes the heart, in issuing from the eyes,
No more may make me seem
A rock of sorrow in a sea of tears.
MICHAEL. Arise, O both arise, you who of God
Are creatures so regarded,
Dismiss your fears of the infernal portent
If your eternal Lord
Corrects you with one hand,
He with the other proffers your protection.
With happy auspices,
He who delivers souls,
On his light wings directs his flight to you,
In God's dread warfare harbinger of peace.
The mighty Fount of life,
The Artificer of souls,
The Architect of worlds,
The mighty Lord of heaven,
Maker of angels and of all things made,
The infinite Creator,
To safety summons you,
And to short war a lasting peace ordains.
Now from those double fountains
The warm and gushing streams
Of sorrow, Eve, restrain!
Thou hast been culpable
In rashly seizing the forbidden fruit;
To man thou hast occasion'd
Anguish and grief; thou hast indeed converted
Peace into war, and life into perdition:
Now by the aid of Him,
Whose handmaid nature is, and servant fate,
Who can restrain the sun,
And motion give to this unmoving mass,
Even yet may Eve enjoy
In prison liberty;
May be unbound, though fetter'd,
And triumph, while she is o'ercome, and vanquish
Now, since there shines in heaven
The star of love and peace,
And to the shame of hell,
The victor to the vanquish'd yields his palm,
Ah now let each, with humble eyes to heaven,
Incline the knee to earth,
And supplicant in prayer, give God the praise

Of goodness infinite;
For you shall find, to recompense your zeal,
That God your father is, your mansion heaven.
ADAM. Thou mighty Lord, who, resting high above,
With regulated errors
And with discordant union guidest heaven;
O of the fair eternal realms of light
Thou Lord immutable, resplendent power,
Thou dazzler and obscurer of the sun!
Now in these weeping eyes
And on this humid cheek
I dry my bitter tears, I cheer my heart.
Now, by thy zealous mercy,
Though spotted, I have safety;
Security in hazard, love in hate;
And sinking into hell,
Am yet a citizen of highest heaven.
EVE. With dissolution life,
With strife and contest peace,
With ruin victory,
With deep offence salvation,
With powers of darkness heaven,
These to unite is not a human talent,
But of the eternal hand,
Omnipotence supreme; hence is it, Lord,
That wounded Eve is whole,
Triumphs in loss, and, though subdued, has glory.
My guide, I will obey thee;
Since, O benignant Lord,
Thy service is dominion,
And to obey thee, glory.
If pain allow not that I speak the pain
Which wounds my heart so deeply,
Thou most indulgent Father
Givest to the heart and soul a new existence:
Awaken'd by affliction,
Raising my voice to heaven,
I'll teach resounding echo
To carry to the sky my humble song,
Devoted to thy praise.
MICHAEL. Ye victims cleansed by tears,
Ye martyrs in affliction,
Amidst your blessed pains,
Ye holocausts of life and of content!
Now call the stars no more
Vindictive; war is now
Converted into peace,
And death turn'd into life.
Hence mortal Adam is now made immortal,
And Eve, though dead in many parts, revives.

The potent fire of love,
In which the tender God of mercy blazes
Inflames him with pure zeal to save the sinner
Contend, resist, and bravely
Wage with the hostile Serpent constant war;
It is man's province now
To conquer hell, and triumph over death.
Creatures of grace! feel deeply now for ever,
That your most gracious Father
Would not direct towards the ground your face,
As he has made the brute, but up to heaven;
So that, for ever mindful of their source,
Your happy souls may point towards their home!
For the high realm of heaven
Is as a shining glass, in which of God
The glories ever blaze.
Inure yourselves to water, sun, and winds,
And in the stony caves,
In the most barren desert
That the sun visits when he blazes most,
There both exert your powers;
There many years and many,
United ye shall dwell in hallow'd love;
And from your progeny henceforth the world
Exulting shall derive fertility.
And now to you, ye mortal pair, I promise,
As ye together sinn'd,
If ye in penitence have join'd together,
Together even in heaven,
In a corporeal veil
Contemplating the sacred face of God,
Ye shall enjoy the bliss of paradise.

ADAM. Greater than my offence I now acknowledge
Your mercy, O my God!
Since you, become the sovereign friend of man,
To him, though ruin'd, now extend your hand!

EVE. As I have known to sin,
So shall I know to weep;
For who in sinning knew forbidden joy,
Humble in punishment, should know to suffer
Be mute, be mute, my tongue;
Speak thou within, my heart,
And say with words of love,
See how to mortals, even in perdition,
The hand of heavenly succour was extended!

MICHAEL. At length, since now with joy
Man, being thus delivered
From hell's keen talon, feels unbounded transport,
And in his rapture deems
Earth turn'd to heaven, this world a paradise;

822

By these pure splendid dazzling rays of heaven,
By these delightful fires,
That in the light of God more lovely blaze,
Rich with new beams, and with new suns this day,
Day of festivity,
The day of paradise, rather a day
Blest in itself, and blessing every other!
Let all with festive joy
Of God's indulgence sing;
Of Adam and of Eve,
Now made on earth the denizens of heaven;
And let your tuneful songs
Become the wonder of futurity.

ANGELS SING.

Move, let us move our feet
There, where this man shall now
Wash out his past offence
With humble, hallow'd drops;
And of the mighty Maker
Praise we the love and mercy,
That in this day to man's envenom'd wound
Suddenly gives his pity's healing aid;
Rejects him and receives,
Deeming his every wrong and error light,
And now at last with more benignant zeal,
And in despite of Satan,
Gives him, redeem'd from hell,
A seat amid the golden stars of heaven.
Ye progeny of Adam,
Whose race we shall behold adorn the world,
Ye shall not pray in vain
To your high Lord, the fountain of all mercy.
Be leaves of that pure branch,
On which the Word Incarnate shall be grafted!
Thunder, infuriate hell,
Be stormy! yet his leaf shall never fall:
To him a joyous offspring
Is promised by the Lord of heaven's great vineyard,
Stricken, transfix'd, enkindled in a blaze,
And burning with eternal love for man.

THE END.

The changes both my heart & my fancy employs
I reflect ~~upon the~~ on frailty of man and his joys
Short-lived as we are, our pleasures we see
Have a still shorter date, and die sooner than we

The changes both my heart & fancy employs
I reflect on the frailty of man & his joys;
Short lived as we are, yet our pleasures we see,
Have a still shorter date and die sooner than we.

www.ingramcontent.com/pod-product-compliance
Lightning Source LLC
LaVergne TN
LVHW011155110826
845150LV00006B/1227

* 9 7 8 1 4 2 5 5 4 6 0 0 7 *